Interdisciplinary Reflections on South Asian Transitions

Bhabani Shankar Nayak
Debadrita Chakraborty
Editors

Interdisciplinary Reflections on South Asian Transitions

Exploring the Rise of Far Right Ideology

Editors
Bhabani Shankar Nayak
University for the Creative Arts
Epsom, UK

Debadrita Chakraborty
University of Petroleum and
Energy Studies
Dehradun, India

ISBN 978-3-031-36685-7   ISBN 978-3-031-36686-4   (eBook)
https://doi.org/10.1007/978-3-031-36686-4

This Palgrave Macmillan imprint is published by the registered company Springer Nature Switzerland AG.
The registered company address is: Gewerbestrasse 11, 6330 Cham, Switzerland

Paper in this product is recyclable.

Acknowledgement

We are thankful to all contributors in the making of this volume. We dedicate this volume to people who are fighting against the wave of right-wing transitions to ensure citizenship rights and establish peace and secularism in South Asia. We are thankful to Wyndham Hacket Pain, Palgrave, for all editorial support in the shaping of this volume.

30th of March 2023   Bhabani Debadrita

About the Volume

Since the past decade, democracies globally have turned towards right-wing leaders, parties and movements that demonstrated traits of xenophobia, nationalistic traits, a tendency towards authoritarianism and aggressive leadership, among others. In South Asia, right-wing populism have thrived on majoritarian politics that sponsored socio-cultural, -religious and -political prejudices and carnages against minority communities. The growing popularity of right-wing ideology continues to have both social and economic implications on South Asian states, more so for India's socially regulated economy. Temporally, such shift is closely correlated to a growing consolidation of wealth in the hands of a few corporations creating a historically unique condition where ethno-nationalism promotes a peculiar brand of capitalism. Right-wing politics has also seen translations within the South Asian public sphere in terms of various right-wing movements that appropriate scientific discourse and uphold age-old religious and cultural theories and in doing so represent right-wing ideology as the only rational alternative to survive within public and private spaces.

The book seeks to interrogate the political and economic transition to the Right and its implications within the South Asian region. It argues that liberal politics of South Asia is the foundation for occasional Rightist turns and prognosis for its retreat. It documents circumstances in which right-wing populism appears and the particulars of the political strategy that the right-wing leaders and movements in South Asia employ. Are right-wing political formations a product of perceived distress or are they a central part of the process of political transformation in the region? How do they relate to the perceived 'democratization'? The book examines different aspects of these complex linkages, seeking to understand and explain the rise of the political Right in the South ASIAN REGION, especially the links between right-wing politics, economic conditions, and socio-cultural and religious formations.

CONTENTS

Notes on Contributors

Dyotana Banerjee is Assistant Professor of Political Science in the School of Science and Humanities at Shiv Nadar University, Chennai. She holds a PhD in Political Science from the Department of Humanities and Social Sciences, Indian Institute of Technology Gandhinagar. Her research interests include politics of urban transformations and remaking of city spaces in India; caste, land struggles and urban migration; identity politics and practices of democracy.

Enrico Beltramini specialises in Christian theology and history, focusing particularly on historical and political theology as well as history and historiography of religion. He is the author of two monographs and numerous book chapters, and he has contributed many peer-reviewed articles to academic journals. He is on faculty at Notre Dame de Namur University, California. Beltramini has been trained as a theologian, historian, and social theorist, and he has earned doctoral degrees in theology, history, and business.

Debadrita Chakraborty is a Charles Wallace Fellow and an Associate Fellow of the Higher Education Academy, UK. Debadrita completed her BA and MA in English Literature from the University of Calcutta and Macquarie University, Australia, respectively, and her doctoral degree from Cardiff University, UK. Her primary research lies at the intersections of Cultural Theory, Gender and South Asian Literary Studies. In her doctoral research, she examined literary and cultural representations of the shifting nature of the construction and performance of South Asian masculine identities catalyzed by major political and socio-cultural events from the 1970s onwards in Britain. She has published articles and essays in the fields of South Asian culture, politics and literature, graphic fiction, gender studies and diaspora studies in reputed journals including *Gender, Work and Organization* and *Wasifiri* and books titled *Graphic Novels as World Literature* and *Living Theories and True Ideas in the Twenty-First Century Reflections on Marxism and Decolonization*. Presently, she is co-editing a two-part volume titled *Right-Wing Politics: Interdisciplinary Reflections on South Asia*. She has won the Sidney Perry Foundation Education grant, Gilchrist Educational Trust grant and the FFWG grant as a doctoral scholar.

Farooque Chowdhury is from Dhaka, Bangladesh. His work covers Bangladesh, capital, climate, democracy and democratic movement, economy, environment, geopolitics, labor, imperialism and imperialist intervention, micro credit, politics, rural development, the War for Liberation in Bangladesh, and war. His books in English are *Micro Credit, Myth Manufactured* (2007), *The Age of Crisis* (2009), *With the Passing Time* (2021), *The Great October Revolution* (2022). His Baanglaa books include *Venezuela, Roopaantarer Laraai* [Venezuela, Struggle for Transformation], *Mahaa Khoodaa* [Great Hunger], *Upamahaadeshe Srameek Aandolener Kaalpanjee* [Chronology of Labor Movement in Bangladesh-India-Pakistan sub-continent], *Khoodra Reen Breehat Khatee* [Micro Credit, Bigger Loss], *Biggaan Dekhee Chaardhaar* [Science for Young Learners]. His translation, from English to Baanglaa, works include Fidel Castro, *Aamaar Kaishor Aamaar Taaroonna* [Fidel Castro, My Early Years], *Mahaa Aarthek Sangkat* [John Bellamy Foster and Fred Magdoff, The Great Financial Crisis], *Biponna Preetheebee* [John Bellamy Foster, The Vulnerable Planet]. His works, as editor/co-editor, include *People's Report on Bangladesh Environment*, vols. 1 and 2 (co. ed., 2001), *People's Report on Bangladesh Environment* (co. ed., 2002–2003), *The Great Financial Crisis, What Next* (ed., 2012), Selected Essays by Paul M Sweezy (in Baanglaa, ed. 2008), Selected Articles from *Monthly Review*, on market and inequality (in Baanglaa, 2009). He has translated, from English to Baanglaa, scores of articles/essays/reports/books. His Baanglaa articles appeared in Baanglaa quarterly *Natun Diganta* from Dhaka; Baanglaa monthly *Aneek* from Kolkata, India; Bangla Journal from Ontario, Canada. His articles, a few hundred, appeared in English national daily *New Age* from Dhaka, teleSUR, weekly *Frontier* from Kolkata, e-journal *Countercurrents*, *Dissident Voice*, *Peoples Dispatch*, *MR Online*, *Venezuelanalysis*, *Pambazuka News*, a number of dailies/weeklies from India, Sri Lanka and a number of Latin American countries.

Abhijit Dasgupta is Assistant Professor of Sociology, GITAM School of Humanities and Social Sciences, Gandhi Institute of Technology and Management (GITAM) University, Visakhapatnam. He received his PhD in Sociology from the Department of Humanities and Social Sciences, IIT Bombay. His area of interest includes anthropology of Christianity, sociology of neighbourhood and migration studies.

Jayanth Deshmukh is an independent researcher based out of Pune, India. His research interests include sociology of religion, political sociology, India, and nationalism. Jayanth has extensively published articles on politics and religion across journals and online media. You can reach him at jayanthdes@gmail.com

Benjamin Duke has research interests in active pedagogy, ageing demography, criticality, corporate business practices, curriculum design, European Green Deal, Europeanisation, experiential learning, gender equality, global social policy, higher education, international development, LGBTIQA++ issues, political science, squatter's social movements and sustainable business. Ben Duke holds a PhD in Social Policy from Keele University (2017), United Kingdom (UK). He currently works or has worked in research positions for University College London (UCL), UK; the University of Leicester, UK; the University of Northampton, UK; and the University of Nottingham, UK. Ben Duke has had twenty-four discussion papers published, including three book chapters, two conference papers and a book review. His most recent article was published in July 2022. He is Deputy Lead Governor for NHS Sheffield, UK, and volunteers for Sheffield Mencap, UK, assisting vulnerable adults and children with learning difficulties. He also does voluntary work for numerous other UK charities.

Muhammed Favaz is from the Azim Premji University, Bangalore, India. He did his bachelors in Sociology Honors from Jamia Millia Islamia, New Delhi, India. His research interests primarily lay on politics of communal violence, urban sociology, structural violence and political anthropology.

Andrea Malji is Associate Professor of International Studies at Hawai'i Pacific University. She was a 2022 Fulbright-Nehru Scholar and was based at the University of Kerala in Thiruvananthapuram. She received her PhD in Political Science from the University of Kentucky, and her research focuses on traditional and non-traditional security issues in South Asia.

Raza Naeem is a Pakistani award-winning researcher, translator and dramatic reader based in Lahore, where he is also the president of the Progressive Writers Association. He has been trained in Political Economy from the University of Leeds in UK, and in Middle Eastern History and Anthropology from the University of Arkansas at Fayetteville, US. He is the recipient of a prestigious 2013–2014 Charles Wallace Trust Fellowship in the UK for his translation and interpretive work on Saadat Hasan Manto's essays. He is currently working on a book *Sahir Ludhianvi's Lahore, Lahore's Sahir Ludhianvi*, forthcoming in 2022.

Bhabani Shankar Nayak is a political economist and works as Professor of Business Management and Programme Director of Strategic Business and Management at the University for the Creative Arts, UK. His research interests consist of closely interrelated and mutually guiding programmes surrounding political economy of religion, business and capitalism, along with faith and globalisation, and economic policies. He is the author of *Political Economy of Artificial Intelligence and Economic Development* (2023), *Intersectionality and Business Education* (2023), *Political Economy of Gender and Development in Africa* (2023), *China: The Great Transition* (2023), *Creative Business Education* (2022), *Political Economy of Development and Business* (2022), *Modern Corporations and Strategies at Work* (2022), *Disenchanted India and Beyond* (2020), *China: The Bankable State* (2021), *Hindu Fundamentalism and the Spirit of Global Capitalism in India* (2018) and *Nationalising Crisis: The Political Economy of Public Policy in India* (2007).

Jessy K. Philip is an assistant professor at Jesus and Mary College, Delhi University, India. Her work has featured in international journals such as *Contemporary South Asia* and *Journal of Agrarian Change*.

Manish Jung Pulami is a lecturer at Nepali Military Academy in Bhaktapur, Nepal, academically instructing the officer cadets of Nepalese Army. He is also a PhD candidate/Research Scholar at the Department of International Relations, South Asian University in New Delhi, India. He was Public Policy Fellow placed at National Planning Commission, Government of Nepal. He has also completed a fellowship in International Relations from Institute of South Asian Studies (ISAS), Sichuan University in Sichuan, China. He completed his Master's in International Relations and Diplomacy from Tribhuvan University in Kathmandu, Nepal. He is the Gold Medallist of the subject for academic session 2018–2020. He has also worked with many research organizations and think tanks inside and outside the country, and similarly assisted many eminent professors in research works. He is active in writing about the international affairs in online media platforms and has published journal articles as well.

INTRODUCTION

RIGHT-WING TRANSITIONS IN SOUTH ASIA

The South Asian regions consist of Afghanistan, Bangladesh, Bhutan, India, Maldives, Nepal, Pakistan and Sri Lanka. Ethnic, cultural, social, religious and linguistic diversities define these countries. However, democratic deficit and attack on multiculturalism by dominant groups are growing in the region. These countries are witnessing a growing environment of democratic deficit with the rise of authoritarian right-wing and reactionary forces. The progressive politics rooted in anti-feudal, anti-colonial, anti-imperialist and anti-capitalist struggles in South Asia is at risk now due to the rise of right-wing waves in politics, society, culture and economy. The governing elites in South Asia are capturing the states and governments with the help of electoral politics linked with hate and intolerance towards minorities and dissenters. The deepening of democracy and expansion of citizenship rights are shrinking with the forward march of reactionary radicalisation of religion, society, culture and politics in different South Asian countries. In the name of nationalism, the flag-waving reactionary forces are becoming popular in electoral politics and gaining state power to patronise and promote right-wing ideology which is concomitant with the requirements of the capitalist markets and corporations. The weakening of welfare state and diminishing democratic cultures are net outcomes of right-wing politics often dominated by majoritarian communities.

The meteoric rise of majoritarian authoritarianism led by the populist right-wing political regimes have consolidated their base in different regions of South Asia. The reproduction of fear, hate, intolerance and market friendly economic policies are four pillars of these reactionary forces. The electoral democracy provides platforms for political prosperity to the reactionary forces to expand their legitimacy in the name of patriotism, nationalism, religion, culture and society based on hierarchical segregation and categorisation of population in terms of religion, culture, language, region, caste, sexuality, gender, localities and territories. These categories were often constructed, institutionalised, sustained and patronised by the British during the colonial rule in South Asia to weaken anticolonial struggles. However, the right-wing narratives are soft on the colonisers but harsh on minorities, when it comes to colonial injuries of partitions, its neoliberal reproductions and other historical injustices within body politic.

The dominance of Hindutva in India, political consolidation of one-party democracy in Bangladesh, marginalisation of linguistic and religious minorities in Sri Lanka, growth of reactionary Islamic politics in Pakistan, return of Taliban to power in Afghanistan, rise of Rastriya Swatantra Party in Nepal, the electoral victory of the Peace and Prosperity Party in Bhutan, and electoral dominance of extremists in Maldives show a common thread of right-wing waves in South Asia. This common right-wing thread is defined by political propaganda based on marginalisation of minorities, populist politics based on nationalism and religion, majoritarian dominance, market friendly neoliberal economy, and diminishing welfare state. The persecution of minorities is another defining feature of the right wing upsurge in South Asia.

The neoliberal economics and right-wing politics move together to uphold the local, regional, national and international variants of crony capitalism in the South Asian region. Neoliberalism facilitates authoritarian right-wing politics and right-wing politics provides shelter and promotes neoliberal economic, social and cultural order as only available alternative. The right-wing, authoritarian and bourgeois transformation in South Asia is very much in line with the requirements of global capitalism. The middle classes and bourgeoisie in the region have been facilitating such a transformation, which was evolving from 1990s onwards, when neoliberalism and right-wing politics started its forward march.

According to Prof. Christophe Jaffrelot, "[in India] economic liberalisation has given rise to a middle class of a different kind. In a way, it is more politicised, partly because salaried people are more sensitive to corruption. But the middle class is very much after growth and the means to get that growth may not matter much to them … the middle class has little problem with rising inequalities. The social democratic Nehruvian project was intended to contain inequality. But that is not the regime the middle class would now favour. They now support economically liberal policies. This new middle class supports the BJP more than the Congress. First, because it wants to grow in status by being recognised as Hindu through a kind of sanskritisation process and balance its growing materialism by some religiosity [...]" (*Business Standard*, 14 April 2014). The other regions of South Asia are witnessing similar transformations that bring together the troika of right-wing politics, religiosity and neoliberalism. Such an embodiment destroys the progressive foundations in postcolonial states in South Asia.

The Eurocentric theories of modernisation, industrialisation, urbanisation, westernisation, secularisation and rationalisation do not help to understand the complex transformations in South Asia. The rise of information technology, science, education and economic prosperity did not diminish the role of religion in public and private sphere. The reactionary traditional culture survived in dominant form to domesticate everyday lives and body polity of the state and governance in South Asia. Therefore, it is important to revisit, rewrite and reject some of the basic premises of these theories within the context of transformations in South Asia.

The first chapter provides a critical evaluation of the rise of right-wing politics in South Asia and its implication for the minority groups in the region. The second chapter documents the forward march of radical Buddhist monks, the core of majoritarian Sinhalese right-wing politics in Sri Lanka. The fourth chapter outlines the resurgence and appeal of monarchy and Hindu-nation in Nepalese political discourse. The fifth chapter critically examines the ideologies of agrarian and religious populism among the other backward caste groups in the South Indian state of Telangana. It creates grounds for Hindu right-wing politics in the region. The sixth chapter summaries the crisis and Hindutva challenges to Indian secularism. The seventh chapter locates different dimensions of Hindutva project as a social contract and its political implications for the state, society, culture and economy in India. The eighth chapter analyses the trajectories of Hindu nationalism and construction of its famine own and Muslim other. The ninth chapter argues about the dominance of exploitative relations in Bangladesh. The tenth chapter examines resistance by marginalised to the biopolitics of Hindutva majoritarianism, which expands its necropolitics by sustaining Brahmanical homogeneous hierarchies. The final chapter is a product of first-time translation of Abdullah Malik's little-known Hajj travelogue, which examines the Hajj in Communist eyes and its Islamic dystopia.

Epsom, UK   Bhabani Shankar Nayak

South Asian Minority Groups Beware: Economic, Political and Social Reasons Driving a Shift to Right-Wing Ideology

Benjamin Duke

INTRODUCTION

In recent times, certainly since the turn of the century the year 2000, there has been an international impetus to integrate South Asia into the global economy (Alamgir et al. 2022: 718). This has led to a welcome increase in foreign direct investment (FDI) and corporate activity. The international development work has been tempered by a lack of focus, on establishing societal buy-in of South Asian populations in the global drive. This has a serious effect upon minority populations living in a South Asian country with a right-wing government (Lim and Khoon Ng, Carnegie Endowment, June 2022, p. 18). In such circumstances, diasporic and immigrant populations find that as non-national people their views are excluded. Indigenous Peoples and minority groups alike have often been sidelined by FDI and/

B. Duke (✉)
NHS Sheffield, Sheffield, UK
e-mail: bd158@leicester.ac.uk

B. S. Nayak, D. Chakraborty (eds.), *Interdisciplinary Reflections on South Asian Transitions*,
https://doi.org/10.1007/978-3-031-36686-4_1

or a South Asian dash for growth fuelled by corporate capitalism (Chettri 2022: 4). The appearance of capitalism at this early juncture has societal resonance in South Asia. The profit motive ethos of capitalism heralds a turn away from cultural orthodoxy and a move towards liberal, secular, modernism in South Asian countries (Kvangraven, Aeon, 15 April 2022).[1] Occurring in tandem with the arrival of capitalism is an increase in right-wing governments elected in South Asian countries. This has critical importance to the populations of South Asian countries, especially their minority groups. This has a serious effect upon minority populations living in a South Asian country with a right-wing government. In such circumstances, diasporic and immigrant populations find that as non-national people their views are excluded (Karatasli and Kumral 2022: 2). The social furniture in many South Asian countries is that of right-wing ideology, which is focussed on one-nation nationalism, coupled with capitalism. The situation becomes more problematical because often right-wing political leaders and their governments are authoritarian and xenophobic. The interaction between right-wing ideology and capitalism creates a cocktail, which has resulted in the formation of right-wing governments, who themselves are essentially a small political elite (Frankel 2020: 89; Mansbridge and Macedo 2019: 59). Dealing with such a small group enables corporatism to progress in South Asian countries with little in the way of consultation. Capitalism is an agent of critical resource allocation; as such its ethos of profit motive affects any social protection programmes being considered for low-income households. The profit-generating and critical resource allocation utility of capitalism is clearly an economic, political and social driver, which results in a shift to right-wing ideology.

RIGHT-WING IDEOLOGY IN PRACTICE

The socio-cultural landscape in a South Asian country includes its ability to negotiate the political relationship with social, cultural and economic elites. In pragmatic terms, this means a government's ability to form allegiances with any social actor, which can influence the wellbeing of the country (Loewe et al. 2021: 9). One such example is foreign direct investment (FDI) from public sources—other international external to South Asian countries; private sources—large corporate investment; or philanthropic voluntary sources—non-government organisations (NGOs) such as Asia Indigenous Peoples Pact,[2] providing climate change mitigation and/or social protection international development projects in impoverished areas. Foreign investment from large corporate bodies has introduced capitalism, free market neoliberalism to South Asian countries; some of which are least developed countries (LDCs) and/or small islands, too weak to control, understand or withstand capitalism influence upon societies. Such countries could become subject to 'elite capture' (Brattberg and Feigenbaum, Carnegie Endowment, 13 October 2021; see also Virdee 2019: 15).[3] State capture can occur if a country becomes too reliant economically or electorally on unelected influential social actors, for example capitalism and/or corporate investment. The socio-cultural landscape in a South Asian country is also shaped by the governments relationship with its internal civil society organisations (CSOs), alongside external international NGOs and academia. CSOs, NGOs and academia carry out the important geopolitical function, of being independent critical observers of a global government's social policies (BTI, Bertelsmann Stiftung's Transformation Index, Mauritius Report 2022: 36). These are non-state-controlled organisations who can independently verify the lived experience of, for example, minority populations living in various South Asian countries.

One cultural elite are religious leaders who represent religions dating back several millennia. Vaishnav (2019) informs us that some South Asian countries where the political leaders are also religious leaders, share a number of common characteristics. They have an evangelical puritanical mindset, which results in them developing an authoritarian nationalist approach to government (Wibisono et al. 2019: 6). As religious nationalists they use moral appeals to advocate for economic austerity, basing government policies on an interpretation of their religious scriptures. In some cases, South Asian political and religious rulers can distract attention from the social landscape, if they are presiding over a failing state (Hopkins, The Lowy Institute, 12 July 2021). Political rulers can use the majority religion practised in their country as a cloak of respectability to justify using their religious scriptures: 'to redefine the basis of national identity in a manner that excludes or marginalizes religious minorities' (Vaishnav 2019).

Kefford et al.'s (2022) 'Nativism' study discusses nationalism, priming and agenda setting, which can make certain societal issues more relevant to some voters. Kefford et al. (2022) provide a definition of nativism which resonates in analysis of the driving force of right-wing ideology. The issue of priming interacts with media manipulation.

> *We argue that nativism should be understood as an exclusionary form of nationalism, or as Mudde (2007) describes it, as 'xenophobic nationalism'. It clearly demarcates society into 'in' and 'out' groups, and opposes, people, ideas, culture, and traditions which are viewed as foreign, or nor reflective of the nation, however defined. In its most extreme forms, such nativism can take the form of ethnic nationalism, whereby only those of a particular ethnic group (or those 'born here') are seen as legitimate citizens and members of the state (Fernandez 2013).* (Kefford et al. 2022: 4)

Kefford et al. (2022: 3) harmonise with Halikiopoulou and Vlandas (2022: 11) and Alamgir et al. (2022: 721), in saying that nationalism drives population views on immigration. South Asian embracement of right-wing politics has brought with it a re-interpretation of citizenship. A person's citizenship is usually obtained by their place of birth or after a government decided period of naturalisation (Alamgir et al. 2022: 718). Under right-wing ideology anyone or anything which is not originally from the country is not fully welcome. This means that in practical terms, South Asian right-wing governments are less likely to grant members of their minority populations' citizenship.

Verkuyten et al.'s (2022) 'Right-wing political orientation' study discusses national identification and its subsequent effect upon immigrants and minority populations. Verkuyten et al. (2022: 1) articulate that national identification can be understood through three different critical lenses, from a civic, ethnic and cultural perspective. National identification can take the form of national attachment or benevolent inclusive supportive patriotism, which makes all member of the population feel welcome (Marzecki 2020: 33). This is quite different from how citizenship is interpreted and implemented by right-wing governments in South Asia. When national identification takes the form of blanket patriotism, hubris or national glorification (Verkuyten et al. 2022: 1), national identification becomes aligned with one-nation nationalism, being exclusionary of non-nationals. The national glorification and hubris disseminate a xenophobic narrative, identifying 'ins' and 'outs' (Kefford et al. 2022: 4), nationals who are welcome, minority populations who are unwelcome. During such hubris, South Asian right-wing political leaders espouse discourse implying the positive aspects of their country exist due to non-national nationalistic purity. This is a form of ethno-nationalism, which appears to be uncaring and un-listening in its right-wing ideology eccentricity (Tamir 2019: 425).[4]

The political messages are delivered in an authoritarian, belligerent way during public speeches. The right-wing ideology political implication is also an act of 'symbolic violence' (Bourdieu and Passeron 1991: 5)—manifest in the form of the non-appearance of minority populations in South Asian government broadcasts. By definition, minority groups not born in a particular South Asian country are unworthy, should be excluded, ignored and never mentioned. The right-wing xenophobic narrative can also be quite nuanced. In the event that minority people are mentioned in political speeches, it's in a negative light, being scapegoated for the South Asian country's social problems. In this sense, right-wing ideology describes non-nationals as being a threat to the civic and social security of the nation (Kiniklioglu, SWP [Stiftung Wissenschaft und Politik] Research Paper 7, March 2022, p. 22). Right-wing politicians provide a mouthpiece for this thought process, articulating a xenophobic, isolationist, nationalistic political rhetoric. This is socially divisive, purporting that people are a danger to the nation, purely on the basis that they weren't born in this country (Robinson(b), Council on Foreign Relations [CFR], 25 May 2022). Right-wing political mantra that minority group populations are either the source of or support insurgency, represents a security and defence justification of nationalism. The threat articulated by right-wing ideology said to be posed by non-nationals can also be pernicious. Acceptance of minority populations could introduce challenges to the orthodoxy, the age-old tradition of things. New cultures could become established, which challenge the religious beliefs and practices of the orthodoxy. For obvious reasons, the chance that minority populations may·not be as supportive of nationalist discourse from political leaders is seen as a threat. Essentially right-wing ideology acts to fuel grievances, which right-wing politicians artificially created and put there in the first place (Flinders and Hinterleitner 2022: 4).

The South Asian county's majority population can feel they are justified to discriminate against minority people, having been told by their political leaders that effectively migrants are not wanted (World Watch Research 2021: 6; Fejos and Zentai 2021: 81).[5] On the back of such polarising political mantra, anti-immigrant South Asian legislation has been introduced (Tamir 2019: 425). For example, Sahoo (2020: 9) informs us that India is approximately 80% Hindu majority and 20% Muslim minority. President Modi of the BJP (Bharatiya Janata Party) introduced legislation to outlaw the Muslim cultural practice of instant divorce. This was a profound change in legislation in India, which affected the citizenship ambitions and status of many Indian minority populations. This created a social landscape which not only denied India-based Muslim people of Indian citizenship; it often denied them equal access to education, healthcare and housing as well.

> *The Modi government's most polarizing decision, however, was the passage of the Citizenship Amendment Act (CAA) in December 2019. The law—which grants religious minorities form Afghanistan, Bangladesh, and Pakistan a speedier path to Indian citizenship but excludes Muslims—sparked nationwide protests. The passage of the CAA has led many Indians to fear that the BJP has seriously eroded the country's constitutional principles of equality and secularism.* (Sahoo 2020: 13)

Cultural or religious orthodoxy has had to adapt to the new social surroundings it finds itself in, to protect itself from ceasing to exist altogether (Farouk and Brown 2021: 8). The latter being the fate which awaits cultural if not religious orthodoxy, as desired by 2020s South Asian secular modernisers. Recent cultural religious adaptations include global, transnation-state alliances partnerships with capitalism, as demonstrated in the rise of political Islam. Political Islam's success is at least partly based on its replication of multinational Islamic empires, alongside an intention to establish a new global caliphate (Kelaidis, Berkley Forum, 30 March 2022). In this sense political Islam reinforces the cultural religious orthodoxy of the Muslim faith, maintaining the status quo (Robinson(a), CFR, 17 December 2021). Another example of the saliency of political Islam can be found in the post-Liberation Tigers of Tamil Eelam period in Sri Lanka.

> *During the Sinhalese-Tamil conflict "Muslims, with their political support for the Sinhalese dominated major parties gained some socioeconomic as well as political concessions from successive ruling parties." These concessions by the Sinhalese government included the establishment of segregated Muslim schools, a training college for Muslims, the provision of Mosques, the institutionalization of holidays, and legal provisions under the marriage act. Having Arab countries economic and military support, and keeping the Muslims on their side against the Tamil struggle was a major policy goal of the Sinhalese government.* (Midlarsky and Lee 2022: 387)

The analysis provided by Midlarsky and Lee (2022) in their 'Distancing the Other' study demonstrates how continuing cultural and/or religious orthodoxy is societally beneficial. The relative success of political Islam also accommodates 2020s South Asian secular modernisers, by embracing socially progressive ideas to be implemented gradually over time (Fakir 2021: 125). Engagement with capitalism by partnership work with large corporate bodies and political representation is clearly key to the continuing success of political Islam. This is particularly poignant because of the ongoing delicate balancing act that political Islam constantly has to navigate. In South Asia, political Islam encounters intrasocietal conflict, being both aligned and alienated to various aspects of Western secular modernity (Kelaidis 2022). For example, regarding political Islam, social protection provision and the status of women, being respectively, intrasocietal conflict cases in point (Maizland, CFR, 14 July 2022b). Political alignment with right-wing ideology would retard development of political Islam significantly, social progress being stalled due to historical and geopolitical factors (Kelaidis 2022).

Right-Wing Ideology, Governments, Capitalism and Corporate Investment in South Asia

Wright et al. (2021) in their 'State capitalism in international context' study critically evaluate grey literature to discuss how capitalism develops in different countries. Wright et al. (2021: 10) inform us that a causal factor which influences a firm's performance in a foreign country is the political ideology of the government. The political institutions present in the country influence the state's relationship with FDI and private corporate investment. There needs to be consideration of state capacity, the government's ability to deliver its policy ambitions. Similarly, there needs to be due diligence regarding political constraints, limitations caused by political institutions, for example the Courts or religious groups (Ginsburg 2020: 230; Greitens 2020: E184). State regulation of business is another political institution which has resonance as it decides the 'rules of the game' (Wright et al. 2021: 10). This means that when governments have become corporate stakeholders, they are affected by the political institutions which they themselves created. A government's choice of political ideology which they choose to implement 'shapes the relationship between state ownership and performance' (Wright et al. 2021: 10). Alami and Dixon (2020) in their 'State capitalism(s) redux?' study provide a global causal factor influencing a shift to right-wing ideology. They inform us 'particularly with the erosion of global liberal institutions and the strengthening if right-wing populism' (Alami and Dixon 2020: 88). When South Asian countries have right-wing political leaders, this changes the nature of their country's business landscape, often to that of low corporate sector responsibility. Free market, laissez faire, neoliberalism is the order of the day, riding on the crest of an authoritarian right-wing ideological wave (Kwan Lee 2022: 23 and 74). There is low taxation, little scrutiny of business practices, recruitment, worker's rights, terms, conditions and wellbeing. Right-wing political leaders in South Asia have little appetite to change their relationship with foreign investors or the corporate sector. Political elites are formed; cultural and/or religious practices reinforcing the existing orthodoxy are maintained. The partnership with capitalism replicates the cash nexus, undermining the will of secular modernisers, asking for socially progressive liberal interpretations of ancient scriptures. Political ideology and the political institutions created by political parties have an interdependent relationship which is reliant upon each other (Wright et al. 2021: 10).

Alami et al. (2022) in their 'Geopolitics and the 'New' State Capitalism' study discuss new state-sponsored entities which enable foreign investment business activity. These state-sponsored entities include policy banks and sovereign wealth funds (Cuervo-Cazurra et al. 2022: 22; Alami et al. 2022: 995). State capitalism is where a country's government actively participates in creating a business landscape, which enables capital accumulation (Kim 2022: 298). Since the year 2000 the nature of capitalism to include state capitalism has changed. Countries have been able to create or engage with state-sponsored business, finance, investment vehicles, for international development and tax reduction purposes (Alami et al. 2022: 995; Dixon 2022: 131). The expansion of right-wing political governments in South Asia has contributed towards an unexpected global effect. There has been a geopolitical reorganisation of global capital accumulation from the North Atlantic to the Pacific rim (Alami et al. 2022: 996). The lack of regulatory or societal scrutiny of state capitalism by right-wing political parties makes South Asian countries profitable places for foreign investment. The manner in which political institutions, for example regulatory bodies or more importantly their absence, as advocated by right-wing ideology; is indicative of Wright et al. (2021: 10). Alami et al.'s (2022) analysis alerts us to another utility of state capitalism. Digital technological advances including crypto currencies can operationalise business activity between corporate bodies based in countries which are at war with each other. This is an under-theorised, under-researched aspect of global cross-border state capitalism.

Halikiopoulou and Vlandas' (2022) 'Understanding right-wing populism' study explains how right-wing political parties and concordant ideology have several common features.[6] Right-wing political parties garner support by promising to re-establish national sovereignty. Similarly, they promise to 'implement policies that consistently prioritise natives over immigrants' (Halikiopoulou and Vlandas 2022: 5). When nationalistic messages of right-wing political parties are coupled with FDI and corporate delivery of major projects, it conveys a powerful message. Right-wing party elites are able to say by working with the corporate sector and capitalism, we can deliver for our people (Karatasli and Kumral 2022: 7). This is the process by which the corporate sector gets access to South Asian governments, often by supplying them with a quick societal win. Essentially there is a symbiotic relationship: where large corporate bodies legitimise the right-wing government, in return South Asian governments allow the corporate sector to grow its foreign business, with little in the way of corporate social responsibility. From this position, right-wing ideology is able to control the political narrative on several fronts, in the event of South Asian population scrutiny (Wagner, SWP Research Paper 2, January 2022, p. 21). Right-wing governments can set the agenda, for example, that minority groups are the cause of crime in an area or COVID-19. Then these governments can suggest and justify nationalist social policies, which discriminate against diasporic communities, migrants and non-nationals. Effectively by being able to control the narrative, right-wing political parties 'employ a civic nationalist normalisation strategy that allows them to offer nationalist solutions to all types of insecurities that drive voting behaviour' (Halikiopoulou and Vlandas 2022: 13). In the long-term justification for a one-nation nationalist approach to social order is established. The right-wing political message also paves the way for a reduction in state welfare provision, targeted against certain minority groups if desired (Saleem et al. 2022: 10).

RIGHT-WING IDEOLOGY POLITICAL MEDIA PORTRAYALS OF SOUTH ASIAN MINORITY GROUPS

Often the media is controlled by South Asian country's state-approved and/or -owned newspaper, radio and television media outlets (United Kingdom Government [GOV.UK], 28 July 2022). Control of the media is a very powerful tool employed by capitalism to disseminate nationalist propaganda (Shahin 2022: 4; Reisach 2021: 908). A political message that the only rational choice to rid South Asian societies of their ills, for example COVID-19, is support of right-wing ideology (Singh 2022: 107). Warburton's (2020) 'Deepening Polarization and Democratic Decline in Indonesia' study discusses how the media has been used to frame a particular visual narrative. The study also provides examples of how anonymous social media accounts and tabloid magazines were utilised as a vehicle for political imagery (Rios, Bloomberg UK, 8 March 2022). A political rival was portrayed as being associated with socially conservative Islamist figures and hardline minority Muslim groups. In addition, the anonymous social media also portrayed the false narrative, a political rival was in reality a member of Indonesia's banned Communist Party (Warburton 2020: 28). There was a similar situation when a political rival joined forces with right-wing ideology, manifest as hardline Islamist groups. These groups were opposed to the possibility of a non-Muslim minority candidate, being elected to high political office in a Muslim majority country, Indonesia. These groups opposed, 'spread a sectarian message through online networks, prayer groups and mosques' (Warburton 2020: 28). During public interviews the political rival expressed an alternative interpretation on the Quran's position on non-Muslim leaders. The socially progressive views put forward by the political rival were misunderstood; they caused outrage in some quarters. 'Hardliners called for Ahok's arrest on charges of blasphemy and rallied hundreds of thousands of Indonesians onto the streets of Jakarta in a powerful display of opposition to a politician who was both a religious and an ethnic minority' (Warburton 2020: 28). The 2020s situation in Myanmar (formerly known as Burma) is geopolitically very worrying. Maizland (CFR, 31 January 2022a) informs us that there was a military coup in Myanmar in February 2021. There is strong resistance to the military junta from an alternative government, factions of which have declared war against the military coup (OHCHR [Office of the High Commissioner for Human Rights], 25 July 2022). There has been a military crackdown in Myanmar of sufficient brutality, which has resulted in global condemnation from the United Nations (UN), foreign governments and international NGOs (Maizland 2022a). Human rights abuses are widespread; few independent verified internet images are available, because Myanmar's military rulers have criminalised critique of their actions on radio, television and their social media. 'Following the coup, the military has amended sections of the criminal code and the Electronic Transactions Law to include provisions criminalizing anti-regime statements' (UK Government, GOV.UK 2022). Due to the Myanmar military government control of the internet, radio, television and social media, there are few media portrayals of academics, CSO or NGO dissenting voices, or minority populations.

CONCLUSION

In large tracts of South Asia right-wing ideologically driven populism is well established and is enacted with fervour by political and religious leaders alike. Using ancient religious scriptures as an excuse, legislative changes have been introduced which positively discriminate against minorities. For example, India's CAA legislation allows the fast-tracking of citizenship applications for virtually every other minority group in India except the Muslim population. Nationalism and xenophobia are prevalent in many South Asian countries who appear to have protectionist psyche in their cultures. This may be because many South Asan countries have had periods of armed conflict with their neighbours during the period 1950–2020. There is a cultural overhang from the country-wide stress of military action; it has been easier for right-wing ideology to engender societal buy-in of a nationalist approach. A nationalist view of society being anything not originally from your country of birth is at best tolerated, if not driven away entirely. If need be, changes should be made in the economic, legislative, social political climate of the country against non-national ethnic minority people. Segregated schools, housing area, healthcare and public transport usage are favoured social policies in South Asian countries with a right-wing government (Welsh 2020: 48–49).

Capitalism, corporate investment, FDI and various forms of state capitalism are established in many urban areas in South Asia. The alignment with capitalism has brought a number of challenges, for example many people living in rural areas are not seeing the benefit of wealth created by capitalism. Undemocratic alliances have been formed between corporate investors and political leaders desperate for foreign currency, with which to buy food, medicines or arms. This has led to the formation of unaccountable, economic, political and religious elites. A growing number of South Asian governments in the 2020s are not subject to any domestic scrutiny or free and fair elections. This is particularly acute in South Asian countries, where the political rulers are also religious rulers. In these circumstances capitalism and corporate investment have been able to seriously damage the environmental habitat of Indigenous Peoples. A significant amount of foreign investment has been in large factory production, hydro-electricity, coal, gas, oil, rare metal and mineral mining operations. Due to the ethos of capitalism enhanced with right-wing political ideology, the profit motive is prioritised over the needs of rural communities. This results in corporate business taking place apace with little in the way of a corporate social responsibility ethos. In the pursuit of profit there are insufficient corporate covenants, which are providing South Asian rural communities with a school and hospital. Right-wing political ideology supports censorship and removal of a free press, which has a number of societal effects. Many educated cosmopolitan people in South Asian countries are not aware of the over reliance of their government on foreign corporate enterprises. Sometimes that reliance extends to being able to remain in power at all. Little wonder that right-wing ideological governments have low regulation, low taxation and rarely ask foreign investors for public goods covenants.

Religions in South Asian countries appear that they will offer some form of relief to right-wing ideology in the long term. Ambedkar's conversion from Hindu to Buddhism in 1956 demonstrates how religious orthodoxy can be effectively challenged (Murphy, Asia Society, 17 July 2022). Religion is sufficiently fluid and independent to change over time. The reality of politics will bite, especially when support of right-wing ideology does not result in tangible societal improvements for South Asian populations. The orthodoxy based on centuries-old religions have had to re-adapt with the times. This has led to effectively a societal pendulum being in operation in South Asian countries. A pendulum which swings between periods where socially progressive liberals are in the ascendancy, alongside times when there is a resurgence of cultural orthodoxy (Hodson et al. 2022: 625). Patriarchal systems which embed gender-inequality are commonplace in South Asian countries; they are becoming increasingly challenged by secular 2020s societies. In the 2020s in the main, capitalist interests hold sway in most South Asian countries' decision-making processes, but there are altering societal expectations (World Bank, 13 April

2022). The day is approaching when sufficient supranational and transnational organisations will be prepared to use the policy lever of conditionality. This is a geopolitical tool which can be utilised by the UN, IMF, OECD and the WTO, to enact socially progressive changes in South Asian societies.

Notes

1. Kvangraven (2022) provides a short precis of some of the work of the economist Samir Amir (1990), who articulated the process of 'delinking' in economic thought. Amin's (1990) analysis of 'delinking' in part explains that it is not possible to reproduce capitalism in other countries globally, beyond Western Europe. Kvangraven's (2022) precis also informs us: 'Delinking does not require cutting al ties to the rest of the global economy, but rather the refusal to submit national-development strategies to the imperatives of globalisation.' In this sense, Kvangraven (2022) alerts non-Western European territories, for example South Asian countries, that how capitalism could develop might not be suitable for them.
2. Asia Indigenous Peoples Pact (AIPP) is a regional NGO based in Thailand. The AIPP delivers environmental projects and period poverty advocacy work in 14 countries in Asia.
3. Virdee (2019) essentially discusses how social processes and mechanisms have worked together in the competitive nature of predatory state building. Virdee (2019) explains how state-sponsored collaborations for commodity production and capitalist accumulation engendered and reproduced racism. Effectively various Western European nations in the seventeenth century allowed themselves to be captured and replicated racial divides all in pursuit of capitalism.
4. Tamir (2019: 425) explains that ethnic nationalism (which is ethnonationalism in its full term), is 'a mystical religious, and ethnocentric mindset predicated on tribal feelings'.
5. Fejos and Zentai's (2021) 'Hate Speech' study analysed social media messages in Europe.
6. Halikiopoulou and Vlandas' (2022) right-wing populism study discusses the main reasons for the electoral success of right-wing politics in Europe in recent years. Halikiopoulou and Vlandas' (2022) analysis of how right-wing ideology and subsequent politics work clearly applies in South Asia.

References

Alamgir, F., Bapuji, H., and Mir, R. 2022. Challenges and Insights from South Asia for Imagining Ethical Organisations: Introduction to the Special Issue', *Journal of Business Ethics*, 177: 717–728, 28 March. Accessed 26 June 2022. https://doi.org/10.1007/S10551-022-05103-3.

Alami, I., and Dixon, A.D. 2020. State Capitalisms(s) Redux? Theories, Tensions, Controversies. *Competition & Change*, 24 (1), 70–84, 1 January. Accessed 9 July 2022. https://doi.org/10.1177/1024529419881949.

Alami, I., Dixon, A.D., Gonzales-Vicente, R., Babic, M., Lee, S-O., Medby, I.A., and de Graaf, N. 2022. Geopolitics and the 'New' State Capitalism. *Geopolitics*, 27(3), 995–1023. Accessed 10 July 2022. https://doi.org/10.1080/1465004 5.2021.1924943.

Bourdieu, P., and Passeron, J-C. 1991. *Reproduction in Education, Society and Culture*. London: Sage Publications, in association with Theory, Culture and Society. Translated from the French by Richard Nice, with a Foreword by Tom Bottomore. Accessed 3 July 2022. https://monoskop.org/images/8/82/ Bourdieu_Pierre_Passeron_Jean_Claude_Reproduction_in_Education_ Society_and_Culture_1990.pdf.

Brattberg, E., and Feigenbaum, E.A. 2021. *Preface: China's Impact on Strategic Regions*. Washington DC: Carnegie Endowment for International Peace. 19 October. Accessed 4 July 2022. https://carnegieendowment.org/2021/ 10/13/china-s-influence-in-south-asia-vulnerabilities-and-resilience- in-four-countries-pub-85552.

BTI (Bertelsmann Stiftung's Transformation Index). (2022). *Country Report— Mauritius*. Gutersloh: Bertelsmann Stiftung. Accessed 6 July 2022. https:// bti-project.org/fileadmin/api/content/en/downloads/reports/country_ report_2022_MUS.pdf.

Chettri, M. 2022. New Jobs, New Spatialised Patriarchy: Creating Factory Workers in a Himalayan Pharmaceutical Hub. *Gender, Place and Culture*. Published online 18 July. Accessed 24 July 2022. https://doi.org/10.1080/0966369X. 2022.2099351.

Cuervo-Cazurra, A., Grosman, A., and Megginson, W. L. 2022. A Review of Internationalization of State-owned Firms and Sovereign Wealth Funds: Governments' Non-business Objectives and Discreet. *Journal of International Business Studies*, 11 May. Accessed 8 July 2022. https://doi.org/10.1057/ S41267-022-00522-W.

Dixon, A.D. 2022. The Strategic Logics of State Investment Funds in Asia: Beyond Financialisation. *Journal of Contemporary Asia*, 52(1), 127–151. Accessed 8 July 2022. https://doi.org/10.1080/00472336.2020.1841267.

Fakir, I. 2021. The Moroccan Monarchy's Political Agenda for Reviving Sufi Orders'. In Wehrey, F. (ed.), *Islamic Institutions in Arab States: Mapping the*

Dynamics of Control, Co-option, and Contention. Washington, DC: Carnegie Endowment for International Peace, pp. 121–132. Accessed 7 July 2022. https://carnegieendowment.org/files/202106-IslamicInstitutions-final-updated.pdf.

Farouk, Y., and Brown, N.J. 2021. Saudi Arabia's Religious Reforms Are Touching Nothing But Changing Everything. In *Islamic Institutions in Arab States: Mapping the Dynamics of Control, Co-option, and Contention*, ed. F. Wehrey, pp. 7–32. Washington, DC: Carnegie Endowment for International Peace. Accessed 5 July 2022. https://carnegieendowment.org/files/202106-IslamicInstitutions-final-updated.pdf.

Fejos, A., and V. Zentai, eds., with the contribution of M. Bladini, N. Igareda, A. Helmstad, A. Pascale, A. Schulze, R. Sette, S. Sicurella, E-M., Svenson, and C. Wilhem. 2021. Anti-Gender Hate Speech in Populist Right-Wing Social Media Communication. Barcelona: GENHA Project. Accessed 27 June 2022. http://genha.eu/sites/default/files/pdf/Anti-Gender%20Hate%20Speech%20in%20Populist%20Right-Wing%20Social%20Media%20Communication_0.pdf.

Flinders, M., and Hinterleitner, M. 2022. Party Politics Vs. Grievance Politics: Competing Modes of Representative Democracy. *Society*, pp. 1–10. PMID: 35308828, [Electronic Publication Ahead of Print] 14 March 2022. Accessed 29 June 2022. https://doi.org/10.1007/s12115-022-00686-z.

Frankel, B. 2020. *Capitalism Versus Democracy? Rethinking Politics in the Age of Environmental Crisis.* Melbourne: Greenmeadows. Accessed 27 June 2022. https://www.researchgate.net/publication/344738408_Capitalism_Versus_Democracy_Rethinking_Politics_in_the_Age_of_Environmental_Crisis.

Ginsburg, T. 2020. Authoritarian International Law? *American Journal of International Law*, 114 (2), 221–260, April 2020. Accessed 5 July 2022. https://doi.org/10.1017/ajil.2020.3.

Greitens, S.C. 2020. Surveillance, Security, and Liberal Democracy in the Post-COVID World. *International Organization* 74 (S1): E169–E190, December 2020. Accessed 6 July 2022. https://doi.org/10.1017/S0020818320000417.

Halikiopoulou, D., and Vlandas, T. 2022. Understanding Right Wing Populism and What to Do About It. Vienna: Friedrich-Ebert-Stiftung, April 2022. Accessed 28 June 2022. https://library.fes.de/pdf-files/bueros/wien/19110-20220517.pdf.

Hodson, G., Earle, M., and Craig, M.A. 2022. Privilege Lost: How Dominant Groups React to Shifts in Cultural Primacy and Power. *Group Processes & Intergroup Relations* 25 (3): 625–641, 20 April. Accessed 17 July 2022. https://doi.org/10.1177/13684302211070524.

Hopkins, D. 2021. Covid Crisis Deepens in Junta-Ruled Myanmar. *The Lowy Institute*, 12 July 2021. Accessed 7 July 2022. https://www.lowyinstitute.org/the-interpreter/debate/good-government-bad-government-politics-public-health.

Karatasli, S.S., and Kumral, S. 2022. Crisis of Capitalism and Cycles of Right-Wing Populism in Contemporary Turkey: The Making and Unmaking of Erdoganist Hegemony. *Journal of Agrarian Change*, Special Issue: Populism, Agrarian Movements and Progressive Politics, First published 30 June. Accessed 5 July 2022. https://doi.org/10.1111/joac.12501.

Kefford, G., Moffitt, B., and Werner, A. 2022. Nativism, Civic Nationalism and the Malleability of Voter Attitudes. *Acta Politica*, Published Online 12 July. Accessed 17 July 2022. https://doi.org/10.1057/S41269-022-00253-8.

Kelaidis, K. 2022. The Third Rome and the Caliphate: Understanding Religious Nationalism as Alternative Modernity. *Berkley Forum.* Georgetown University Berkley Center for Religion, Peace and World Affairs, 30 March. Accessed 6 July 2022. https://berkleycenter.georgetown.edu/responses/the-third-rome-and-the-caliphate-understanding-religious-nationalism-as-alternative-modernity.

Kim, K. 2022. Locating New 'State Capitalism' in Advanced Economies: An International Comparison of Government Ownership in Economic Entities. *Contemporary Politics,* 28 (3): 285–305, 28 December 2021. Accessed 5 July 2022. https://doi.org/10.1080/13569775.2021.2022335.

Kiniklioglu, S. 2022. Eurasianism in Turkey. *SWP (Stiftung Wissenschaft und Politik).* Research Paper 7, March 2022. Accessed 27 June 2022. https://www.swp-berlin.org/publications/products/research_papers/2022RP07_EurasianismInTurkey.pdf.

Kvangraven, I.H. 2022. Beyond Eurocentrism. *Aeon,* 15 April. Accessed 27 June 2022. https://aeon.co/essays/if-you-want-decolonisation-go-to-the-economics-of-samir-amin.

Kwan Lee, C. 2022. Hong Kong: Global China's Restive Frontier, First published online July 2022. London: Cambridge University Press. Accessed 24 July 2022. https://doi.org/10.1017/9781108914895.

Lim, G., and Khoon Ng, K. 2022. *How Malaysian Politics Shaped Chinese Real Estate Deals and Economic Development.* Washington, DC: Carnegie Endowment for International Peace, June 2022. Accessed 3 July 2022. https://carnegieendowment.org/files/202206-GuanieLim_KengKhoon Ng1.pdf.

Loewe, M., Zintl, T., and Houdret, A. 2021. The Social Contract as a Tool of Analysis: Introduction to the Special Issue on "Framing the Evolution of New Social Contracts in Middle Eastern and North African Countries. *World Development,* 45, article 104982, September 2021. Accessed 4 July 2022. https://doi.org/10.1016/j.worlddev.2020.104982.

Maizland, L. 2022a. Myanmar's Troubled History: Coups, Military Rule, and Ethnic Conflict. *Council on Foreign Relations (CFR): Backgrounder,* 31 January. Accessed 5 July 2022. https://www.cfr.org/backgrounder/myanmar-history-coup-military-rule-ethnic-conflict-rohingya.

———. 2022b. India's Muslims: An Increasingly Marginalized Population. *Council on Foreign Relations (CFR): Backgrounder,* 14 July. Accessed 17 July 2022. https://www.cfr.org/backgrounder/india-muslims-marginalized-population-bjp-modi.

Mansbridge, J., and Macedo, S. 2019. Populism and Democratic Theory. *Annual Review of Law and Social Science,* 15, 59–77, October 2019. Accessed 28 June 2022. https://doi.org/10.1146/annurev-lawsocsci-101518-042843.

Marzecki, R. 2020. Constructive Emotions? Patriotism as a Predictor of Civic Activity in Poland. *Italian Political Science Review/ Rivista Italiana di Scienza Politica* 50 (1): 33–51, March 2020. Accessed 6 July 2022. https://doi.org/10.1017/ipo.2019.15.

Midlarsky, M.I., and Lee, S. 2022. Distancing the Other: Religious Violence and Its Absence in South Korea. In *From Beyond the Death of God: Religion in 21st Century International Politics,* eds. S. Raudino and P. Sohn, pp. 380–410. Michigan: University of Michigan Press, May 2022. Accessed 7 July 2022. https://doi.org/10.3998/mpub.11866503.

Murphy, A. 2022. The Religions of South Asia. Asia Society: Centre for Global Education. Accessed 17 July 2022. https://asiasociety.org/education/religions-south-asia.

OHCHR (Office of the High Commissioner for Human Rights). 2022. UN Special Rapporteurs Appeal for Strong International Response in the Wake of 'Devastating' Executions by Myanmar Junta. *OHCHR Press Releases: Special Procedure,* 25 July 2022. Accessed 31 July 2022. https://www.ohchr.org/en/press-releases/2022/07/un-special-rapporteurs-appeal-strong-international-response-wake-devastating.

Reisach, U. 2021. The Responsibility of Social Media in Times of Societal and Political Manipulation. *European Journal of Operational Research* 291 (3): 906–917, 16 June. Accessed 27 June 2022. https://doi.org/10.1016/j.ejor.2020.09.020.

Rios, L. 2022. How a Feminist Uprising Reshaped Mexico City. *Bloomberg UK,* 8 March. Accessed 29 June 2022. https://www.bloomberg.com/news/features/2022-03-08/the-legacy-of-mexico-city-s-feminist-protest-movement.

Robinson, K. 2021. Understanding Sharia: The Intersection of Islam and the Law. *Council on Foreign Relations (CFR): Backgrounder,* 17 December. Accessed 28 June 2022. https://www.cfr.org/backgrounder/understanding-sharia-intersection-islam-and-law.

———. 2022. What Is Hezbollah? *Council on Foreign Relations (CFR): Backgrounder,* 25 May. Accessed 27 June 2022. https://www.cfr.org/backgrounder/what-hezbollah.

Sahoo, N. 2020. Mounting Majoritarianism and Political Polarization in India. In *Political Polarization in South and Southeast Asia: Old Divisions, New Dangers,* eds. T. Carothers and A. O'Donohue, pp. 9–232. Washington, DC: Carnegie Endowment for International Peace. Accessed 3 July 2022. https://carnegieendowment.org/files/Political_Polarization_RPT_FINAL1.pdf.

Saleem, R.M.A., Yilmaz, I., and Chacko, P. 2022. Civilization Populism in South Asia: Turning India Saffron. *Populism & Politics* (European Center for Populism Studies), article 9, 24 February 2022. Accessed 6 July 2022. https://www.populismstudies.org/wp-content/uploads/2022/03/Civilizationist-Populism-in-South-Asia-Turning-India-Saffron.pdf.

Shahin, S. 2022. News, Nations, and Power Relations: How Neoliberal Media Reproduce a Hierarchical World Order. *Critical Sociology*, pp. 1–16, 27 January. Accessed 27 June 2022. https://doi.org/10.1177/08969205211072455.

Singh, P. 2022. How Exclusionary Nationalism Has Made the World Socially Slicker from COVID-19. *Nationalities Papers* 50 (1): 104–117, January. Accessed 28 June 2022.

Tamir, Y. 2019. Not So Civic: Is There a Difference Between Ethnic and Civic Nationalism? *Annual Review of Political Science* 22: 419–434, May 2019. Accessed 26 June 2022. https://doi.org/10.1146/annurev-polisci-022018-024059.

United Kingdom Government (GOV.UK). 2022. Country Policy and Information Note: Critics of the Military Regime, Myanmar (Burma), July 2022 (accessible). *UK Visas and Immigration, Guidance Note*, Version 4.0, Updated 28 July. Accessed 31 July 2022. https://www.gov.uk/government/publications/burma-country-policy-and-information-notes/country-policy-and-information-note-critics-of-the-military-regime-myanmar-burma-july-2022-accessible#Freedom-of-speech.

Vaishnav, M. 2019. *Religious Nationalism and India's Future*. Washington DC: Carnegie Endowment for International Peace, 4 April. Accessed 5 July 2022. https://carnegieendowment.org/2019/04/04/religious-nationalism-and-india-s-future-pub-78703.

Verkuyten, M., Kollar, R., Gale, J., and Yogeeswaran, K. 2022. Right Wing Political Orientation, National Identification and the Acceptance of Immigrants and Minorities. *Personality and Individual Differences*, 184, article 111217, January 2022. Accessed 28 June 2022. https://doi.org/10.1016/j.paid.2021.111217.

Virdee, S. 2019. Racialized Capitalism: A Account of Its Contested Origins and Consolidation. *The Sociological Review* 67 (1): 3–27, 7 January. Accessed 27 June 2022. https://doi.org/10.1177/0038026118820293.

Wagner, C. 2022. India's Rise: on Feet of Clay? *SWP (Stiftung Wissenschaft und Politik)*. Research Paper 2, January 2022. Accessed 5 July 2022. https://www.swp-berlin.org/publications/products/research_papers/2022RP02_Indias_Rise.pdf.

Warburton, E. 2020. Deepening Polarization and Democratic Design in Indonesia. In *Political Polarization in South and Southeast Asia: Old Divisions, New Dangers*, eds. T. Carothers and A. O'Donohue, pp. 25–39. Washington, DC: Carnegie Endowment for International Peace. Accessed 4 July 2022. https://carnegieendowment.org/files/Political_Polarization_RPT_FINAL1.pdf.

Welsh, B. 2020. Malaysia's Political Polarization: Race, Religion, and Reform. In *Political Polarization in South and Southeast Asia: Old Divisions, New Dangers*, eds. T. Carothers, and A. O'Donohue, pp. 41–52. Washington, DC: Carnegie Endowment for International Peace. Accessed 10 July 2022. https://carnegieendowment.org/files/Political_Polarization_RPT_FINAL1.pdf.

Wibisono, S. Louie, W.R., and Jetten, J. 2019. A Multidimensional Analysis of Religious Extremism. *Frontiers in Psychology* 10, article 2560, 18 November. Accessed 6 July 2022. https://doi.org/10.3389/fpsyg.2019.02560.

World Bank. 2022. *South Asia: Overview*, 13 April. Accessed 26 June 2022. https://www.worldbank.org/en/region/sar/overview.

World Watch Research. 2021. *Bangladesh: Full Country Dossier*. Ermelo and Washington, DC: Open Doors International and World Watch Research, December 2021. Accessed 29 June 2022. https://www.opendoors.org.au/wp-content/uploads/2022/01/Full-Country-Dossier-Bangladesh-2022.pdf.

Wright, M., Wood, G., Musacchio, A., Okhmatovskiy, I., Grosman, A., and Doh, J.P. 2021. State Capitalism in International Context: Varieties and Variations. *Journal of World Business* 56 (2), article 101160, February 2021. Accessed 8 July 2022. https://doi.org/10.1016/j.jwb.2020.101160.

CHAPTER 2

Radical Monks and Rajapaksa: An Overview of Right-Wing Politics in Sri Lanka

Andrea Malji

INTRODUCTION

Sri Lanka is an island situated approximately 55 kilometers south of India. While many are quick to group Sri Lanka with its much larger neighbor to the north, one must be careful to transpose either nation upon one another. Not only will this comparison earn the ire of many Sri Lankan citizens, but it oversimplifies the island country. Like India, Sri Lanka is a complex and diverse country with a history of discord among ethnic and religious lines. Unlike India, Sri Lanka's transition into independence was notably peaceful and the newly independent country was considered a model for inclusive multi-ethnic governance (Wriggins 2011). However, the peaceful, inclusive nature of early independent Sri Lanka quickly faded and later escalated into a protracted civil war. Both India and Sri Lanka have seen an adoption of populist rhetoric and politics albeit both distinct to their respective homes. In Sri Lanka, populist majoritarianism mostly

A. Malji (✉)
Hawai'i Pacific University, Honolulu, HI, USA
e-mail: amalji@hpu.edu

B. S. Nayak, D. Chakraborty (eds.), *Interdisciplinary Reflections on South Asian Transitions,*
https://doi.org/10.1007/978-3-031-36686-4_2

coincided with linguistic and ethnic identity (Sinhalese/Sinhala); however, over time the movement increasingly adopted Buddhist nationalism as well.

The Sinhalese are an ethno-linguistic group that constitute approximately 74% of the population, around 96% of Sinhalese people are also Buddhists. The Tamil population are 15% of the remaining population, with 73% of them known as Sri Lankan Tamils who are concentrated in the north and eastern part of the island. The other 25% of Tamils are known as Indian Tamils and arrived during the colonial period primarily to work on tea plantations; most Indian Tamils live in the central provinces. Most Indian and Sri Lankan Tamils are Hindu. The remaining 9% of the population are known as Moor and are predominantly Muslim and speak Tamil.

Sri Lanka gained its independence from the United Kingdom in 1948. As the country, then known as Ceylon, moved toward self-governance in the previous decades, it adopted various British-influenced styles of governance, including a parliamentary style of democracy. The 1946 constitution, known as the Soulbury Constitution after the British-led royal commission, made Sri Lanka a commonwealth of the United Kingdom. The constitution was relatively progressive for its time and reinforced principles such as universal suffrage, protection of minorities, and secularism (DeVotta 2010). Sri Lanka was considered a relatively wealthy country at independence. Ceylon had served as a key provider of rubber to the allied forces during the Second World War and used the increased revenue to invest in education and healthcare (Holt 2011). Thus, at independence and presently, Sri Lanka has the highest literacy rate and life expectancy in South Asia (ibid.).

A key contention by Sinhalese advocates at the time, however, was that Sri Lankan institutions were historically unfair and favored Tamils (ibid.). They argued that the British colonial administration had prioritized the minority Tamil population for educational opportunities, which led to their dominance in colonial civil service and elite occupations, including education, law, and medicine. By doing so, this favoritism, they contend, led the majority population to be less successful than its minority counterparts. English-medium schools were disproportionately located in Tamil dominant areas, leading to Tamils speaking English at a higher rate compared to Sinhalese. Many had even traveled to study in the United Kingdom. Knowledge of English was especially favored and helped speakers secure jobs within the colonial bureaucracy. Because Tamils spoke

English at greater rates, this meant they had higher representation in many high-end professions compared to Sinhalese. Conversely, many Sinhalese felt upset that despite being the majority demographic, they had lower representation. This was seen as inequitable and thus was the driving force behind the rise in ethno-linguistic populist rhetoric by the Sinhalese population.

By 1955, S.W.R.D. Bandaranaike (1899–1959) and his newly formed Sri Lanka Freedom Party (SLFP) exploited this Sinhalese frustration and campaigned on making Sinhala the only official language. Bandaranaike was perhaps one of the most influential figures that integrated Sinhalese nationalism into Sri Lankan politics. He was a founder of the Sinhala Maha Sabha (SMS), which sought to promote Sinhalese Buddhist culture and language (Rambukwella 2017). The SMS originally joined the centrist United National Party (UNP) as part of a coalition but left the coalition in 1951 to form the Sri Lanka Freedom Party, a left-leaning Sinhalese nationalist party (Verite 2017). Following the SLFP's successful election in 1956, the Sinhala Only Act was passed in parliament, much to the disdain of the Tamil and leftist parties who, not surprisingly, opposed the bill. The ruling parties sought to codify these changes into the constitution shortly after.

CONSTITUTIONAL CHANGES IN SRI LANKA

Some of the progressive ideals put forth in the first Sri Lankan constitution began to quickly erode in the decade following independence. By 1949, the citizenship and voting rights of Indian Tamils, 12% of the population, were revoked (Shastri 1999). Parties like the SLFP, with pressure from many Buddhist organizations, including the *Sangha*, sought to further institutionalize these changes to increase Sinhalese representation across the board. In addition to passing the Sinhala Only Act in 1956, the government also allowed *pirivenas*, Buddhist centers of learning, to be converted into universities (Morrison 2001). By 1971, under the leftist United Front coalition, led by S.W.R.D. Bandaranaike's widow Sirimavo Bandaranaike, the government introduced the policy of standardization at universities. The policy of standardization introduced quotas that sought to reduce the number of Tamil students while increasing the proportion of Sinhalese (Wickramasinghe 2012).

Although the previous decades were eventful, the 1970s served as an instrumental shift. Two new constitutions were promulgated during the decade, one in 1972 and the other in 1978. These changes nurtured Sri Lanka's descent into conflict and gradual embrace of "Sinhalatva", or Sinhalese Buddhist nationalism. However, it should be noted this was not done at the hands of a right-wing government. In fact, the United Front was a coalition of leftist parties (Verite 2017). Thus, socialist ideals that were already embedded in the language of Sri Lanka's constitution were reinforced. Along with a commitment to free education and free health-care, the 1978 constitution changed the country's name from the Free, Sovereign, and Independent Republic of Sri Lanka to the Democratic Socialist Republic of Sri Lanka. The 1978 constitution also gave Buddhism special status (Schonthal 2016). This meant the minority Tamil commu-nity, which was not consulted prior to the constitutional changes, would face significant disadvantages in all walks of life. The 1978 constitution would become one of the trigger events that escalated ethnic tensions into a full-blown civil war and would incalculably change the trajectory of Sri Lanka's future.

The Rise of Sinhalese Nationalism and Ethno-nationalist Conflict

Although Sinhalese nationalism had been present since even before inde-pendence, it became more organized in the 1970s, especially as the Buddhist clergy became increasingly active in Sri Lankan politics. Under the banner of *Jathika Chintanaya* (National Ideology), various Buddhist movements justified violence and militancy toward non-Buddhists (Goonewardena 2020). At the same time, over 37 Tamil militant groups formed in the 1970s. Groups such as the Thangathurai-Kuttimuni, Tamil United Liberation Front (TULF), and Tamil New Tigers (predecessor to LTTE) began carrying out acts of arson and even assassinations in their quest for a sovereign state of Tamil Eelam (Richards 2014). While spo-radic violent resistance by Tamil militants occurred in the 1970s, the watershed moment that drastically shifted the intensity of violence occurred in July 1983, in what came to be known as Black July (Tambiah 2017).

On July 23, 1983, an LTTE cadre ambushed the Sri Lankan army in the northern city of Jaffna, killing 13 soldiers. Following the ambush, a five-day period of riots exploded throughout the country targeting Tamil communities throughout the country. The riots started in Colombo and spread throughout the country, killing 2000–3000 with especially brutal violence (Harrison 2003). Tamil homes and businesses were destroyed and nearly 200,000 Tamils became displaced. In Colombo alone 100,000 Tamils, more than half of the city's Tamil population, became homeless (Aspinall et al. 2013). This event marked the beginning of nearly three decades of ethnic violence that inundated the northern and eastern Tamil majority areas of the island. Although the LTTE existed prior to Black July, the groups' organizational capabilities and recruitment skyrocketed afterward and escalated the ethnic tensions into a full-blown civil war between government forces and the LTTE. Not surprisingly, the Tamil militancy fed into Sinhalese Buddhist nationalism as the quest for Tamil Eelam presented an existential threat to one of the only remaining homes of Theravada Buddhism.

The civil war proceeded in four stages of varying intensity: Eelam War I (1983–1987), Eelam War II (1987–1990), Eelam War III (1995–2002), Eelam War IV (2006–2009). During the civil war the LTTE targeted multiple Buddhist sites and figures, including bombing some of the Buddhism's holiest sites such as the Jaya Sri Maha Bodhi Buddhist shrine in 1985 and the temple of the tooth in 1988 (DeVotta 2007). In 1987 a bus carrying Buddhist monks was also attacked in Aranthalawa, killing 37 (ibid.). Together, these attacks were seen as a further attack upon Buddhist and Sinhalese identity and widened popular support for Sinhalese Buddhist nationalism and hardline tactics by the government. This increasing support helped spearhead new Buddhist monastic political parties such as the Sinhala Veera Vidhana (SVV), Sinhala Urumaya (SU), and Jathika Hela Urumaya (JHU) (DeVotta 2021a). Each of these movements sought to tie Buddhism more closely to the state.

Although the monastic parties were never quite successful, failing to win more than a few seats, their influence in state affairs continued to grow. This became especially true with the candidacy of Mahinda Rajapaksa in 2005. The monastic support of Rajapaksa was transformational for Sri Lankan politics and the civil war (Malji 2022a). Although previous leaders had expressed sympathy with Buddhist nationalist sentiment, it was Rajapaksa's embrace of hardline approaches, including ending the war by any means, that marked a shift in the political landscape. Within a year of his election, the fourth and final phase of the civil war commenced and as promised, Rajapaksa used unprecedented levels of violence. By 2009 the war ended and with it were allegations of widespread human rights violations, including civilian deaths, rape, torture, and disappearances, by Sri

Lanka's government. The exact number is unknown, but between 40,000 and 140,000 non-combatants may have died just in the final months of the war (Lalwani 2017). However, the government's official numbers are much lower at 8649 (Enumeration of Vital Events 2011).

The end of the civil war was a relief for many throughout the country and with it came the promise for a new beginning, especially for ethno-religious reconciliation. For Sinhalese Buddhists, Rajapaksa was seen as a war-hero for his role in ending the war. His popularity soared despite allegations of human rights abuses by the international human rights associations and a war crimes investigation by the UNHCR (OHCHR 2015). With the war now over, however, many Sinhalese nationalists saw this new era as an opportunity to fix previous errors and do everything possible to ensure the survival of the Sinhala language and Theravada Buddhism.

Sinhalatva Groups

The political dynamics of Sinhalese nationalism are complicated and don't easily fit into a left-right spectrum. For example, the SLFP and its leftist allies were the parties responsible for the 1978 exclusionary constitution. The SLFP became more centrist and closely tied with Buddhism over time (Verite 2017). The key opposition party to the SLFP, the UNP, was founded as a non-communal party (ibid.). Despite this, the UNP was responsible for the Ceylon Citizenship act that denied citizenship to most Indian Tamils living in Sri Lanka. The UNP was also in power during Black July and was criticized for its lack of action to quell the riots (ibid.). As an anti-Communist party, the UNP was ideologically more centrist than the SLFP and drew its primary support from the Sinhalese.

Despite their association with anti-minority policies, neither of the two key parties were explicitly nationalist in their platforms. Instead, figures from their respective parties, such as Bandaranaike and Rajapaksa, became known for their pro-Sinhalese ideologies. It wasn't until 2016 that an explicitly Sinhalese nationalist party became mainstream. The Sri Lanka Podujana Peramuna (SLPP) was established by Mahinda Rajapaksa and defines itself as a socially conservative populist party, although the SLPP maintained the left-leaning economic policies of the SLFP. The SLPP quickly became the face of Sinhalese Buddhist nationalism and its ties to radical Buddhist groups like the Bodu Bala Sena (BBS) made that link very clear (Subedi 2022).

The BBS is a far-right Sinhalese Buddhist nationalist organization that is openly anti-pluralist and wants to ensure Buddhism is protected and holds the foremost status in Sri Lanka. The organization consists of lay members and clergy and is led by Buddhist monk Galagoda Gnanasara. Like most of its hardline predecessors, the role of the BBS is to safeguard the status of Theravada Buddhism (Malji 2022a). Unlike its predecessors, the BBS has been more successful at mobilizing Sinhalese people throughout the country and speaking about the urgency of defending one of Buddhism's last remaining homeland. Whereas the BBS sees Sri Lanka as one of the last Buddhist homelands, they claim there are dozens of Christian and Muslim majority countries to protect Christianity and Islam. Therefore, the need to protect Sri Lanka's Buddhist identity is seen as urgent. Although the BBS maintains that Tamil extremism remains a problem, it's now seen as more of a secondary concern. Instead, the BBS focuses on what it considers threats from Islamic extremism and Christian missionaries. The BBS claims that Christian and Muslim groups, specifically those that evangelize and reject traditional Sri Lankan (i.e. Sinhalese) culture, are the greatest threat because they move the country further away from its Buddhist roots.

Following the establishment of the BBS, the group worked quickly to build a presence throughout the island. Rallies led by Buddhist monk Galagoda Gnanasara featured divisive and fiery messages that often escalated into violence and in some instances communal riots (Hay 2014). The BBS led a campaign to oppose what they consider any Islamization efforts and to reclaim Buddhist historical and heritage sites. At the forefront was a campaign against halal certification, which the group contended was a harmful slaughter method that imposes Islamic ways onto the Buddhist population (BBC 2013). The group also sought to ban the *niqab* (face veil) which they contend is a rejection of Sri Lankan culture (Malji 2021).

Social media also played an increasingly influential role from 2009 onward. The lack of content moderation for the Sinhalese language, especially on Facebook, meant that many harmful rumors were able to proliferate without intervention. In 2018, a Facebook video showed a Muslim restaurant owner in the eastern city of Ampara being confronted by a group of Sinhalese men asking in Sinhala if he put "Sterilization pills" in the food (Borham and Attanayake 2018). The man, who spoke Tamil, appeared to agree with the accusations. Once the allegations spread rapidly on social media, the man's business was burnt down by a mob (ibid.).

Four days later, violence erupted in the central city of Kandy following the death of a Buddhist taxi driver attributed to Muslim youth. The man's death led to some of the worst post-conflict violence in Sri Lanka with multiple mosques and Muslim businesses destroyed or vandalized. The attacks led the government to declare a state of emergency, which included a temporary shutdown of major social media sites (Rameez 2018). The riots were purported to be a crystalizing moment for some of the extremist elements in the country (Amarasingham 2019). One year later, on Easter 2019, the previously unknown National Tawheed Jamaat carried out one of the worst attacks in Sri Lanka's history.

On the morning of April 21st, Christian families throughout the country went to attend Easter services. At the same time, tourists were waking to attend breakfast at Colombo's most popular hotels. What should have been a joyful day was interrupted by eight suicide bombings throughout the country, primarily targeting churches and hotels. Over 250 people were killed in the attack (ibid.). By the end of the day, a sense of uncertainty and chaos enveloped Colombo. Once it became clearer that the attacks were carried out by an Islamic group, a sense of rage and a desire for justice also developed throughout the country. Within a week of the attack, Gotabaya Rajapaksa announced his candidacy for President (Gunasingham 2019). With the highest level of fear in more than a decade, Rajapaksa found a way to frame his Presidential campaign as one that would fight Islamic extremism and bring stability and justice to Sri Lanka.

When Rajapaksa announced his candidacy his focus and framing centered around anti-terrorism. He also relied on anti-minority tropes and Sinhalatva rhetoric to rally voters (ibid.). As former Secretary of Defense during Eelam War IV, Rajapaksa was known for his hardline stance against militancy. As Sinhalese fear of a new wave of violence was emerging, many sought a return to those same hardline policies as a means of protection from future possible violence. Rather than fight another protracted conflict, many wanted to squash any growing terrorist movement before it became more established. Rajapaksa certainly exploited that fear and made sure to embrace hardline Buddhist figures like Gnanasara during his candidacy (Klem and Samararatne 2022). Not surprisingly, Rajapaksa easily won the election, dominating in Sinhalese areas while performing poorly in Muslim and Tamil majority areas.

THE RAJAPAKSA REGIME

Within a year of Gotabaya Rajapaksa's election as President, his brother Mahinda was elected as Prime Minister, consolidating control of the government within one family and bringing the new SLPP party into power. Once in power, the early days of the Rajapaksa regime behaved predictably. Monks and family members were added to key government positions and panels (DeVotta 2021b), Sri Lanka withdrew from the UN Human Rights Council's justice and reconciliation process (ibid.), and the Tamil national anthem, which had been added as a show of solidarity in 2016, was removed from Independence Day events (ibid.). Sri Lanka further descended into instability once the Covid pandemic began.

The country was only a couple of months into the new Rajapaksa presidency when Covid began. The pandemic meant that Sri Lanka's government, like everywhere, had to change priorities and focus on public health management. Nevertheless, the Rajapaksa government used the pandemic to implement exclusionary policies, often in the name of public health and safety. One of the most controversial measures implemented by the government was the mandatory cremation of those that died with Covid (Marsoof 2020). Although cremation of the dead is widely practiced by both Hindus and Buddhists, it is considered forbidden by Muslims. This practice continued for nearly one year despite global outcry and insistence from global health agencies that cremation is not necessary to stop the spread of Covid (ibid.). The government also chose to implement a *niqab* (face veil) ban, citing security concerns (Gunasingham 2019). Tamil and Muslim areas also saw an increased security presence in their neighborhoods. During the first week of the lockdown, Rajapaksa also gave a Presidential pardon to Sunil Ratnayake, a soldier who had been sentenced to death by the Supreme Court for the torture and murder of Tamil civilians (Malji 2022b).

The Covid pandemic took a major toll on Sri Lanka. Sri Lanka's reliance on tourism meant that one of the main revenue streams, which was just starting to recover following the Easter attacks, was completely devastated. The potentially promising future that emerged in the first years following the cessation of the civil war had completely dissipated by 2020. Sri Lanka's economy was struggling and the Rajapaksa regime had failed to address a number of pressing economic and political issues, instead choosing to focus on appeasing nationalist sentiments, like increasing Sinhalese resettlement in Tamil areas.

Within two years a devastating financial crisis hit Sri Lanka and the country defaulted on multiple foreign debts. This default was for several reasons, but first and foremost because the country did not have enough revenue. Not only did Covid drastically reduce revenue and foreign remittances, but the consequence of Rajapaksa's drastic 2019 tax cuts meant the country was in an even more dire condition. When the Rajapaksa government came into power, it implemented the largest tax cuts in the country's history, which cut state revenue even more making the government further unable to pay its debts (ibid.). Rajapaksa also made catastrophic decisions such as an organic agriculture scheme that required farmers to quickly adopt organic fertilizer without providing easy access to it (ibid.). This failure meant that Sri Lanka had to import much of its food, including its staple rice crop (Jadhav and Jayasinghe 2022).

Protests gained momentum throughout the country and frustration with the Rajapaksa regime grew exponentially along with increasing misery for citizens. Residents waited in long queues for gasoline, school was cancelled for long stretches of time, and there was widespread food and medication shortages. Even the most loyal of SLPP and Rajapaksa supporters began to turn against him. As Sri Lanka advanced toward collapse in summer 2022, protests and fury continued to grow throughout the country. Key members of the government submitted resignations and a growing number also called on Rajapaksa to resign. In a scene that made Sri Lanka a household name throughout the world, protestors raided and occupied the Presidential palace, leading Rajapaksa to subsequently flee the country to Maldives and then Singapore (BBC 2022).

It is yet unclear if the support for Sinhalese Buddhist nationalism has diminished alongside the Rajapaksa legacy. At the time of this publication, Sri Lanka remains unstable as it attempts to recover from the 2022 economic collapse. The current President Ranil Wickremesinghe of the UNP was elected by the parliament following Rajapaksa's exile. Wickremesinghe is seen by many as a Rajapaksa ally and part of the establishment. However, Wickremesinghe and the parliament have taken some important steps to potentially change Sri Lanka's course and potentially diminish authoritarian tendencies. For example, in October 2022 a constitutional amendment was approved to limit Presidential powers (Jayasinghe 2022). Expanded Presidential powers were repeatedly exploited under previous Sri Lankan Presidents, especially during the civil war. The limitation of powers will hopefully lead Sri Lanka to a more democratic and inclusive future.

CONCLUSION

Sri Lanka is now a far cry from the newly independent picturesque country analysts once praised. Its progressive ideals were traded for exclusionary policies and nationalism. The government of Sri Lanka has continued to reject opportunities to establish a more inclusive government. Instead, the promise of security and retribution for historical inequities toward Sinhalese Buddhists has been the defining and powerful political force. Although this nationalist political stance has not always aligned with right-wing politics, the rise of the SLPP, BBS, and the Rajapaksa clan in the mid-2010s meant an adoption of hardline and divisive militaristic approaches.

Despite the instability it unleashed, the summer 2022 crisis provided an opportunity for a reset. For most of its post-colonial history, Sri Lanka's lawmakers have embraced exclusionary Sinhalese Buddhist nationalist policies. Decades of evidence demonstrate that these divisive policies have failed to benefit most citizens. The dramatic rise and fall of the Rajapaksa family brings the opportunity for an investment in a more inclusive, non-dynastical, future government. However, as long as extremist clergy continue to hold influence within the government, this future will not be possible. A stable opposition party that rejects identity politics is essential, Sri Lanka's future depends upon it.

REFERENCES

Amarasingham, A. 2019. Terrorism on the Teardrop Island: Understanding the Easter 2019 Attacks in Sri Lanka. *CTC Sentinel* 12 (5): 1–10.

Aspinall, E., R. Jeffrey, and A.J. Regan, eds. 2013. *Diminishing Conflicts in Asia and the Pacific: Why Some Subside and Others Don't.* Vol. 13. Routledge.

BBC. 2013. The Hardline Buddhists Targeting Sri Lanka's Muslims. https://www.bbc.com/news/world-asia-21840600

———. 2022. Sri Lanka: President Gotabaya Rajapaksa Flees the Country on Military Jet. https://www.bbc.com/news/world-asia-62132271

Borham, M., and D. Attanayake. 2018. Tension in Ampara After Fake 'Sterilization Pills' Controversy. *Sunday Observer.* www.sundayobserver.lk/2018/03/04/news/tensionampara-after-fake-'sterilization-pills'-controversy.

DeVotta, N. 2007. Sinhalese Buddhist Nationalist Ideology: Implications for Politics and Conflict Resolution in Sri Lanka. *East-West Center. Policy Studies* 40.

———. 2010. Politics and Governance in Post-Independence Sri Lanka. In *Routledge Handbook of South Asian Politics*, 118–130. Routledge.

———. 2021a. The Genesis, Consolidation, and Consequences of Sinhalese Buddhist Nationalism. In *When Politics Are Sacralized: Comparative Perspectives on Religious Claims and Nationalism*, 187–212. Cambridge University Press.

———. 2021b. Sri Lanka: The Return to Ethnocracy. *Journal of Democracy* 32 (1): 96–110.

Enumeration of Vital Events (Northern Province). 2011. *Department of Census and Statistics, Sri Lanka.*

Goonewardena, K. 2020. Populism, Nationalism and Marxism in Sri Lanka: From Anti-Colonial Struggle to Authoritarian Neoliberalism. *Geografiska Annaler: Series B, Human Geography* 102 (3): 289–304.

Gunasingham, A. 2019. Sri Lanka Attacks. *Counter Terrorist Trends and Analyses* 11 (6): 8–13.

Harrison, F. 2003. Twenty Years on-Riots that Led to War. *BBC News.* http://news.bbc.co.uk/1/hi/world/south_asia/3090111.stm.

Hay, M. 2014. Meet the Violent Monks Starting Riots in Sri Lanka. VICE. www.vice.com/en/article/av4jye/meet-the-violent-buddhists-starting-riots-and-killing-muslims-in-sri-lanka.

Holt, J. 2011. Introduction. In *The Sri Lanka Reader*, ed. J. Holt, 607–617. Durham: Duke University Press.

Jadhav, R., and Jayasinghe, U. 2022. India Starts Supplying Rice to Sri Lanka in First Major Food Aid. *Reuters.* https://www.reuters.com/world/asia-pacific/india-starts-supplying-rice-sri-lanka-first-major-food-aid-2022-04-02/.

Jayasinghe, U. 2022. Sri Lanka Passes Constitutional Amendment Aimed at Trimming Presidential Powers. *Reuters.* https://www.reuters.com/world/asia-pacific/sri-lanka-passes-constitutional-amendment-trim-presidential-powers-2022-10-21/.

Klem, B., and D. Samararatne. 2022. Sri Lanka in 2021: Vistas on the Brink. *Asian Survey* 62 (1): 201–210.

Lalwani, S. 2017. Size Still Matters: Explaining Sri Lanka's Counterinsurgency Victory Over the Tamil Tigers. *Small Wars & Insurgencies* 28 (1): 119–165.

Malji, A. 2021. Gendered Islamophobia: The Nature of Hindu and Buddhist Nationalism in India and Sri Lanka. *Studies in Ethnicity and Nationalism* 21 (2): 172–193.

———. 2022a. *Religious Nationalism in Contemporary South Asia.* Cambridge University Press.

———. 2022b. The Covid-19 Pandemic and Deepening Marginalization in Sri Lanka. In *The Covid-19 Crisis in South Asia*, 38–54. Routledge.

Marsoof, A. 2020. The Constitutionality of Forced Cremations of COVID-19 Victims in Sri Lanka. *People's Rights Group of Sri Lanka* 8.

Morrison, B. 2001. The Transformation of Sri Lankan Society, 1948–1999: The Fragmentation of Centralism. *Journal of Asian and African Studies* 36 (2): 181–202.

OHCHR. 2015. *Report of the OHCHR Investigation on Sri Lanka.*

Rambukwella, H. 2017. Locations of Authenticity: SWRD Bandaranaike of Sri Lanka and the Search for Indigeneity. *The Journal of Asian Studies* 76 (2): 383–400.

Rameez, A. 2018. Resurgence of Ethno-Religious Sentiment Against Muslims in Sri Lanka: Recent Anti-Muslim Violence in Ampara and Kandy. *Journal of Politics and Law* 11 (4).

Richards, J. 2014. An Institutional History of the Liberation Tigers of Tamil Eelam (LTTE). *The Centre on Conflict, Development, and Peacebuilding.*

Schonthal, B. 2016. Securing the Sasana Through Law: Buddhist Constitutionalism and Buddhist-Interest Litigation in Sri Lanka. *Modern Asian Studies* 50 (6): 1966–2008.

Shastri, A. 1999. Estate Tamils, the Ceylon Citizenship Act of 1948 and Sri Lankan Politics. *Contemporary South Asia* 8 (1): 65–86.

Subedi, D.B. 2022. The Emergence of Populist Nationalism and 'Illiberal' peace-building in Sri Lanka. *Asian Studies Review* 46 (2): 272–292.

Tambiah, S.J. 2017. The Colombo Riots of 1983. In *The Sri Lanka Reader*, ed. J. Holt, 641–647. Durham: Duke University Press.

Verite Research. 2017. Mapping Sri Lanka's Political Parties: Actors and Evolutions. https://www.veriteresearch.org/wpcontent/uploads/2018/06/Mapping_Sri_Lanka_s_Political_Parties_Actors_and_Evolution.pdf.

Wickramasinghe, N. 2012. Democracy and Entitlements in Sri Lanka: The 1970s Crisis Over University Admission. *South Asian History and Culture* 3 (1): 81–96.

Wriggins, H. 2011. After Forty-Five Years. In *The Sri Lanka Reader*, ed. J. Holt, 607–617. Durham: Duke University Press.

CHAPTER 3

Nostalgia of Monarchy and Contemporary Right-Wing Politics in Nepal

Manish Jung Pulami

INTRODUCTION

South Asia has witnessed the rise of right-wing politics in the first two decades of the twenty-first century. Many point out this *democratic erosion* to the faulty lines and crisis of the neo-liberal order (Chacko and Jayasuriya 2018; Levitsky and Ziblatt 2018). Additionally, the increased populist political practices based on religion, caste, language, geography, and ethnicity have played a critical role in the growth of right-wing populism in the region. The creation of the rigid hierarchies based on the criteria mentioned above, further enhanced by the traumatic experience of colonialism, wars of independence, and internal conflicts, has intensified the body of right-wing politics. A different perspective in studying the contemporary right-wing politics in the region is the nostalgic memories created in the past. A different outlook towards the popular study of right-wing politics in the region might be the nostalgic monarchical ideology prevalent in Nepal.

M. J. Pulami (✉)
Nepalese Military Academy, Bhaktapur, Nepal

B. S. Nayak, D. Chakraborty (eds.), *Interdisciplinary Reflections on South Asian Transitions*,
https://doi.org/10.1007/978-3-031-36686-4_3

It is not always true that monarchy ought to be an authoritarian rule by a single 'divine' individual. However, throughout the political history of civilised humankind, there has been the development of the monarchical system, which has fit themselves with the liberal and neo-liberal values (Tridimas 2021). The idea of a constitutional monarchy practised in the countries like the United Kingdom, Denmark, Bhutan, Bahrain, and others has proven to place the *divine* and the people perfectly in the same political system (Stepan et al. 2014). Many left-wing political parties with Marxist or Leninist perspectives have contestation about this form of a political system, but many prefer this *divinity*. The number of monarchies around the globe primarily decreased with time, but the presence of the two perspectives has divided the people into the two sides of the political spectrum and equally has kept right-wing politics breathing in contemporary times.

The monarchy and church have always been coupled with religion. The studies relating to European Kings and church are plenty. Nevertheless, it is essential to know about how the monarchies in other places of the globe are associated with religion. In South Asia, Nepal was the only country with a Hindu King, and in Bhutan, the King is said to be the protector of the state religion of Mahayana Buddhism (Aris 1994). Thus, more than 80 per cent of the people follow the Hindu religion in Nepal, among which more than half of the population are with a nostalgic memory of the monarchy, which has been jogged by political instability and failure after officially ousting the King in 2008.

As a result, the popularity among the Nepalese has increased regarding the monarchy and state religion as Hinduism. The political parties, particularly Rastriya Prajatantra Party (RPP), which supports Hindu nationalism and constitutional monarchy, have tremendously gained support. Although the Communists and the Socialists have more considerable support among the people in Nepal, this right-wing agenda cannot be discarded from the Nepalese political discourse. The study of Nepalese right-wing politics shall provide a different outlook on the right-wing discourse in South Asia. How did the Nepalese perceive King? What is the image of the King in contemporary Nepalese society? Why do people in the country want the King as the Head of the State? What is the role of religion in Nepalese politics? Moreover, how can we relate monarchy with Hinduism? What are its implications? This set of questions is fundamental in order to understand the emergence of nostalgic memory of monarchy, which is the cause for the increase in the degree of right-wing politics in Nepal.

Thus, this chapter focuses on providing answers to the crucial but undermined aspects of Nepalese politics. With the political change, many have missed these aspects, but this study believes that these are among the crucial aspect of Nepalese politics and for the study of the pattern of the rise of right-wing politics in South Asia.

The Ideas of 'King' in Nepalese Society

The monarchs have always been placed at the highest value in any society. They were called to be a *divine* individual with royal and political legitimacy. However, this divinity is thought to be a western concept or Christian values, later called a divine theory or divine rights of King (Straka 1962). Nevertheless, the idea of a monarch, in almost all societies, originates from the attributes of God's will (Straka 1962). From the beginning, this *divinity* of the individuals from a specific family or dynasty has been questioned and challenged. However, the monarchy has been an enduring institution and a symbol of societal stability (Woodford 2013).

The idea of monarchy and Kings may not appeal to the people who have not experienced themselves, or anti-monarchist modernists may have apprehensions about this idea. Many people might think, 'how does an idea of a single individual becoming King because of birth make sense?' Even in South Asia, the idea of monarchy may be a *thing* of the past; however, for the people in Nepal and Bhutan it was a recent but gone phenomenon or ongoing political system, respectively. In Nepal, the idea of monarchy still appeals to many people against the Federal Democratic Republic system. The initiation of monarchy in Nepal, as the modern nation-state, can be dated back to King Prithvi Narayan Shah, who started the unification campaign in 1799 (Stiller 2017). Before that as well, the petty states used to be ruled by monarchs of their own.

Neither history nor politics particularly mention the people's perception of their monarch, but through a sociological view, the idea of a monarch before the nation-building stage for Nepal was associated with a powerful, wealthy, and Godly person. Regarding the justification of the unification campaign by King Prithvi Narayan Shah, an evangelical legend is prevalent among the Nepalese that Guru Gorakhnath (a Hindu Yogi) blessed the King to unify the country (Acharya 1966). As such, the Kings of Nepal (descendants of King Prithvi Narayan Shah) have been thought to be the God themselves or the *avatars* of God (Acharya 1994). In Hindu mythology, the Kings are considered to be the forms of Narayan or Vishnu (the Protector) (Appleton 2016). Thus, the Kings of Nepal were also considered to be the forms of Lord Vishnu. In this manner, in a country of the majority of followers of Hinduism, the idea was that King was not a human but a Godly figure who could protect and feed them.

Moreover, the history of politics of Nepal has mainly revolved around the Kings. This might be the politics of historiography or could be confirmed as the politics used to revolve around the King because of the powers vested in him. The King of Nepal has mostly been portrayed as a stable figure or a figure of stability. Previous to 1950, which was before the introduction of democracy, they have been attributed mainly to a Godly figure, essential for the country at that time. However, with the introduction of democracy and the vital role of King Tribhuvan in that process, the Kings of Nepal have been considered saviour figure. With the unstable nature of domestic politics of the country, the Kings were considered to be stable political figures. This symbol of stability played a considerable role in the Nepalese consciousness. This reflected the trustworthiness, dependability, and reliability among the citizens.

After King Tribhuvan, his son Mahendra became the King of Nepal in 1955. In 1960, King Mahendra introduced a party-less Panchayat system alleging the governments to have been involved in corruption, failed to promote national interests and maintain law and order in the country (Shaha 1990). This portrayed King Mahendra to be a strong and powerful monarch of the nation who was righteous at the same time. He promoted the three pillars of Nepalese identity, which were Hinduism as religion, Nepali as a language, and monarchy. This essentially indoctrinated into the Nepalese consciousness. This has a huge role to play in the contemporary nostalgia of monarchy. His many reforms in diverse areas during this Panchayat system also established him as a figure of action rather than words and promises. So, King Mahendra's reign has been a landmark in developing the idea of 'King' in Nepalese society.

After his death, King Birendra ascended the throne of King of Nepal. During his reign, there was the reintroduction of democracy and the end of the Panchayat system, introducing a constitutional monarchy in Nepal. This led to King Birendra being admired by both monarchists and supporters of democracy. His decent and humble stature made him the people's King. However, he and his family were massacred in 2001 (Jha 2014). This traumatic incident induced a series of emotions in the country. It started more hatred towards the political parties and admiration for the royal family. After his death, his brother King Gyanendra became the ruling monarch. His reputation was shattered in public by anti-monarchists, but the perception of the people also changed when he took over power from a democratically elected government and became the *absolute* ruler of the country (Jha 2014). This defamed the idea of monarchy in Nepal. After 2008, Nepal was no more a monarchy, and the country became the Federal Democratic Republic of Nepal and a secular country.

Nevertheless, the idea of secularity and tremendous change in the state religion of Nepal was a massive blow to the Hindu people. Since 2008, the country has been subject to political instability, turmoil, and underdevelopment. The deteriorating political situation in Nepal has changed the mood of the Nepalese people and lured them to seek a more stable, reliable, and dependable figure. This has turned them again towards the monarchy. With this, some political parties have advocated the reinstating of monarchy in the country along with Hinduism. This has been the rise of right-wing politics in Nepal. The idea of a King in the Nepalese society plays a vital role in the right-wing politics of the country.

Democratic Changes and Voices for Monarchy

The democratic movements in the early 1950s in Nepal against the autocratic Rana regime led to the introduction of democracy in Nepal. King Tribhuvan announced the end of the 104 years of the Rana regime and promised a democratically elected government in the country. However, although he was a leading figure in the introduction of democracy, he could not hold elections and died. His son, King Mahendra, introduced a new constitution in 1959 and, in the same year, held the elections for the national assembly (Joshi and Rose 2004/1966). Bishweshwar Prasad Koirala became the first democratically elected Prime Minister of Nepal. However, King Mahendra dissolved the parliament and started a direct and political party-less system in the country, citing the incapability of the Government to rule the country (Joshi and Rose 2004/1966).

Although a direct rule from the King, his rule is much remembered because of the development works in the country and the enhancement of its image among the international community. He is known as a strong King who did not submit himself to the hegemonic behaviour of the Southern neighbour. Thus, he is known as an influential political figure in Nepal amidst the geopolitical changes in the region. However, there was a strong will among the people to overthrow the 'controlled democracy'.

In 1990, the political parties started a People's Movement and reintro-
duced democracy in Nepal with the King as the Head of the State and the
Prime Minister as an executive (Pathak 2012). In 2001, there was a Royal
Massacre which wiped out the whole family of King Birendra, and his
brother Gyanendra became the King of Nepal (Jha 2014).

Moreover, the Maoists launched a People's War against the Nepalese
monarchy and the Government in 1996, referring to caste-based discrimination, oppression, and social exclusion (Chhetri 2018). This led to a
decade-long war between the Maoists and the Government, which can be
characterised by a massive change in the political system but also by war
crimes and human rights violations (Chhetri 2018). When King Gyanendra
started an *absolute* rule in 2005, about a year later, the People's Movement
was started, which eventually led the King to reinstate the parliament
(Pathak 2012). On 21 November 2006, Prime Minister Girija Prasad
Koirala and the Chairman of the Maoists signed a Comprehensive Peace
Agreement (CPA) promising peace and democracy in the country (Jha
2014). The Constituent Assembly elections were held in 2008, and the
newly elected Constituent Assembly ended the 240-year-old monarchy in
Nepal and established the country as a Federal Democratic Republic (Jha
2014). With the change in the political system of the country, it declared
Nepal as a secular country ending Hinduism as the state religion
(Bishwakarma 2019). In 2015, Nepal promulgated a constitution through
the Constituent Assembly.

After such tremendous democratic changes in the country, why are
there voices for the return of monarchy along with Hinduism as a state
religion? The question is very critical to answering the rise of right-wing
politics in Nepal. The supporters of monarchy and removal of secularism
in the country are increasing. The appeal for the return to monarchy actually comes from a huge dissent and dissatisfaction with the current
Nepalese politics. The 'political instability' is the word that could define
the current political situation in Nepal. The frequent changes in the
Government and leaders involved in the power politics have created discontent among the Nepalese citizens (Einsiedel et al. 2012). This has
trashed the Nepalese hopes for economic rejuvenation and infrastructural
development. The promises made during the People's War and People's
Movement have been shattered by political instability. The political disorder has led to the failure to strengthen federalism in the country. The
shrinking space of Nepal in the international community, increasing corruption in bureaucracy and judiciary, deteriorating health and education

sectors, inflation, unemployment, and degrading quality of life among the people have induced frustration. This has come as a psychological shock to the Nepalese.

Amidst this, the people have started to seek political stability and hopes for the country to change from this instability and chaos. The appeal for the return of the monarchy to the country has been a psychological phenomenon for the Nepalese. The shock among the Nepalese caused because of political instability and disorder has induced nostalgia for stability in the country. The people, while seeking such, have turned to the monarchy, as in the past, the monarchs have been the symbol of stability, protection, and hope. This support for the return of the monarchy in Nepal among a particular group of people comes as a nostalgia for stability and security in Nepal, which they have been missing from the political parties. The shift in the public perception of monarchy ignites right-wing politics, and acceptance of some hierarchies is essential and natural (Bobbio and Cameron 1996).

Moreover, the nostalgia for monarchy in contemporary times comes with the attachment to the notion of Hinduism. Before the declaration of Nepal as a secular country, Nepal was the only Hindu Kingdom in the world. This has been portrayed as the symbol of pride in the international community by right-wing politicians (Sherpa 2021). They assume the image of the country is deteriorating among the international community. The right-wing politics in Nepal portray the failure of the governments in the foreign policy and diplomatic domain as a humiliation. Thus, Nepal, as the only Hindu Kingdom, is taken as a matter of identity and pride. Establishing Nepal as the Hindu Kingdom mainly focuses on instituting an identity of the country based on religion rather than founding Hindu fundamentalism (Dahal 2016). The desire for a Hindu nation has coexisted with the need for the monarchy to be restored. The reason for this is because the monarchy and Hinduism have merged, and the King is thought of as the *avatar* (form) of the Hindu deity Vishnu.

The essence of the Hindu nation has become much more alluring in recent years. The desire to return to the past is shared by many people, not only royalists. The growth of Hindu nationalism and the desire for the establishment of a Hindu state can be attributed to a number of factors. The Hindu nationalist Bharatiya Janata Party (BJP)'s power in India has had a significant impact on Nepal as well. Hindu nationalists in Nepal have found an ally in the BJP (Poudel 2021). The Hindu nationalists on both sides of the border have united in this matter despite the Nepalese propensity to express their own identity by frequently 'othering' India. The changes taking place in Nepal, in some ways, mirror a worldwide phenomenon. The majority groups that had historically held sway in many nations are resisting so-called progressive policies meant to advance the interests of minorities (Poudel 2021). Hindus are the ones at the forefront in Nepal.

CONTEMPORARY RIGHT-WING POLITICS IN NEPAL

One of the exceptional features of the constitutional monarchies is the separation of monarchy and the Government, who, however, act responsibly for the crown (Bulmer 2017). Walter Bagehot states that the monarchy is the dignified one, whereas the Government is the efficient one (Douglas-Home and Kelly 2000). Nevertheless, the efficient part of the crown, the Government, should always protect the dignified part of the monarchy and preserve its primal role in the system (Douglas-Home and Kelly 2000). The monarchist is referred to as the right wing in the political spectrum (Bulmer 2017). The monarchists' view on the inevitable hierarchy and order essential for society places them on the right side of the political spectrum. Their justification of the monarchical hierarchy on the basis of natural law and tradition further supports their stand. Moreover, the rise of religion as a factor in right-wing politics is increasing (Lienesch 1982). The monarchy is portrayed as the right-wing force for national greatness by the religious reactionaries (Upadhyaya 2017). These right-wing politics not only focus on following a single religion but also on certain cultural, social, and religious norms of the general populace (Upadhyaya 2017). These conservative forces want to impose the concept of national, linguistic, regional, cultural, and religious chauvinism on everything (Ganguly 2008).

Unlike any South Asian country, a different wave of right-wing politics can be observed in Nepal. There are political forces in the country who have been campaigning to reinstate the traditional hierarchical order of monarchy and, along with it, the Hindu nationalism among the Nepalese populace. One such right-wing political party is Rastriya Prajatantra Party (RPP). The formation of this political party by the ruling elites in 1990 depicts its position as the right-wing political party. It was established as an alternative force to the major political parties after the reintroduction of democracy in Nepal. The RPP is ideologically based on the idea of establishing a constitutional monarch (Republica 2017). Although the

Constituent Assembly 2008 officially ousted the monarchy and declared Nepal a secular country, the RPP has been in support of the monarchy and reinstating the country as a Hindu state (Republica 2017). However, the party also promises to provide religious freedom. This party is now led by Rajendra Lingden. Looking at the history of the party in the democratic election shows some support of people for the party's ideology.

Nevertheless, the party has been negatively affected because of splits (The Himalayan Times 2016). Presently, the former Chairman of the RPP has split and reformed a separate party called Rastriya Prajatantra Party-Nepal (RPP-N) (Republica 2022). This has created instability among the supporters of the agenda of monarchy and Hindu nationalism in Nepal. The other right-wing parties emphasising Hindu nationalism are Akhanda Nepal Party, Shivsena Nepal, Hindu Prajatantrik Party, Nepal Rastrabadi Gorkha Parishad, and Shanti Party Nepal (some are not registered with Election Commission Nepal). However, RPP and RPP-N are the political parties with national prominence. Hence, it can be observed that there are right-wing political parties supporting the monarchy and Hindu state in Nepal.

The idea of Hindu nationalism in Nepal has always been afloat in the political discourse from 2008 and after the promulgation of the constitution in 2015. The political protests and demonstrations in Nepal in support of the Hindu state have been a common phenomenon. Religious leaders have supported the cause of these political right-wings in several instances. Notably, the aim of the right-wing political parties has been to re-establish the Hindu identity for Nepal. Analysts predict that when some groups within Nepal's political parties, which were instrumental in the country's conversion to a republic state, show signs of wanting to return to the former status, calls for a Hindu state may intensify (Lal 2022). Moreover, while analysing contemporary right-wing politics, it is vital to observe some of the incidents that have spurred Hindu nationalism in the country. The former Prime Minister K.P. Sharma Oli, who is a Communist leader, visited Pashupatinath and spelt out that 'thori' (a place in Parsa District of Nepal) as the birthplace of Lord Ram (Giri 2021). These incidents have also increased Hindu nationalism in Nepal at the present time.

Moreover, the increase in Hindu politics, which many point out as 'saffron politics' in India, has also played a more significant role in Nepal's right-wing politics (Poudel 2021). The rise of the Hindu fundamentalist party, the Bharatiya Janata Party (BJP), in India has supported the rise in Nepal as well. The BJP has acted as an ally for the Hindu nationalists in

Nepal. In a letter to the Nepali Prime Minister in 2015, BJP leader and Chief Minister of Uttar Pradesh Yogi Aditya Nath claimed that Nepal had to become a Hindu state and outlawed conversion to another faith (Srivastava 2014). At that time, the draft of the Nepali constitution was about to be completed. Aditya Nath has previously stated that a Hindu ruler and Hindu culture were an integral part of Nepal's spirit and that Nepal would fall apart without them (Nepali Times 2007). In 2016, he accepted the former King Gyanendra Shah's invitation to a religious gathering in Nepal. He has often declared the desire for Nepal to be converted back into a Hindu state (Poudel 2021).

The Prime Minister of India, Narendra Modi, has also visited Nepal on a pilgrimage and paid visits to Janakpur, Muktinath, and Pashupatinath during his two-day stay in Nepal in 2018. He stressed Nepal's and India's shared religious and cultural heritage. The visit, according to many opponents back then, was primarily intended to shore up Hindu voters' support in India (Adhikari 2018). Hindu Janajagruti Samiti and other Indian Hindu organisations have supported the revival of the Hindu state through internet campaigns (Sarkar 2021).

Future of Right-Wing Politics in Nepal: The King and the Hindu Nation

Although there have been contestations and dissatisfactions by a specific group about Nepal turning to federalism and republicanism along with secularism, the future of monarchy and Nepal as a Hindu nation seems improbable. Returning back to the previous model of the political system has no space after a huge political change made possible through a decade-long People's War and People's Movement. After splitting the RPP, the Chairman of the RPP-N, Kamal Thapa, declared that the party had left the agenda of restoration of the monarchy in Nepal. He repeated that the King had no place in the present political scenario (Khabarhub 2022). He even formed an alliance with the Communist Party of Nepal-Unified Marxist-Leninist (CPN-UML) in the recent local elections (Khabarhub 2022). Although the right-wing political party, the Rastriya Prajatantra Party (RPP), has been continuously present in the elections and has won several seats in the parliament, its presence has been negligible. In the 2017 elections, the RPP only won 1 seat out of 275 seats in the House of Representatives (Baral 2019). The right-wing party has been crucial at various times for forming a coalition government but has not been able to put forward its agenda of monarchy and a Hindu nation.

Some argue about the possibility of the likely return of the monarchy and Hindu nationalism in Nepal because of the rise of such forces in India. The major leaders of the BJP have pointed out the inevitability of the monarchy in Nepal (Pillalamarri 2014). The supporters of the monarchy and Hindu nationalism indicate the presence of parliamentarians in the parliament from RPP as a sign of people wanting the right-wing's agenda. However, the functionality of the parliamentarians on the core agenda of the party has not been satisfactory; instead, they have been more involved in power politics. The conspiracy about secularism that it was never an agenda of the people to wipe out Nepal's identity as a Hindu nation but a western construction has been widespread among the mass. This conspiracy has been only limited to talks among the people, but none has been able to prove so. Considering the increase in the people's perception of the monarchy and Hindu nationalism, the upcoming elections will provide the pathway to the future of right-wing politics in Nepal. However, although right-wing politics may have an uncertain future, they shall be a constant force in Nepalese society and politics.

CONCLUSION

There has been a constant rise in right-wing politics around the globe. South Asia is among the reason why there has been a significant increase in right-wing politics. Many people focus on the study of India, Pakistan, and Bangladesh; however, Nepal is an exceptional case to study. Nepal, as a monarchy for more than two centuries, was turned into a federal republic and secular country a few years back. A larger populace has witnessed the rule under the monarchy, and the knowledge of politics has indoctrinated some people with monarchy as a symbol of stability, power, and reliability. The idea of a King in Nepal is as exact and different from the same time as in any part of the world. He has been portrayed as a Godly figure and a symbol larger than life. The appeal for the return of monarchy comes from the nostalgic memory of monarchy in contemporary times of political instability and the incapability of the state to develop and prosper.

Moreover, along with the monarchy asked for the Hindu state to be inter-connected. Nepal was the only Hindu Kingdom in the world with a Hindu monarch. It was a part of the national identity of Nepal. Today, the right-wing people claim that this was a part of national pride and thus should be reinstated along with monarchy in the country, with more than 80 per cent of the population being Hindu. Thus, there are several right-wing political parties, among which the Rastriya Prajatantra Party (RPP) is among the most influential in the country. It has been putting forward the idea of a constitutional monarchy and Hindu nation for Nepal. Furthermore, there have been rising protests and demonstrations with support for the religious leaders for this agenda. There are many internal and external factors which have spurred Hindu nationalism and the idea of constitutional monarchy in Nepal.

However, the question about the future and sustainability of right-wing politics drives future research. There are dual arguments about the future of the monarchy in Nepal. However, the future is uncertain and ambiguous. Although it has been a popular discourse in Nepal, the electoral votes show otherwise. The instability among the right wings in Nepal has created further uncertainty among the supporters. The democratic voting shows significantly less support for the right-wing agenda.

References

Acharya, B.R. 1966. *Nepal ko Samkshipta Brittanta.* Kathmandu: Pramod Shamsher and Nir Bikram' Pyasi'.

Acharya, Y. 1994. *An Outline History of Nepal.* Kathmandu: Ekta Books.

Adhikari, D. 2018. *India's Modi Uses Cultural Ties to Mend Ties with Nepal.* [Online]. https://www.aljazeera.com/features/2018/5/13/indias-modi-uses-cultural-ties-to-mend-ties-with-nepal. Accessed 5 July 2022.

Appleton, N. 2016. *Shared Characters in Jain, Buddhist and Hindu Narrative: Gods, Kings and Other Heroes.* Oxon: Routledge.

Aris, M. 1994. *The Raven Crown: The Origins of Buddhist Monarchy in Bhutan.* London: Serindia Publications.

Baral, B. 2019. *Despite Stirrings, Revival of Nepal's Monarchy and Hindu Character Unlikely.* [Online]. https://thewire.in/south-asia/nepal-hindu-state-agenda-monarchy-secularism. Accessed 5 July 2022.

Bishwakarma, M. 2019. *Political Transformations in Nepal: Dalit Inequality and Social Justice.* London: Routledge.

Bobbio, N., and A. Cameron. 1996. *Left and Right: The Significance of a Political Distinction.* Chicago: University of Chicago Press.

Bulmer, E. 2017. *Constitutional Monarchs in Parliamentary Democracies.* Stockholm: International Institute for Democracy and Electoral Assistance (International IDEA).

Chacko, P., and K. Jayasuriya. 2018. Asia's Conservative Moment: Understanding the Rise of the Right. *Journal of Contemporary Asia* 48 (4): 529–540.

Chhetri, T.B. 2018. Federal Democratic Republic Nepal: Deepening Problems and Prospects. *Journal of Political Science* 18: 114–142.

Dahal, K. 2016. *Secular Nepal: Understanding the Dynamics of Religious Nationalism and Secularism.* The Arctic University of Norway.

Douglas-Home, C., and S. Kelly. 2000. *Dignified & Efficient: The British Monarchy in the Twentieth Century.* Brinkworth: Claridge Press.

Einsiedel, S., D.M. Malone, and S. Pradhan, eds. 2012. *Nepal in Transition: From People's War to Fragile Peace.* Cambridge: Cambridge University Press.

Ganguly, S. 2008. Ethno-Religious Conflict in South Asia. *Global Politics and Strategy* 3: 88–109.

Giri, A. 2021. *How Hindu State Idea is Trying to Gain Ground in Nepal.* [Online]. https://kathmandupost.com/national/2021/08/22/how-hindu-state-idea-is-trying-to-gain-ground-in-nepal. Accessed 30 May 2022.

Jha, P. 2014. *Battles of the New Republic: A Contemporary History of Nepal.* London: Hurst and Company.

Joshi, B.L., and L.E. Rose. 2004/1966. *Democratic Innovations in Nepal: A Case Study of Political Acculturation.* Kathmandu: Mandala Book Point.

Khabarhub. 2022. *No Space for Monarchy in Nepal: RPP Chairman Thapa.* [Online]. https://english.khabarhub.com/2022/16/247344/. Accessed 15 June 2022.

Lal, C. 2022. *The Fire of Hindutva Upsurge.* [Online]. https://kathmandupost. com/columns/2022/01/05/the-fire-of-hindutva-upsurge. Accessed 5 July 2022.

Levitsky, S., and D. Ziblatt. 2018. *How Democracies Die.* New Year: Crown Books.

Lienesch, M. 1982. Right-Wing Religion: Christian Conservatism as a Political Movement. *Political Science Quarterly* 97 (3): 403–425.

Nepali Times. 2007. *Nepal Should be a Hindu Rastra Again.* [Online]. http://archive.nepalitimes.com/news.php?id=13940#.YuUN_nZBzIV. Accessed 3 July 2022.

Pathak, S.P. 2012. Political Instability in Nepal: Examining the Roles of the Parties and Monarchy in the Second Democratic Period (1990–2002). *The Journal of Social Science* 73: 149–170.

Pillalamarri, A. 2014. *Could Nepal Return to Monarchy?* [Online]. https://the-diplomat.com/2014/06/could-nepal-return-to-monarchy/. Accessed 28 March 2022.

Poudel, S.S. 2021. *In Nepal, Calls Grow for the Restoration of a Hindu State.* [Online]. https://thediplomat.com/2021/12/growing-calls-for-restoring-hindu-state-in-nepal/. Accessed 28 June 2022.

Republica. 2017. *RPP Manifesto: Support for Restoration of Constitutional Monarchy.* [Online]. https://myrepublica.nagariknetwork.com/news/30275/. Accessed 25 March 2022.

———. 2022. *Kamal Thapa Quits RPP*. [Online]. https://myrepublica. nagariknetwork.com/news/kamal-thapa-announces-to-separate-from-rpp/. Accessed 8 July 2022.

Sarkar, S. 2021. *India's Hindu Nationalists see Nepal's Political Chaos as Chance to Boost Royalist Calls, Target Secular State*. [Online]. https://www.scmp.com/ week-asia/politics/article/3118355/indias-hindu-nationalists-see-nepals-political-chaos-chance. Accessed 15 June 2022.

Shaha, R. 1990. *Modern Nepal: A Political History, 1769–1955*. New Delhi: Manohar Publishers and Distributors.

Sherpa, A.S. 2021. *The Struggle Between Hindutva and Secularism in Nepal*. [Online]. https://hir.harvard.edu/the-struggle-between-hindutva-and-secularism-in-nepal/. Accessed 30 June 2021.

Srivastava, R. 2014. *Nepal Must Declare Itself a Hindu Rashtra: Adityanath*. [Online]. https://timesofindia.indiatimes.com/india/nepal-must-declare-itself-a-hindu-rashtra-adityanath/articleshow/48194975.cms?utm_source=contentofinterest&utm_medium=text&utm_campaign=cppst. Accessed 20 June 2022.

Stepan, A., J.J. Linz, and J.F. Minoves. 2014. Democratic Parliamentary Monarchies. *Journal of Democracy* 25 (2): 35–51.

Stiller, L.F. 2017. *The Rise of the House of Gurkhas*. Kathmandu: Education Publishing House.

Straka, G. 1962. The Final Phase of Divine Right Theory in England, 1688–1702. *The English Historical Review* 77 (305): 638–658.

The Himalayan Times. 2016. *RPP Merges with RPP-N*. [Online]. https://thehimalayantimes.com/nepal/rastriya-prajatantra-party-merges-with-rastriya-prajatantra-party-nepal/. Accessed 2 July 2022.

Tridimas, G. 2021. Constitutional Monarchy as Power Sharing. *Constitutional Political Economy* 32: 431–461.

Upadhyaya, S.P. 2017. Secular Democracies, Governance and Politics of Religion in South Asia. *Society and Culture in South Asia* 3 (2): 244–261.

Woodford, B. 2013. *Perceptions of a Monarchy Without a King: Reactions to Oliver Cromwell's Power*. Montreal: McGill-Queen's University Press.

CHAPTER 4

Revisiting History and Society: Understanding the Impact of British Era Policies in Shaping Present-Day Hindu Right-Wing Ideology

Jayanth Deshmukh and Muhammed Favaz

INTRODUCTION

The British rule in India has been hailed as one of the darkest periods of times in Modern Indian History. The British Raj heralded a time of uncertainty and transformed the shared religious beliefs of communities into political interests. The mistrust that this moment garnered among Indians led to the demise of collective nationalism. While many believe that the Independence struggle in India was an act of unison, this is far from true. This chapter aims to highlight three policies of the British that led to the death of a united India and eventually led to resulting communal

J. Deshmukh (✉)
Pune, India

M. Favaz
Bangalore, India

49

B. S. Nayak, D. Chakraborty (eds.), *Interdisciplinary Reflections on South Asian Transitions*,
https://doi.org/10.1007/978-3-031-36686-4_4

disharmony in present-day India. The policies—Divide and Rule, Partition of Bengal, and the Indian Councils Act (1909)—have led to the exponential rise of a relatively new phenomenon—political Hindutva which morphs into Hindu nationalism. Findings of the chapter suggest that there has been a significant rise of communal disharmony, and present-day Indian politics partly runs on the same ideology that the British operated in India. The chapter also argues that the current imagined reality of India as a Hindu nation and the rise of BJP are a result of colonialization. The chapter also argues that communalism in India was constructed during the British era and also reconstructed the notion of society from an unorganized community into a fuzzy community divided by enumeration. The chapter concludes by arguing that the British rule has successfully constituted India into sets of homogenous communities riddled with religious conflict.

Communalism in India has been a long-standing issue and a threat to the social fibre of the country. The word can trace its origin to the early twentieth century where Viscount Melgund, the fourth Earl of Minto, attempted to elucidate on the existing conflicts between religious communities in India while formulating the Indian Councils Act (1909). At the time, the main political religious interests were put forth by the Hindu Mahasabha and the All-India Muslim League while the Indian National Congress (INC) took a backseat by adopting a nationalistic stance. The rift between religions eventually led to the Partition, whose effects are still felt till date. Today, political India remains divided across religious and social identities while being held together by the secular Constitution of the country. The strong emergence of Hindutva politics at the turn of the twenty-first century underscored the division of India along religious lines. However, this is not a new phenomenon and can be traced back to the British and its divisive policies. This chapter aims to outline three such policies and their impact on present-day politics in India.

Muzzy Creation of Community Identities During Colonial Era and Its Impact on Modi's India

The Imperial knowledge system that existed during the Colonial era successfully reconstructed the notion of a community. What previously consisted of a commune of different religions was successfully demarcated into an apotheosis of "enumerated" communities (Kaviraj 2010). This was only possible through the implementation of the Census which started in the second half of the nineteenth century. The Census was an act of social engineering—an act that aimed to rigidly define a diverse India on the principle of difference—that would enable the colonizers to further their agenda in the subcontinent (Mann 2015). Even today—analogous to the British Census—the enumerated communities are appositely circumscribed. However, in the process, they end up creaming different castes, sects, and devotional groups that pursue distinct styles of worship under the banner of Hinduism (Zavos 2000). The subsequent failure of the British in organizing India into a community that defined itself for its diversity led the creation of an enumerated community that accelerated religious bigotry in Independent India.

The reconstruction of a fuzzy community led to the homogenizing of heterogenous practices into standardized models as prescribed by British officers. Ergo, a Hindu or a Muslim had to fit into the definitional traits as outlined by the Census record. Bhagat (2001) states that this resulted in a decline population of multiple communities, thereby giving an impetus to creating a feeling of antipathy. Creating them into homogenous groups did not limit its impact to creating animosity, but it also created a narrative that their past was ridden with discord. The creation of a barbaric Hindu-Muslim relationship in Northern India during the Colonial era is an eidolon of this statement. The class conflict between a Hindu zamindar and a Muslim peasant eventually encompassed the strife narrative (Pandey 1990). This further augmented the British's claim of India as a barbaric and uncivilized land that was intolerant of the Western lifestyle, therefore requiring "Britain to civilize India" (Tunick 2006).

In pre-Modi India, the nationalist engagement with the definition and redefinition of the communities remains confused. National secular parties such as the INC and All India Trinamool Congress (TMC) vacillated in thought to engage in communal articulations. Secular parties, unlike right-wing religious parties like the Bharatiya Janata Party (BJP), felt that aggravating their religious community vote banks in the run-up to the elections would hurt their chances. This is a historic trend, especially for the INC that saw its initial members oscillate between Hindutva, soft Hindutva, and secularism (Bhagavan 2008).

The nationalist reconstruction of the Indian past as a response to counter the colonial construction is flawed. Pandey (1990) articulates that the nationalist reconstruction aimed to undo the negative effects of the colonial narrative through the invocation of a historic syncretism that existed in a pre-British India. The ambivalence of initial INC members between soft Hindutva and secularism and the inability to commit to one direction has led to the burgeoning of communal tensions. It is precisely this tension that has enabled the BJP to capitulate itself to power in key state and national elections. The rhetoric of the BJP, unlike secular parties, has been the same—to create *Akhand Bharat* and a nation that acts as a safe haven for Hindus. The absence of indecisiveness has enabled it to focus on consolidating its members and working towards its agenda.

The reconstruction of communities under the British Census has also led to the rise of right-wing politics. The grouping of multiple minorities regardless of their mode of worship has resulted in the creation of a larger Hindu base. It has now become achingly difficult for scholars to dissect who is a Hindu and who isn't. The paradox of creating a homogenous community marked by heterogeneity in characteristics has resulted in an increased ability of right-wing political parties to reach a wider audience. This has enabled the BJP to drive a narrative that they are fighting for the good of a larger population than they really are. The enumeration undertaken by the British has effectively enabled the BJP to create a communion that is bound by common religious practices and blurring individuality (Sarma 1993).

DIVIDE AND RULE TO BREAK INDIA

Colonial British used three major strategies on their colonized people to sustain power: colonial settlement, assimilation of local elites, and *divide et imperia* (Divide and Rule) (Morrock 1973). Among these, the Divide and Rule policy was the most detrimental and its effects are still felt in Independent India. Divide and Rule, according to Morrock (1973: 129), is "the conscious effort of colonialists to create differences, augment the differences existing between communities and politicize differences, so that it would be carried over to the post-colonial period". This divide was usually along ethnic or religious lines and not along the lines of ideologies. The strategy was mainly used by the British to create strife among the different ethnic or religious identities, and eventually, their colonies were known for strong inter-communal conflicts (Ray 2018). Furthermore, colonial India had undergone several social changes. For instance, it was during this era that Hindutva and Hinduism emerged as a political identity. In the aftermath of the Sepoy Mutiny, the Britishers engaged in selective recruitment to the British troops from different communities and identities in the aftermath and strived to enhance differences among different communities (Morrock 1973).

Similar to the British, the BJP has used the *divide et imperia* to establish a firm ground in Indian politics. BJP has never tried to acknowledge the caste differences unless for sentimental political rhetoric. During the campaign for 2014 election, when Modi commented on Priyanka Gandhi's politics as a daughterly attribute, she replied it as 'low' politics, which he suddenly connected with his caste status. According to Jaffrelot (2015), Modi has never relied on his caste until the run-up to the 2014 General Elections. BJP had always deflected caste questions by romanticizing Hindu unity in the fear that, if addressed, the divisions along the lines of caste would cost them their votes. This strategy is evident from the Mandal-Mandir politics of the 1990s. In response to the implementation of the Mandal Commission Report, the BJP used the Babri Masjid as a political tool to mitigate the divisions created by the Report among the Hindus (Seshia 1998).

The rise of BJP from the fringe of Indian politics to the centre was orchestrated with the decline of cross-cutting cleavages that existed in Indian society (Seshia 1998). The Partition of India and the violence associated with it was not enough to completely dilute the secular fabric of the Indian state. India remained one of the largest Muslim populated country in the world even after the vivisection on the lines of religion. The political manifestation of Jinnah that Muslims and Hindus cannot be seen as different communities in a nation, but rather both should constitute two different nations, was not welcomed by many Muslims who chose to stay in India over theocratic state of Pakistan. Muslims rallied behind the INC after Independence for their commitment towards secularism (Gayer and Jaffrelot 2012).

The political system that existed under the National Democratic Alliance (NDA) rule was different than that of the United Progressive Alliance (UPA) rule. Secularism, even though it had limitations while being practised under the INC system, was an ideological hallmark of the Indian state. However, the UPA government has failed to allegiance to secularism and has in turn engaged in communal strategies during election campaigns. In other words, the growth of BJP in India owes largely to the communal Divide and Rule tactics played by it to set Hindus against Muslims and benefit from the resulting polarization.

During Modi's campaign for 2014 parliamentary elections, supporters of BJP unleashed a number of bigotry attacks on Muslims. Visiting Hindu temples, meeting Hindu priests, and wearing saffron clothes in stages to attract majoritarian sentiment were common during his campaign. He referred to the UPA government as "Delhi Sultanate" and Rahul Gandhi as "Shehzada" and eventually creating an understanding that the country was ruled by Muslim appeasers (Jaffrelot 2015).

The threat on the Hindus was never acceptable to the BJP, for which they started to bring in a religious binary. Hindu migrants from neighbouring states were referred to as 'asylum seekers' and Muslim migrants were labelled as 'infiltrators' (Saikia 2020.) From this premise, the UPA government sought to grant citizenship to persecuted minorities who were Hindus, Christians, Sikhs, Jains, Buddhists, and Parsis, from Afghanistan, Pakistan, and Bangladesh. Since Muslims are 'infiltrators', conscious efforts were made to exclude Muslims. Another example is the bifurcation of Jammu and Kashmir, the only Muslim-majority state, into two union territories (Jammu and Kashmir and Ladakh) by revoking Article 370 of Indian Constitution is another incident of Divide and Rule. While the Kashmiris saw it as a humiliation, the rest of the country saw it as a victory over the region (Apoorvanand 2022). Disruption and dissonance have hence become the two main strategies to effectively create BJP's Hindu Rashtra.

Discrimination against Muslims by the state in the pretext of secularism, progressiveness, and law has flared up over the last year (Maizland 2022). The *Hijab* (head covering) ban in colleges of Karnataka which was upheld by the apex court purportedly to promote uniforms was deeply criticized for being an attack on religious freedom of Muslims (Al Jazeera 2022). However, Hindus are allowed to sport *tilaks*—a religious symbol—with no hindrance (Indo-Asian News Service 2022). Bulldozing of houses across the country in the name of evicting illegal settlements is another tactic to alienate individuals. Those opposing policies of the governments or engaging in protests often find their houses demolished. The demolition is selective and targets only Muslim illegal settlements while Hindu illegal settlers in the same vicinity remain unaffected (BBC 2022).

THE INDIAN COUNCIL ACT (1909): THE PAST OF PRESENT

With the growing aversion and militant opposition towards British rule since the passing of the Act of 1892, which expanded the size of legislative councils in India, the British government took measures to include the participation of Indians in governance. Since including Indians in the governance could pose a threat to their supremacy, the British made sure that the Indian participation would be limited. They refused to recognize the INC as the sole representative of India. Their move to oppose the INC stemmed from the fact that the British felt that the INC did not reflect the concerns of the underprivileged of the country (Kooiman 1995). This was evident from a growing concern among Muslims in India when the INC proposed that political representation and popular elections should be along ownership of property (Kooiman 1995). This schism in understanding among communities created a national movement which the British took advantage of.

Muslims with property rights wanted to voice the concerns to the British. A group of 35 Muslim leaders who had 'property and influence' headed by Sir Agha Khan III met Lord Fourth Earl of Minto in his lodge in Shimla to convince him the need of special protection for the political rights of Muslims in 1906. They had also demanded reservation for Muslims in government jobs. The intent of the Muslim leaders were to gain fine share of political representation which was in threat due to the upper-caste Hindu-dominant INC. Syed (1962) argues that the demand for separate electorate by Muslims was not planned by the British but was a demand put forward by intellectually capable Muslim leadership who had better political aspirations. Lord Minto favourably considered their claim for representation through the enactment of Minto-Morley reforms of 1909—formally called the Indian Councils Act (1909). The reform was brought about to gain the support of moderates led by Gopala Krishna Gokhale, former extremists, and Muslims with political clout. For the first time, under the Indian Councils Act (1909), Indians were included in the highest government decision-making body. A seat was reserved for Indians in Viceroy's Council and the Council began to include Indians in provincial councils. Along with the expansion of the legislative council, the law intended to offer separate electorates for Indians based on their religion. This eventually led to the evolution of multi-religious nationalism in the country (Arivarasi 2016).

The Act worked effectively for the British, in that it led to divisions among communities. It resulted in the failure of a common nationalism and led to the rise of separate Hindu and Muslim nationalism in the country. Koss (1967) states that people like MN Das saw Lord Minto as a Machiavellian schemer, whose attempt to bring communal reforms was a deliberate strategy to divide Indian nationalist movement, thereby prolonging the British rule over the country. MN Das also assumed that

Secretary Morley, who was against Divide and Rule policy in his earlier station Ireland, failed to recognize the consequences of the Act imposed in India. However, Morley never let the communal divisions limit the rights of minorities. He believed that it was the duty of the British, in communally divided places, to safeguard the rights of minorities, yet he had no plan to create a strife between Hindus and Muslims (Koss 1967).

The British played a communal card in governance affairs and also did the same in educational institutions. The major drawback of the reformed Act was that it did not confer real administrative power. The reformed councils remained as mere advisory bodies. The communal electorate was further extended in the centre and provinces giving separate electorates for Sikhs, Christians, Anglo-Indians, and Europeans. A major problem with the separate electorate was that it restricted routine ground-level interactions with people from different communities. In effect, it meant that a Hindu would have to vote for a Hindu. If people from different communities live as neighbours, both of their representatives in the local body, assembly level, and parliamentary level would be different. Interactions in their day-to-day political affairs hence become difficult. If there was room for any dialogues, it would only be possible on the legislature level between the elected representatives. In case of communal tensions, the communities involved would be institutionally and politically powerful to combat each other.

Another serious drawback with a communal electorate is that demographic changes over the period of time could lead to more conflicts. An increase in population of a community over time would mean an increase in representation in the councils. This would come at the cost of sacrificing another community's representation. This would further strengthen the notion that citizenship and political rights of a person in a separate electorate are directly based on the affiliation and size of the community and not on the rights of the individuals.

The separate electorate system for institutionalizing the religious differences had faced a lot of criticisms from nationalists and historians (Kooiman 1995). Chandra et al. (1988: 122) referred to the communal electorate as "one of the poisonous trees which was to yield a bitter harvest in later years". Sarkar (1983) argued that separate electorate made politicians create their own religious vote banks which hardened the division along the lines of religion. Gopal opined that the separate electorate has created two imagined religious communities which are waging against each other rather than fighting their common enemy. Kothari (1970) argued that the communal electorate had finally ended up in the two-nation theory.

Though the separate electorate idea was not incorporated in Independent India, it had done its damage. The idea had created a notion of religious nationalism. Hindu nationalism was propagated by Hindu Mahasabha, Muslim nationalism was propagated by All-India Muslim League, and Sikh nationalism was propagated by the Akalis. The Indian Union Muslim League which was formed in Independent India had a politics different from Jinnah's All-India Muslim League. Since the Partition, Indian Muslim who were politically less powerful and economically poor who never were represented by Muslim League in pre-Partition Era, rallied behind the INC for the sake of secularism. On a parallel track, the Hindu Mahasabha who were trying to occupy powerful political positions in administration even before Independence, continued with their project of Hindu nationalism. Savarkar (1949: 16) implored,

> Up with Sanghatan for the consummation of which it is simply imperative for non-Hindus to capture what ever political power has been wrung out by our efforts in the past under the present Reforms Act. The Mohammedans only vote for those who openly and boldly pledge to guard and aggressively secure rights for the Mohammedan people. But we Hindus commit the suicidal blunder of voting for those who openly declare that they are neither Hindus nor Mohammedans and yet are never tired of recognizing Mohammedan organizations and dealing with them and of adjusting compromises in the name of the Hindus, ever against Hindu interests and to unbearable humiliation of the Hindus. You must henceforth vote for those who are not ashamed themselves of being Hindus, openly stand for the Hindus and pledge themselves not to keep burning incense, always at the cost of the Hindus before the fetish of a dishonourable unity—cult.

Since Muslims supported the INC, Hindu Mahasabha tried to polarize voters further, who were voting along communal lines in separate electorates. Savarkar (1949: 62) also asked Hindus not to trust a Hindu who is a supporter of INC, a party he referred to as "pseudo-nationalistic". His attacks were mainly driven on the lines that the INC betrayed India for Muslim votes in order to appear 'nationalistic'.

The BJP, since its inception in 1980, following the tactic experimented by Hindu Mahasabha, portrayed the INC as a Muslim bloc and themselves as Hindu bloc. Nationalism of the INC were often equated with that of erstwhile Muslim kingdoms like Mughals. BJP showed themselves as the gatekeepers of Hindurashtra, where 'aware' and 'awakened' Hindus who would support Hindu nationalism would be primary citizens. Muslims, who would vote for the INC and secular parties, since they belonged to a separate bloc, would be treated as secondary citizens. In Maharashtra, the Shiv Sena also laid stake in the guardianship of 'Hindu land' of Maratha. The BJP and Shiv Sena had also relied on renaming the cities to make them 'proper' Indian. Places with English names or Muslim names were 'Hinduized' (Frayer 2019a). In the case of Bombay, a name that resonated with the cosmopolitan character of the city was changed to 'Mumbai', which had origins in 'Mumbadevi', a Maratha goddess. The renaming of Bombay by Shiv Sena with the support of BJP in 1995 was aimed at alienating Muslims and other 'enemies' in the city (Hansen 2001).

The Partition of Bengal: Ideology, History, and Implications

Before delving into the process of the Partition of Bengal, it is worth understanding why the province was chosen by the British over others. The British were aware of the animosity between the Hindu kings and the Mughals. This was evident through their *divide et imperia* policy. Stewart's (1951) seminal article on the Divide and Rule policy of the British outlines how various British officials leveraged animosity amongst communities. For instance, the letter of an unnamed Chief of Staff of India stated,

> I am strongly of the opinion that Mussulmans should not be in the same company or troop with Hindus or Sikhs, and that the two latter should not be mingled together. I would maintain even in the same regiment all differences of faith with the greatest of care. There might be rivalry or even hatred between two companies. (Stewart 1951: 54)

The report of the Punjab Commissioners played a pivotal role on Sir John Lawrence—one of the staunchest supporters of the Divide and Rule policy—and Colonel Durand while addressing the question of Bengal. Stewart's (1951) paper stated that Colonel Durand was in favour of the Partition of Bengal:

> That presidency [Bengal] may be divided into two or three great areas, in which the people are very distinct, and in which there is a very considerable degree of that sort of jealousy and animosity which exists between conter-

minous people. It is advisable for us to take advantage of that sort of feeling. (Stewart 1951: 55)

It is also worth reminiscing that the June 3 Plan regarding the Partition of Bengal demarcated the parameters under which the Partition would take place. According to the proposed plan, the Bengal Legislative Assembly would form two separate and distinct blocs, one consisting of Muslim-majority districts and the other consisting of Hindu-majority districts. The two voting groups, though divided on religious beliefs, were in fact divided on territorial assertions. However, the Hindu and Muslim blocs were not invited to discuss their communal will individually and all meetings took place in presence of each other.

The inability of the two voting blocs to effectively meet the British and solve dilemmas resulted in the British successfully defining nationalism in West Bengal to be based on religious grounds. The Hindus began complaining that the division would make them a minority despite Lord Curzon stating that the division would enable administrative efficiency (Chandra 2001). The Partition of Bengal had far greater acceptance in East Bengal. Hindu-Muslim unity was sought on lines of linguistic nationalism and not religion. The imagined nation for Muslims was more likely in East Bengal as they would no longer be subjugated by the Hindu majority. West Bengal faced different concerns as its residents worried that Bangla would decline with the proliferation of Hindi in the region. Effectively, the British engaged in administrative strategies that heightened communal anxieties and converted pluralism into rancour.

In post-Independence era, while the INC sought it fit to contain Hindu-Muslim differences within the boundaries of democracy and representation, certain Hindu sections found the democratic grounds to be fertile to argue for an aggressive ideology—establish a concrete form of Hindu nationalism. This definition of Hindu nationalism rests on the decree of M.S. Golwalkar that defined the Indian state as:

In Hindusthan exists and must needs exist the ancient Hindu nation and naught else but the Hindu Nation. All those not belonging to the national i.e. Hindu Race, Religion, Culture and Language, naturally fall out of the pale of real 'National' life ... So long as they maintain their racial, religious and cultural differences, they cannot but be only foreigners, who may be either friendly or inimical to the nation ... There are only two courses open to the foreign elements, either to merge themselves in the national race and adopt its culture, or to live at its mercy so long as the national race may allow them to do so … [Muslims and non-Hindus] must lose their separate existence to merge in the Hindu race, or may stay in the country, wholly subordinated to the Hindu Nation, claiming nothing, deserving no privileges, far less any preferential treatment -not even citizen's rights. (Golwalkar 1939: 26, 99, 104, 105)

For the BJP, the time succeeding the 2002 Gujarat riots was the archetype to realize Golwalkar's dream. They began establishing the narrative of Muslims as the 'Other', much akin to the British. Realizing the change in tide, the Congress reduced its campaigning in Muslim areas in the fear of being portrayed as a party appeasing minorities. Attesting to this statement, the party did not even field a single Muslim candidate in the 2014 elections (Tewari 2014). Eventually, much like the 10% of Gujaratis who are Muslims, the Congress along with its vote bank was becoming invisible in the larger political discourse in Gujarat.

With the successful religious Partition of Gujarat, Hindutva ideologues hope to replicate the same on a national level. Since its ascendence to power in 2014, the BJP has been covertly pushing Hindutva by capturing apparatuses of state power and concurrently imposing cultural and religious hegemony by mobilizing Hindu youths on knots such as beef consumption, cow slaughter, threats posed by Pakistan, and terrorism and violence in Kashmir (Hasan 2005; Noor 2007; The Indian Express 2016; Tripathi 2019). The Partition of the Indian subcontinent has, in a way, helped the party promulgate its views. Right-wing ideologues now view Bangladesh and Pakistan as countries that are safe havens for Muslims. The bloody aftermath of the Partition and the frequent raiding of India by Mughals have also enabled these ideologues to portray Muslims as inheritors of violence. Historians who have unequivocally refuted these claims are now brushed aside as "secular" historians who are distorting real history (Anand and Lall 2022).

For extreme right-wing Hindutva supporters, the existence of Pakistan and Bangladesh effectively meant that the Muslims who stayed back in India after the Partition have forfeited their Indian citizenship. According to them, the Partition had been agreed on religious lines. If two nations are dominated by Muslims, at least one nation must protect the rights of Hindus. This agenda—present since 1930s—has decorously resulted in the calls for implementing the National Register of Citizens (NRC)-the Citizenship Amendment Act (CAA) in India. The marginalization of Muslims and the possibility of losing their Indian citizenship are partly fuelled by the ideology that the Hindus in India need to be protected and that Muslims—even those that are Indians—have to return to their original safe havens created by the Partition.

The long-term impact of the Partition is the creation of a perpetual psychological mindset that Hindus and Muslims cannot live together. Today, the fact that both communities can reach a consensus on political and developmental agendas seems absurd. The upping of this psychological schism over multiple generations has created tremendous political auras seated on violence and mobilization of the masses. The communal tensions that were sowed by the Partition of the Indian subcontinent continue to create a dichotomous political arena—secular parties that decry right-wing ideologies and religious parties that decry faux secularism.

Today, there are clear indications in India that Muslims are no longer a part of the country. Violent youth vigilante groups have begun springing up in various parts of the country and continue to raise slogans *Mussulmans ke liye keval do jagah, Pakistan ya toh Kabristan* (there are only two places for Muslims—either Pakistan or the graveyard) (Siddiqui 2019). Incidents of mob lynching against Muslims by saffron-clad youth have become commonplace, sending a message that Muslims are second-class citizens and must know their place (Frayer 2019b; Pandey 2021; Parth 2020).

Conclusion

The impact the British policies have had in Colonial era continue to resonate till date. The damages done have defined the relationship between communities across India and its political implications are for all to see. This chapter has also examined how the BJP were able to leverage on the differences created by the British and ensured the meteoric rise of Narendra Modi to power. The demolition of the Babri Masjid was in part a shockwave felt by the divisive policies of the British and is an assault on the fabric of the Indian state. The emergence of a new India depends on how the government and community navigate differences among communities. Indians must hope that the tense situation among religions does not last for long. Indians need to hope that the shockwaves sent by the British reduce over the years. Without this, the longer impact of creating a secular state would always hang in the balance.

REFERENCES

Al Jazeera. 2022. Hijab Ban in Indian State Violates Religious Freedom: US Official. *Al Jazeera*, February 12.

Anand, K., and M. Lall. 2022. The Debate Between Secularism and Hindu Nationalism—How India's Textbooks Have Become the Government's Medium for Political Communication. *India Review* 21 (1): 77–107.

Apoorvanand. 2022. Divide and Rule, BJP style. *The Wire*, June 21.

Arivarasi, V. 2016. Minto-Morley Reforms of 1909 in Madras Presidency. *Indian Journal of Research* 5 (12): 217–220.

BBC. 2022. Nupur Sharma: Houses of Muslims demolished in Uttar Pradesh after protests. *BBC*, June 13.

Bhagat, R.B. 2001. Census and the Construction of Communalism in India. *Economic and Political Weekly* 36 (46): 4352–4356.

Bhagavan, M. 2008. The Hindutva Underground: Hindu Nationalism and the Indian National Congress in Late Colonial and Early Post-Colonial India. *Economic and Political Weekly* 43 (37): 39–48.

Chandra, B. 2001. *History of Modern India*. New Delhi: Orient Blackswan.

Chandra, B., M. Mukherjee, A. Mukherjee, S. Mahajan, and K.N. Panikkar. 1988. *India's Struggle for Independence: 1857–1947*. New Delhi: Penguin.

Frayer, L. 2019a. India is Changing Some Cities' Names, and Muslims Fear Their Heritage is Being Erased. *NPR*, April 23.

———. 2019b. 'This is it. I'm Going to Die': India's Minorities are Targeted in Lynchings. *NPR*, August 21. https://www.npr.org/2019/08/21/751541321/this-is-it-im-going-to-die-indias-minorities-are-targeted-in-lynchings

Gayer, L., and C. Jaffrelot. 2012. *Muslims in Indian Cities: Trajectories of Marginalisation*. London: Hurst and Company.

Golwalkar, M. 1939. *We or Our Nationhood Defined*. Nagpur: Bharat Publications.

Hansen, T.B. 2001. *Wages of Violence: Naming and Identity in Postcolonial Bombay*. Princeton, NJ: Princeton University Press.

Hasan, S. 2005. India and Pakistan: Common Identity and Conflict. *Refugee Survey Quarterly* 24 (4): 74–80.

Indo-Asian News Service. 2022. 'Why Not Turban, Bindi, Cross': Hijab Arguments Play Out in Karnataka HC. *Business Standard*, February 16.

Jaffrelot, C. 2015. The Modi-Centric BJP 2014 Election Campaign: New Techniques and Old Tactics. *Contemporary South Asia* 23 (2): 151–166.

Kaviraj, S. 2010. *The Imaginary Institution of India: Politics and Ideas*. New York: Columbia University Press.

Kooiman, D. 1995. Communalism and Indian Princely States: A Comparison with British India. *Economic and Political Weekly* 30 (34): 2123–2133.

Koss, S.E. 1967. John Morley and the Communal Question. *The Journal of Asian Studies* 26 (3): 381–387.

Kothari, R. 1970. *Politics in India*. New Delhi: Orient Blackswan.

Maizland, L. 2022. India's Muslims: An Increasingly Marginalized Population. *Council For Foreign Relations*, July 14.

Mann, M. 2015. *South Asia's Modern History*. New York: Routledge.

Morrock, R. 1973. Heritage of Strife: The Effects of Colonialist 'Divide and Rule' Strategy Upon the Colonized Peoples. *Science & Society* 37 (2): 129–151.

Noor, S. 2007. Pakistan-India Relations and Terrorism. *Pakistan Horizon* 60 (2): 65–84.

Pandey, G. 1990. *The Construction of Communalism in Colonial North India*. Oxford: Oxford University Press.

———. 2021. Beaten and Humiliated by Hindu Mobs for Being a Muslim in India. *BBC News*, September 2. https://www.bbc.com/news/world-asia-india-58406194

Parth, M.N. 2020. Palghar Lynching: Saffronisation of Tribal Areas and Islamophobia Behind the Curtain. *Newsclick*, August 13. https://www.newsclick.in/palghar-lynching-saffronisation-tribal-areas-islamophobia-behind-curtain

Ray, S. 2018. Beyond Divide and Rule: Explaining the Link Between British Colonialism and Ethnic Violence. *Nationalism and Ethnic Politics* 24 (4): 367–388.

Saikia, S. 2020. Saffronizing the Periphery: Explaining the Rise of the Bharatiya Janata Party in Contemporary Assam. *Studies in Indian Politics* 8 (1): 69–84.

Sarkar, S. 1983. *Modern India 1885–1947*. New Delhi: Prabhat Prakashan.

Sarma, J. 1993. Changes in Tribal Culture in India. *Anthropos* 88 (4/6): 504–508.

Savarkar, V.D. 1949. *Hindu Rashtra Darshan: A Collection of the Presidential Speeches Delivered from the Hindu Mahasabha Platform*. Bombay: Syt. Laxman Ganesh Khare Print.

Seshia, S. 1998. Divide and Rule in Indian Party Politics: The Rise of the Bharatiya Janata Party. *Asian Survey* 38 (11): 1036–1050.

Siddiqui, I.A. 2019. You've Only Two Places, Pakistan or Kabristan. *Telegraph India*, December 26. https://www.telegraphindia.com/india/youve-only-two-places-pakistan-or-kabristan/cid/1730395

Stewart, N. 1951. Divide and Rule: British Policy in Indian History. *Science & Society* 15 (1): 49–57.

Syed, R. 1962. *Lord Minto and the Indian Nationalist Movement, with Special Reference to the Political Activities of the Indian Muslims, 1905–1910*. Doctoral thesis, SOAS University of London.

Tewari, M. 2014. Lok Sabha Polls: 25 Years, Zero Muslim MPs from Gujarat. *The Times of India*, April 16. https://timesofindia.indiatimes.com/

news/lok-sabha-polls-25-years-zero-muslim-mps-from-gujarat/article-show/33833828.cms

The Indian Express. 2016. Beef row: Where it is Illegal and What the Law Says. *The Indian Express*, July 27. https://indianexpress.com/article/india/india-news-india/beef-madhya-pradesh-video-cow-vigilantes-gau-rakshaks-2938751/

Tripathi, B. 2019. We Will Ban Cow Slaughter in States Where it is Still Legal. *India Spend*, September 11. https://www.indiaspend.com/we-will-ban-cow-slaughter-in-states-where-it-is-still-legal/

Tunick, M. 2006. Tolerant Imperialism: John Stuart Mill's Defense of British Rule in India. *The Review of Politics* 68 (4): 586–611.

Zavos, J. 2000. *The Emergence of Hindu Nationalism in India*. New Delhi: Oxford University Press.

CHAPTER 5

Peasant Populism and Hindu Imagery: A Case Study from Gadwal, Telangana State of South India

Jessy K. Philip

INTRODUCTION

The language of populism is a handy ideological position for instituting the hegemony of the 'upper groups'. Populism brings together groups that occupy contradictory caste and class positions (Hall 1985). Populist ideologies construct narratives of injustice to 'undifferentiated' people by 'corrupt' elites who occupy independent institutions and mobilise emotions more than interests (Harriss 2000; E. Laclau 2005). Populism is a thin-centred discourse rooted in the idea of popular will and aligns with an ideology that could appeal to the majority (Hall 1985). It is a flexible model of persuasion (Michael Kazin 1995).

These ideas work well to consolidate right-wing agendas. Populist narratives of mistrust of liberal institutions and valorisation of elections as a manifestation of popular will push authoritarian ideas that undermine

J. K. Philip (✉)
Jesus and Mary College, Delhi University, New Delhi, India

B. S. Nayak, D. Chakraborty (eds.), *Interdisciplinary Reflections on South Asian Transitions*,
https://doi.org/10.1007/978-3-031-36686-4_5

individual rights and institute social and legal exclusionary practices (Jessop et al. 1984). The appeal to strong leaders than to independent liberal and modern institutions also furthers an authoritarian agenda. Hall (1985) points out that the strength of authoritarian populism lies in 'the way it addresses real problems, real and lived experiences, real contradictions—and yet is able to represent them within a logic of discourse which pulls them systematically into line with policies and class strategies of the right' (ibid.: 185–186; see also Hall 1985: 138–146).

The populism of the left has a long legacy in the Indian context and is often conflated in journalistic writing with fiscal policies of handouts to the poor (welfare policies) (Wyatt 2013). However, 'populism of the right' appeals to the religiously or ethically constituted majority rather than the economic majority (Palshikar 2015). Hence, populism of the right often takes the form of majoritarian nationalism.

Creating a religiously constituted majority with a grievance towards a homogenised minority community is a fraught process in India, considering caste cleavages within the 'majority' religion. Other Backward Class (OBC) communities have less attraction for confessional politics due to their low position in the Hindu hierarchy. Hence, Hindu right-wing groups use aggressive nationalism and hostility towards Muslims as the most favoured strategy for their mobilisation (Gudavarthy 2019b; Sanjay Kumar and Gupta 2020). While the existence of a vilified minority accelerates the creation of a homogenised Hindu community, this could be achieved by other means. Accommodating elements of socio-political demands of 'lower' caste groups or offering transactional gains and symbolic accommodation are other strategies used to mobilise opinion in these groups in favour of Hindu majoritarianism.

Scholars engaged in ascertaining the degree of the consent of social groups lower in caste hierarchy for the Hindu authoritarian right-wing project for caste supremacy tend to conciliate between two contradictory views. On the one hand, scholars attribute support of these groups to transactional gains while simultaneously pointing out a fundamental ideological shift of subaltern classes from caste radicalism to a project aimed at creating a 'Hindu' community (Badri Narayan 2021, 2022). Scholars note positive attempts made by the Hindu right-wing to create a community through accommodation of lower caste gods and attempt at ameliorating social status by rewriting caste histories (Badri Narayan 2021). These overtures by the Hindu right-wing are often seen as a concession given to 'lower' groups due to the politically assertive agency of the lower castes. However, such 'plebianization' of political Hinduism could move these groups from 'caste to faith' (Chadha 2018) and facilitate groups with 'diverse social experiences to speak to one another' (Rodrigues 2017), enabling an ideological shift to authoritarianism among these groups. Thus, religious populism and symbolic accommodation are conceptualised in these studies as effective weapons deployed by right-wing organisations to ride over caste and class contradictions. However, if the electorate's support largely hinges on transactional gains, it could not be taken as the agreement of the electorate with the ideological framework of Hindu majoritarianism.

Scholars examining the symbolic integration of lower caste groups to a Hindu community have primarily based their studies in the North of India. For various reasons, such political processes of creating a Hindu political community are often observed in their complete form in North India. Christopher Jaffrelot (2000) argues that the presence of a large Dvija (twice-born Brahmin Kshatriya and Vaishya) population who directly gain from the consolidation of Hindu identity, a caste society that comes closest to the Varna Model, and the resilience of the ethos of Sanskritisation among OBCs and Dalits provides a favourable environment for the creation of a pan-Hindu identity.

In the South of the Vindhya, such symbolic politics is also being deployed to create a Hindu identity. Scholars report that Hindu right-wing organisations also deploy similar moves to accommodate lower caste gods in a pan-Hindu imagination in parts of Telangana. On the back of these reports, Gudavarthy believes that Telangana will be the second state in South India that the BJP will breach (Gudavarthy 2019a). However, the politics of socio-political accommodation is far more developed in these parts of the country. These regions offer an ideal ground to examine the interaction between ideologies of economic populism and religious populism and the balance of political allegiance of the electorate to these ideologies. In this chapter, we ask the following questions. How does the contemporary discourse of symbolic distribution work with ideologies of economic populism or welfarism reported to have been entrenched in Indian politics due to an expansion of democratisation? What socio-economic processes shape the formation of such ideologies that represent a particular relationship between caste groups, parties and the state?

This chapter explores religious symbolism used in the political movement to create Telangana and its echo in the field site, a village in the Gadwal district of Telangana. This ideological project is conceptualised as a probable and possible antecedent to the creation of Hindu imagery in this region. Examining the articulation of political churns and socio-economic grievances among small peasants from an OBC caste in a village I call Desharajupalli, I show that a new politics based on symbolic redistribution and accommodation using religion has dawned in the state of Telangana. However, the socio-political base of this symbolism among small peasants belonging to OBC castes remains agrarian populism undergirded by caste radicalism. The chapter traces the interconnections between cultural populism and economic populism in the politics of Telangana to assess the likely success of attempts to create a Hindu community for political mobilisation.

In 2009, I conducted field research into caste and agrarian relations in a village. This data set describes significant economic processes interacting with political mobilisation and the state. I conducted a second round of field research in 2015 to map emerging peasant subjectivities, peasant organisational activities and changes in state politics. This data set was complemented with interviews taken with the Member of the Legislative Assembly (MLA) of the constituency and various leaders belonging to civil society at Gadwal town. The second section of the chapter is a theoretical discussion on the relationship between shifts in political economy, populist politics and democratisation.

POLITICAL ECONOMY, TRANSACTIONAL POLITICS AND 'DEMOCRATISATION'

Scholars believe that despite 'the ideological turn' in Indian politics evidenced by the election of the BJP, the mass support for this ideological project is often shaped by transactional politics (Deshpande et al. 2019). Some scholars consider such transactional politics as an outcome of the spread of aspirations for mobility among the mass of Indian society. Many scholars have observed a new kind of assertive political agency among the Indian electorate, which has consequently shaped national and state party politics, competition and policies (Yadav and Palshikar 2014; Yogendra 2010).

Changes in political economy have historically shaped the political agency of social groups and their involvement in ideological projects of the post-colonial Indian state. Land reforms, green revolution, consequent depersonalisation of labour relations and decline of traditional authority have resulted in significant changes in political morality, party system, regimes and state operation (Manor 2004, 2010; Lerche 1999). In this context, the decline of agriculture and village society post-liberalisation of the Indian economy has decisively contributed to shaping a more assertive and entrepreneurial political agency (Gupta 2005; Jodhka 2014). This has altered the political interaction between social groups, parties and the state (Price 2006; Price and Dusi 2014).

Political ideologies that mediate relations between groups, parties and the state are often the result of such sociological processes. One such political ideology which has gained prominence after the globalisation of economy and society in mediating state-society relations is populism (Wyatt 2013). Many factors are believed to have contributed to the pre-eminence of the ideology of populism. As the rural electorate gets freed from a traditional authority, they use the resultant agency to gain from political action. The competitive populist offerings by different political parties have often been located in this shift in nature of the political agency of the Indian electorate (Carswell and De Neve 2014; Gorringe 2010). A restive electorate gets impatient with political regimes and has dispensed with party loyalties in pursuit of immediate benefits. On the converse, the electorate also rewards governments that deliver welfare effectively (Yadav and Palshikar 2014).

South Indian politics has a long history of populist leaders and policies. The genesis of the political power of many dominant groups belonging to ritually inferior Shudra castes in the South lies in their participation in the movement against Brahmin dominance and feudalism (Parthasarathy 2015). The contemporary dominance of these groups can be traced to the social capital they earned through caste alliances stitched during such movements. This anti-caste ideological environment encouraged the populism of MGR in Tamil Nadu, encapsulated in policies such as the mid-day meal scheme and strategies of power-sharing with non-dominants as junior partners perfected by The Telugu Desam Party (TDP) in erstwhile Andhra Pradesh (Subramanian 2007; Krishna Reddy 2002). Economic populism with limited redistributive policies and power-sharing with other oppressed castes were the hallmarks of the accommodative politics of the South Indian state (Elliott 2011; Wyatt 2013). In Andhra Pradesh, large-scale government distribution of material benefits in exchange for electoral support termed populism began with the scheme of subsided rice and reduced electricity rate for farmers started by the TDP government in 1985 (Elliott 2011).

Such populism or turn to welfarism has gone hand in hand with increasing political representation for OBCs and Dalit groups. Shudra dominant caste has historically held power in the erstwhile Andhra region by progressive accommodation of economic and political demands of OBCs and Dalits (Harrison 1956). The affiliation of lower groups with such parties representing dominant castes such as TDP (with Kammas) and Congress (with Reddies) has combined welfarism with such politics of representation. Theorists argue that lower groups seek preferential access to government benefits by placing members of their caste in a decision-making position (Chandra 2004). Hence, politics of representation becomes a logical corollary to the politics of welfarism in the South. Improvement in state revenue due to economic growth led to increased populist politics in South India. Congress regime (2004–2014) in Andhra Pradesh could increase the scope and extent of such a scheme on the back of enhanced state revenue (Wyatt 2013; Elliott 2011).

A decade before the contemporary shift to authoritarian populism, scholars argued that this turn to 'populism' and transactional politics indicates 'democratisation' of political competition and access (Manor 2004, 2010). Policies of welfarism undertaken by United Progressive Alliance (UPA) and right-based legislation clearly introduced a potential significance for subaltern claim-making and created political agency capable of mobilisation (Ruparelia 2013). However, such state discourses enlarge scope in hindsight, and such pronouncement of 'democratisation' seems far-fetched. It is to be noted that scholars argued that a 'democratisation' is underway without considering shifting forms of social power in Indian society and political 'access' to the state. Dominant castes have enlarged their wealth and social power through efficient utilisation of the market as well as state protection (Parthasarathy 2015; Alam 2009). The growth of the power of the erstwhile rural elites as a regional power and provincial capital on the back of privileged access to state for export agriculture, real estate and informal industrial units is particularly noteworthy in this regard (Guérin et al. 2015; Picherit 2012). In cities, while the hold of twice-born and dominant Sudra castes over public institutions declined a little due to reservation policies, these castes could also effectively capture employment and investment in the emerging corporate sector. Alam (2009) warned that such regrouping of priviligentsia will have harmful consequences for democratisation.

Village studies from states of South India report that such populism works politically in the context of alliance relations between upper and lower caste groups in village society (Picherit 2012; Pattenden 2011). While dominant groups draw significant rent from gatekeeping access to the state and use state benefits to control labour, lower groups seek this alliance to ensure a stake in villages and development funds. Populist schemes, which are long term, were not mere handouts and replaced, to some extent, clientelist politics that targets a minimal number of people. While the earlier clientelist politics based itself on allegiance relations between rural elites and working masses through connections of debt and dependency, populist methods make relations less exploitative (Berenschot 2014). However, such welfarism is combined with clientelism, as reported by several studies from South India (Elliott 2011; Pattenden 2011). I (Philip 2017) argued elsewhere that there are limits to democratisation as relations of dominance continue in village society and dominant groups consolidate their hold on the regional state.

More importantly, this turn to transactional politics embedded in populist policies adopted by the UPA regime and other state government welfare policies often occurs in the context of the state's retreat from social protection (Nilsen 2018; Chatterjee 2008). The neo-liberal populist policies are often based on various exclusionary criteria and attempt to discipline the poor (Fischer 2020). Socially weaker groups empowered by the decline of older traditional types of authority structures discover a new kind of political agency. But they find that it cannot be directed to bring fundamental changes in social policy due to the enthronement of the neo-liberal state and dominant sections that command it. Studies of democratisation overemphasise gains of agency of lower groups without considering structures limiting the full expression of such agency.

In sharp contrast to such an assessment of the political agency of lower groups, the electoral victory of the BJP and the formation of a Hindu right-wing government have promoted a radical rethinking among political scientists on the long-term trajectory of the Indian political system. Political scientists who argue that lower castes look for advancement in socio-economic parameters through populist routes and are exposed to caste radical alternatives point out a right-wing sway among the Indian electorate.

Badri Narayan (2011) elaborated on the emergence of a Dalit public in North India, democratising society. His recent works map the expansion of a new Hindu public among the same caste group (Narayan 2021). Such views do not reckon that an individual cannot rapidly replace world views without doing epistemic violence to oneself. Some call it a conciliatory subalternity that is friendly to Hindutva, heralding a subaltern Hindutva phenomenon (Sajjan Kumar 2020). These studies argue that Hindutva appeals to the non-dominant OBC and Dalit castes due to its promise of making them members of a powerful Hindu community against just being a socially and politically weaker caste. However, these studies also argue that these groups see transactional politics and demands for political representation as salient ideas. But such ideas are either subordinated to the attraction of symbolic accommodation within the Hindu community or form a seamless continuity with Hindu majoritarianism (Palshikar 2015).

In this chapter, we argue for a method that unpacks the strategies for political power used by the dominant sections from the political viewpoint of the subaltern castes and map the balance of power between them to comprehend the sway of such ideas among subaltern caste groups. We view symbolic and material transactions as attached to different types of populism, hence distinct ideologically. Views that consider the seamless movement of oppressed castes from socio-economic transactions to symbolic accommodation ignore the role of political ideas in their political lives. In the next section, we examine the movement for the Telangana state and policies of the newly formed state as the first instance of a frontal usage of religious imagery in the politics of this region. We ground such usage in the compulsions of political rule under neo-liberal conditions felt by dominant caste elites.

Agrarian and Religious Populism and Formation of Telangana State

The movement for regional autonomy and subsequent regional and sub-regional formation in Telangana and Gadwal has followed political trends until 2014. Pani (2017) points out that varied experiences of regions as 'region of interests', 'region of aspirations' and 'region of culture' come together in movements for regional autonomy. One could argue that region-making in Telangana is informed by the political agenda of various castes of the region articulated through 'populism' which dictated the political process before the successful agitation for Telangana.

The imagination of the region of Telangana before and after the formation of the state is located in the historical struggle of the people of Hyderabad state against the economic and political oppression of outsiders (Nizam government, Coastal Andhra interests), culminating ultimately in statehood (Srikanth 2013). Hence, the common struggle of all castes (populism) against 'backwardness' and their aspirations for prosperity inform Telangana region-making. Foundational songs of the Telangana state showcase this populist and aspirational region-making.[1]

One could observe the peasant moorings of this populist movement for regional autonomy from the slogan of a 'golden Telangana' (colour of paddy fields before harvest) advertised by the movement as the outcome of possible regional sovereignty and the promise to use the coal and water resources of the region for the prosperity of the peasantry. Another movement slogan was 'neelu, nidhi, niyamakalu' (water, resources and employment). Within this populist compact, mother worship among the majority of castes of the region is highlighted as the region's unique identity (Srikanth 2013). Telangana Thalli (mother) is promoted as the region's mascot in contrast to Telugu thalli, the official mascot of the erstwhile Andhra. The goddess with a crown holds maize corn (harvest) in one hand, reflecting the region's prosperity, while Bathukamma, the unique cultural symbol of Telangana, is in the other. Bathukamma is a Hindu goddess of the region; the word translates to life and mother. Bathukamma celebrates the inherent relationship between earth, water and human beings and is associated with the non-Brahmanic caste groups of the region. The new state also promotes non-Brahmanical festivals such as Bathukamma and non-Brahmanical pilgrimage such as Sammakka Sarakka as regional culture (Kancha Ilaiah Shepherd 2022). A new scheme called 'Rythu Bandhu' (cash transfer to peasants) was implemented (Amrit 2018). Thus, a political agenda of populism and democratisation and a larger thrust of 'aspirations' inform region-making in the Telangana state.

However, as Telangana Rashtra Samithi (TRS) consolidate its rule, progressive efforts are made to drain the radical and democratic content of the political and cultural assertion for regional autonomy. Support was given to caste-based occupations such as barber, washermen and shepherds (Kancha Ilaiah Shepherd 2022). The narrative used by the government emphasised the desirability of caste-based occupations. Education advancement has suffered under the TRS regime. TRS regime also has centralised power, weakened the opposition and created new districts to consolidate power (Rao 2017). TRS chief promoted Brahmanic rituals such as Sudarshana, Chandi and Rajashyamala Yagams and liberally patronised Brahmins and temples (Kancha Ilaiah Shepherd 2022, 8 February).

At the cultural plane, there has been a switch and bait politics. While subaltern gods, goddesses and festivals were initially promoted, overtly Brahmanic gods and goddesses were promoted later. Chief Minister, K Chandra Sekhar Rao from a Velama landlord (Shudra dominant caste) family, is a follower of Vaishnava *peetadhipathi* (head of a Vaishnava mutt) Chinna Jeeyar. Chinna Jeeyar installed a 216-feet statue of Ramanujacharya dubbed the 'Statue of Equality', inaugurated by Prime Minister Narendra Modi (Kancha Ilaiah Shepherd 2022). His remarks against the Sammakka Sarakka festival, considered a symbol of Telangana's statehood struggle, made news in Telangana recently. In some instances, an attempt was made to install Brahmanic traditions in subaltern spaces, and the state highlighted the pilgrimage routes of these temples. Non-Brahmanic festivals such as Bathukamma have seen a change with Brahmanic practices imposed on celebrations. These economic, political and cultural interventions have led to the charge that the TRS government is a Dora Rajayam (landlord government). These interventions of the TRS government put in place a new kind of populism that combined programmatic populist intervention with cultural populism that attempted to bring together Brahmanic and non-Brahmanic cultures in a facile manner. This could easily give way to the right-wing authoritarian populism of the BJP.

Scholars have often pointed out that since proponents of the new state attempt to gain economically and politically from the global city region of Hyderabad through global flows and networks, it is improbable that the aspirations of the people of the state would be met. These scholars point out that ruling elites are more likely to rely on neo-liberal populism to manage the region politically. In this ideology, the earlier strategy of appeasement of popular discontent through welfare benefits is partially abandoned in favour of symbolic redistribution and empowerment (Srikanth 2013).

METHODOLOGY AND FIELD SETTING: VILLAGE AND THE REGION

I conducted fieldwork in Desharajupalli village, Ghattu Mandal of Gadwal district, Telangana state, in two tranches, in 2009 and 2015. I conducted personal interviews with political leaders in 2009 and 2015 at Gadwal town to map the political architecture of the region. The region is a backward district with low economic growth and literacy. It is a dry track with canal irrigation available only in villages near Gadwal town as there is a significant irrigation project called Jurala.

Gadwal town was the capital of Gadwal Samsthanam, a vassal of the Nizam of Hyderabad. After the integration of Hyderabad into the Indian union, the Raja of Gadwal lost power and shifted to the capital city of Hyderabad. However, the employees of Rajas went on to become the power centre of the region up until now. The region's politics revolves around a single family called DK. Family members were elected to the Assembly at least nine times, starting with DK Satya Reddy's victory in 1957. Gadwal town expanded in the 1980s due to the shift of landed elites from villages. Radical assertions undercutting the authority of the landlords impelled many local elites to shift their base to town. These traditional elites congregated around the influential family controlling the region's politics. These elites economically prospered on the back of privileged access to the state through state contracts.

The late 1980s also witnessed a 'backward class assertion' in the region for political power. TDP, a political party, made its debut in this region by promoting OBC leaders. It also promised a change in the village power system hitherto controlled by a traditional arrangement called Patel–Patwari system, which enjoyed juridical support from the state. This assertion culminated in the election of the first-ever OBC MLA of the region Gattu Bheemudu in 1999, breaking the hold of one family rule in the region.

In the 2004 elections, the DK family could claw their way back to power on populist promises to the peasantry of free electricity, loan waiver and The Mahatma Gandhi National Rural Employment Guarantee Act 2005 (MGNREGA). From 2004 to 2014, a Reddy elite grew in Gadwal town with the political patronage of the government consolidating Reddy's rule. Movement for Telangana was not observed much in the region, and the formation of the state has led to some movement of sub-regional leaders and local leaders aligned with them. D. K. Aruna, then belonging to the Congress party, was the MLA during the first and second rounds of fieldwork. News Minute reports the operation of the provincial capital in Gadwal town under the patronage of the DK family. Toddy shops, bars, gas, petrol bunks, godowns, it is all theirs. For every road that is laid, the gravel is theirs, and so is the sand. The DK family controls everything in the town and takes commissions on everything. Contractors are their people, and so are the engineers. If they spend Rs 100 in election campaigning, they earn Rs 99 back, alleged an aide of Gadwal's BJP candidate, Venkatadri Reddy.

Investigations into regional dynamics were a prelude to an in-depth investigation of rural dynamics in 2009 and 2015. The village studied called Desharajupalli falls in Gattu Mandal of Gadwal district. It is situated on the Deccan plateau and is bereft of canal irrigation. The village is in a rain shadow region on the lower slope of the plateau. The region's histori-cal name lives on through migratory labour, referred to as 'palamur' labour. Desharajupalli is a multi-caste village with a full contingent of peasant/pastoral castes and occupational and service castes. And 50% of the village households are from peasant and pastoralist castes of Boyas and Kuruvas. Occupational castes such as carpenter, blacksmith, toddy tap-pers, fisherfolk and service castes such as barbers and washermen consti-tute 21% of the households. These two sets of caste groups are classified as backward class/caste by the government of India (OBC). Dalits, or ex-untouchable communities of Malas and Madigas, constitute 19% of the village, and other castes (castes considered 'forward' in socio-economic indicators) 8%.

Economic Processes and Political Attitudes

Boyas are the more numerous OBC caste of the village. Boyas were ten-ants and servants of big landlords during the times of princely Hyderabad. The decline of the power of landlords consequent to the integration of Hyderabad into the Indian union and the extensive land reforms under-taken by the post-independent state government reduced land monopoly and juridical power of landlords. The decline of big landlords' political power also released Boyas's political agency, facilitating the clearing of for-est lands for cultivation. However, the post-independent state govern-ment retained the hereditary Patwari system of local government, ensuring the centrality of the landlords to the village system. This sets the stage for a long struggle between the old elites and the Boya caste. From 1980 to 1995, Boya peasants could markedly enlarge their status due to a shift in production from traditional subsistence agriculture to intensive agricul-ture. Peasants from backward castes emerged as large-scale employers of casual labour leading to a decline in the prestige of traditional elites built on a monopoly of land-based assets, facilitating a power shift. The region-wide movement for democratisation in the 1990s, often referred to as a 'backward class assertion', aggregated such micropower shifts in the vil-lage and deepened the trend towards democratisation of village power structures. OBC castes gained access to the state to the sub-district level. The regional- and national-level movements enabled the retention of pop-ulist policies such as occasional loan waivers by national and state govern-ments. In this period, a well-developed ideological position of caste radicalism and agrarian populism developed among the Boya caste.

From the mid-1990s, commercial penetration under unfavourable eco-logical and market conditions caused a class differentiation and pauperisa-tion among this group. Neo-liberal conditions have brought a more significant squeeze on farming incomes. Farming households can repro-duce themselves only with some component of wage work leading to a circular migration among this group. Some theorists of agrarian change have been pointing out that due to competitive pressure, many smallhold-ers are losing hold on cultivation. The village has a large proportion of what agrarian theorists characterise as classes of labour: small farmers and farmer-labourers whose primary income is cultivation but who must engage in nonfarm labour to reproduce the family.

An ongoing process of repeasantisation is observed in the village whereby peasants plough migration proceeds to purchase land and assets. Repeasantisation could only be accomplished by widening the provisions of externally provided productive infrastructure such as electricity connec-tions, credit, seed, fertiliser and pesticides. Such provisions could only be secured by capturing the state or finding accommodation within state apparatus controlled by dominant groups. I noticed in my fieldwork a stringent critique among OBC peasants of dominant sections perceived as exploiters of peasants as money lenders, merchant and commission agents, and a pragmatic rapprochement with them to secure state provisions. Such a balance of power has historically engendered allegiance relations between peasants and their overlords of Reddy Brahmin elite interests in the region. Till 2009, both Congress and TDP represented the varying allegiance of OBC peasants with dominant castes of Reddies at the Gadwal town for strategic gain from the latter's access to the state. The state is perceived as a collaborator of dominant interests. Globalisation is not perceived as an amorphous influence of the external market but as mediated by dominant castes of the region. Thus, although entangled in allegiance relations for transactional gains, peasants from backward caste keep the dream of autonomous politics of peasants and oppressed castes alive in them.

Pauperisation of OBC peasants also has other social consequences. Due to the economic levelling of social groups, Dalits refuse to offer ranked transactions to OBC peasants in the village. Thus, a decline in economic status also affects social status. This has engendered a status conflict between OBC peasants and Dalits, who are now vying with them for equality. This status conflict has also produced a conservative attitude among them. Politics in this Telangana village that once witnessed pitched between OBC and dominant castes of Reddies for the democratisation of village power structures are seeing a conflict between OBC and Dalits. Such agrarian change impacts political subjectivities and the formation of ideologies among OBC caste groups. The formation of a Telangana state on the back of a movement for regional autonomy has provided legitimacy to such political ideologies of radicalism and conservatism among peasants.

POLITICAL IDEOLOGIES AND ALLEGIANCE RELATIONS POST FORMATION OF THE TELANGANA STATE

The coming of the Telangana state excited hopes for 'rythu Raj' (peasant rule) and has spurred the growth of organisational activities among peasants in the Gadwal region. These associational activities culminated in a siege at the district secretariat for a loan waiver in 2015. However, officials refused to meet peasant representatives. Several peasants who participated in this protest expressed their political helplessness in the usual caste idiom of 'superiors shooing them away without respect'.

The Boyas I interviewed categorised the contemporary model of development as 'city-based development', and the TRS regime was dismissed as 'Velma Dora rule' (TRS chief belonged to Velama, an upper caste and a feudal rentier group of 'Dora'). TRS regime was identified with the upper castes' urban real estate and industrial interests and was accused of pushing pro-industrialisation policies. The efforts of the TRS government towards land record digitalisation were perceived as the first step towards land grab by industries and real estate. There were rumours of De beers, the global diamond agglomerate, prospecting the area.

Peasants followed the discourse of claiming radical difference with urban interests with an articulation that connects national identity with 'peasantness' and sovereignty with local control of resources. My arguments for liberalisation of markets were countered with this comment, 'if parties in power are willing to import food, then those parties should be prepared to import their votes too!'

However, the region's ruling elites attempt to domesticate this radical agrarian discourse of populism. District political class has moved to contain peasant discontent by addressing the issue of cultural territory without having to address the demand for economic and political territory. In 2017, a district of Gadwal called 'Jogulamba Gadwal' named after the temple of goddess Jogulamba at Gadwal was formed, carving it out of Mahbubnagar district.[2] This move gives a cultural and religious expression to aspirations of sub-regional autonomy.

Goddess Jogulamba is considered the fifth shakti peeta among 18 shakti peetams in the country. She represents Goddess Shakti and is part of the regional Hinduism of the local Sudra upper castes. While upper caste in origin, Jogulamba also resonates with the prevalence of mother worship among the backward caste peasants. Hence, the choice of Jogulamba also gives the appearance of a democratic content to this expression of regional autonomy. An effort is also made to promote and connect two diverse types of mother worship, namely the worship of 'Jogulamba' by castes such as Reddy and the cult of 'Jammulamma' more firmly associated with Boyas. Serving MLA has advised the tourism department to advertise Jammulamma temple as a major tourism site in Gadwal. The temple management authority has also allotted funds for ramping up services in the temple.[3] In short, the coming together of these two goddesses is designed to heal the rift between upper caste elites and OBC small peasants.

Jammulamma worship of the Boyas emerged as a regional cult with a dedicated temple in the heart of the Gadwal town from 1980 onwards, dwarfing the upper castes' Brahmanic temples. The growth of the Jammulamma temple was due to the growing prosperity and independence of the Boya caste after the abolition of Raja rule, land reforms, the decline of the Patel and Patwari system, and the subsequent democratisation of the regional state. The bringing together of Jammulamma and Jogulamba as a distinctive regional culture thereby imitates the first instance of backward class assertion in the 1990s. The acceptance of Jammulamma as the region's icon also soothed identity anxieties and fears of loss of worth felt by Boya peasants.

Certain tendencies of Hindu authoritarian populism are visible in the formation of Jogulamba Gadwal. In a mimetic action, the ruling elites in Gadwal follow the Chief Minster of the state, KCR, and accommodation of OBC goddesses is followed by a reassertion of relational divinity.

A deliberate effort to efface class difference and highlight selective unified features which are distorted could be observed in the religiously imagined autonomous region of 'Jogulamba Gadwal'. However, these actions of 'Hindu populism' is followed by bold association of a region as the property of the dominant Reddy caste. The Reddy ruling group in Gadwal has also proposed the renovation of Chennakeshava Swamy temple, the private temple of the erstwhile Reddy ruler. The brochure of Jogulamba Gadwal is replete with pictures of Brahmanic consecration of the Kshatriya rule.

While actions of regional elites craft a religious populism, OBC peasants remained entangled with their ideologies. Boya peasants were more interested in benefiting from allegiance relations. A section of Boya peasants was involved in the movement for the creation of the Gadwal district. Still, their concern was improving access to the state and using the district formation to push the demand for categorising Boyas as a scheduled tribe. Thee saw the exercise of asserting the supremacy of Jogulamba as a cultural expression of prevailing power equations between OBC peasants and Reddy provincial capital.

However, religious populism in the district is also matched by a new awareness among Boyas of their Hindu leanings. This has to do with the Boya's disquiet at the recent assertions of Dalits for equality in the village than with their agreement with elite-crafted ideologies. Due to Boya's demands for ritual services perceived as humiliating by Dalits, they have begun to mount a stringent critique of theological elements of the caste system. Boya peasants have installed across the region statues of Valmiki, believed to be the original ancestor of Boyas, in direct competition with Dalits. The latter have similarly installed statues of Dr B. R. Ambedkar. These acts of Boya of instrumental use of Hindu identity as a weapon against Dalit assertions have enabled a return of the infrastructure of Brahmanic Hinduism in the villages of Gadwal. Temples were in disrepair earlier due to the assertion of other backward castes are being renovated. Ratholsavam, a Brahmanic form of the temple festival, has returned to the region. The return of Brahmanical infrastructure benefits the peasants in their efforts to control socially assertive Dalit labour. Dalits, correctly perceiving the nature of religious and political change and the emergence of Boyas as clerks and muscle men of Sanskritic Hinduism, were converting to Christianity. The construction of Brahmanic temples and processions by the caste Hindu elite is a parallel process which rivals the construction of new Christian churches by Dalits.

CONCLUSION

The chapter pointed out that peasants of the village articulated discourse of agrarianism which employed a trope of rural/urban distinctions. The agrarian discourse articulated by the peasants was also found to be progressive. It raised questions of citizenship and economic and social justice and often pointed out the regressive caste agenda of globalisation that benefits rural and regional elites. However, the chapter pointed out that calculations of gains of political inclusion under conditions of the hegemony of rural and provincial elites make right-wing politics of relative mobility attractive to peasants.

Peasants and workers de-territorialised by intensive agriculture and globalisation have aspirations for 'territory' (as a place of identity, self-recognition and historical occupation or practices of land use) and strive for political democratisation (Sauer 2012). However, given the nature of the political agency of Boya peasants shaped by imperatives of repeasantisation and allegiance relations with regional elites, these expressions for territory-based identity often do not overtly question populism that benefits elite groups.

The chapter pointed out how the sub-regional elites attempted to yoke agrarian populism with religious populism to soothe peasant angst' at economic decline, lack of political representation and low esteem. As argued by others, the strength of right-wing populism is its ability to articulate different subject positions and interests in an unfiled system of discourse. The chapter argued that the boundaries between Hindu populism and agrarian populism remain porous, blurred and malleable. Sub-regional elites attempt to efface the sharp contradictions between peasant classes and elite groups. Issues of asset inequality, citizenship and social justice at the core of progressive agrarian discourses were attempted to be jettisoned for a politics of cultural assertion.

However, the success of such a project sponsored by the upper caste Hindu elite remains uncertain, considering the strength of a radical anti-caste discourse of agrarian populism. Calculations of transactional gains yoke OBC peasants with regional elites rather than a similarity of world view. At the same time, imperatives of repeasantisation involving a subordination of Dalit labour could cultivate a Hindu identity among OBC peasants more durable than such elite constructions. Studies of right-wing authoritarianism in India (Gudavarthy 2018, 2019b) have pointed out how the right-wing has become the face of corporate globalisation and articulate group anxieties that are triggered due to the undermining of the community by the same process. The shift in peasant politics from an attack on dominant elites to a focus on Dalits could feed into politics for relative mobility that provides ample ground for religious mobilisations. Peasant disquiet at the destruction of caste and village community could find accommodation in right-wing discourses which articulate these anxieties.

The changes in the socio-political sphere could pave the way for right-wing mobilisation based on Hindu identity and set the stage for a politics of religious polarisation associated with the BJP. It is pertinent that the Reddy Congress leader who initiated these changes in the region has defected to BJP in the 2019 elections.[4] The last round of parliamentary elections in 2019 witnessed the growth of the BJP in Telangana. OBCs have shown some inclination towards the party (Vageeshan 2019). Shifts in the party system in Telangana could provide a space for a more virulent form of authoritarian populism in communal politics, primarily found in towns which could provide a more durable ideological base for moving towards Hindu identity among peasants. The ascendant upper castes of Telangana find their class interests protected by the project of Hinduisation. At the same time, agrarian distress could provide a breeding ground for Hindu right-wing mobilisation among land-holding OBCs.

However, considering the balance of strength of ideologies of agrarian populism and caste conservatism, it is unlikely that OBC peasants could be mobilised only on the plank of relative mobility without significant accommodation of their socio-economic demands. It is crucial to distinguish between pragmatic alliances of OBCs with regional elites from ideological consensus. It is more important to highlight the role of political ideas in the electorate's lives. Such a view will not read the political actions of oppressed castes from the strategies of containment used by the caste elites. It is vital to highlight agency and foreground it in the political economy of a region.

Scholarly work on the peasants and the Hindu right-wing in India focuses on rich peasants (Brass 2019; Lindberg 1995; Ramakumar 2017). The rich peasant movements articulated a form of agrarianism which contained ideas of conservatism, nationalism and populism (Brass 2015, 2019; Ramakumar 2017). Hence, Brass (2015, 2019) considers the rightward shift of farming communities as a continuation of long-term trends in post-colonial peasant movements in India. However, scholars indicate that the growth of right-wing hegemony will depend on its spread among other backward castes that have traditionally resisted or are indifferent to the overtures of Brahmanical Hindu right-wing (Gudavarthy 2019a, 2019b; Rodrigues 2017). Until a new political imagination brings together Dalits and OBC peasants on a common discourse of citizenship and combines the quest for economic justice (fight against neo-liberalism and internal class exploitation) with questions of dignity, recognition and political representation, politics of the peasantry will remain vulnerable to ideologies sponsored by the regional elites. This is evidenced by the political importance of movements inspired by 'a narrative of agrarian distress'.

NOTES

1. Songs are available on YouTube and websites of different Telugu TV channels. https://www.deccanchronicle.com/140526/nation-current-affairs/article/jaya-jaya-he-telangana-be-new-state-song.
2. https://www.thenewsminute.com/article/gadwal-mla-alleges-kcr-deliberately-ignoring-demand-separate-district-trs-refutes-charge.
3. https://www.thehansindia.com/telangana/jammulamma-jatara-begins-in-gadwal-602855.
4. https://www.news18.com/news/politics/in-big-jolt-to-telangana-congress-dk-aruna-switches-over-to-bjp-2072541.html.

REFERENCES

Alam, Javeed. 2009. Democracy in India and the Quest for Equality. *Community Development Journal* 44 (3): 291–304. https://doi.org/10.1093/cdj/bsp021.

Amrit, B.L.S. 2018. In Telangana, TRS's Flagship Farmers' Welfare Scheme Could Be Its Downfall. *The Wire*, December 6.

Berenschot, Ward. 2014. Political Fixers in India's Patronage Democracy. In *Patronage as Politics in South Asia*, ed. Anastasia Piliavsky, 196–216. Cambridge: Cambridge University Press. https://www-cambridge-org.ezproxy.jnu.ac.in/core/books/patronage-as-politics-in-south-asia/political-fixers-in-indias-patronage-democracy/EE84502815140BD8EBE85BCC8520DA3C.

Braj Ranjan Mani. 2016. The RSS Brahmantva Versus Dalit-Bahujans. *Countercurrents.Org*, April 26.

Brass, Tom. 2015. Peasants, Academics, Populists: Forward to the Past? *Critique of Anthropology* 35 (2): 187–204. https://doi.org/10.1177/0308275X15569853.

———. 2019. Is Agrarian Populism Progressive? Russia Then, India Now. *Critical Sociology*. https://doi.org/10.1177/0896920519878488.

Carswell, Grace, and Geert De Neve. 2014. Why Indians Vote: Reflections on Rights, Citizenship, and Democracy from a Tamil Nadu Village. *Antipode* 46 (4): 1032–1053. https://doi.org/10.1111/anti.12081.

Chacko, Priya. 2018. The Right Turn in India: Authoritarianism, Populism and Neoliberalisation. *Journal of Contemporary Asia* 48 (4): 541–565. https://doi.org/10.1080/00472336.2018.1446546.

Chadha, Kalyani. 2018. From Caste to Faith: Contemporary Identity Politics in a Globalized India. *Journalism & Communication Monographs* 20 (1): 84–87. https://doi.org/10.1177/1522637917750132.

Chandra, Kanchan. 2004. *Why Ethnic Parties Succeed: Patronage and Ethnic Head Counts in India*, Cambridge Studies in Comparative Politics. Cambridge: Cambridge University Press. https://doi.org/10.1017/9781108573481.

Chatterjee, Partha. 2008. Classes, Capital and Indian Democracy. *Economic and Political Weekly* 43 (46): 89–93.

Deshpande, Rajeshwari, Louise Tillin, and K.K. Kailash. 2019. The BJP's Welfare Schemes: Did They Make a Difference in the 2019 Elections? *Studies in Indian Politics* 7. https://doi.org/10.1177/2321023019874911.

Elliott, Carolyn. 2011. Moving from Clientelist Politics Toward a Welfare Regime: Evidence from the 2009 Assembly Election in Andhra Pradesh. *Commonwealth and Comparative Politics* 49 (1): 48–79. https://doi.org/10.1080/1466204 3.2011.541111.

Fischer, Andrew M. 2020. The Dark Sides of Social Policy: From Neoliberalism to Resurgent Right-Wing Populism. *Development and Change* 51 (2): 371–397. https://doi.org/10.1111/dech.12577.

Gorringe, H. 2010. The New Caste Headmen? Dalit Movement Leadership in Tamil Nadu. In *Power and Influence in India: Bosses, Lords and Captains*, ed. P. Price and A.E. Ruud, 119–143. London: Routledge.

Gudavarthy, Ajay. 2018. *India After Modi: Populism and the Right*. New Delhi: Bloomsbury.

———. 2019a. Can the BJP Breach the South? *The Wire*, June 19.

———. 2019b. Why OBCs Hold the Key to the Future of Indian Democracy. *The Wire*, September 27.

Guérin, Isabelle, G. Venkatasubramanian, and S. Kumar. 2015. Debt Bondage and the Tricks of Capital. *Economic and Political Weekly* 50 (26/27): 11–18.

Gupta, Dipankar. 2005. Whither the Indian Village. *Economic and Political Weekly* 40 (8).

Hall, Stuart. 1985. Authoritarian Populism: A Reply. *New Left Review* I/151: 115–124.

Harrison, S. 1956. Caste and the Andhra Communists. *The American Political Science Review* 50 (2): 378–404.

Harriss, J.C. 2000. Populism, Tamil Style: Is It Really a Success? *Review of Development and Change* 5 (2): 332–336.

Jaffrelot, Christophe. 2000. Sanskritization vs. Ethnicization in India: Changing Identities and Caste Politics Before Mandal. *Asian Survey* 40: 756–766.

Jessop, Bob, Kevin Bonnett, Simon Bromley, and Tom Ling. 1984. Authoritarian Populism, Two Nations, and Thatcherism. *New Left Review* 147 (January).

Jodhka, Surinder S. 2014. Emergent Ruralities. *Economic and Political Weekly* XLIX (26/27): 5–17.

Kancha Ilaiah Shepherd. 2022. Telangana CM's Idea of a 'new Constitution' is Self-Destructive. It Echoes RSS Propaganda. *The Print*, February 8. https://theprint.in/opinion/telangana-cms-idea-of-a-new-constitution-is-self-destructive-it-echoes-rss-propaganda/824342/.

Krishna Reddy, G. 2002. New Populism and Liberalisation: Regime Shift under Chandrababu Naidu in AP. *Economic and Political Weekly* 37 (9): 871–883.

Kumar, Sajjan. 2020. The Waning of Subaltern Solidarity for Hindutva. *The Hindu*, May 31. https://www.thehindu.com/opinion/lead/the-waning-of-subaltern-solidarity-for-hindutva/article62107988.ece.

Kumar, Sanjay, and Pranav Gupta. 2020. BJP's Ideological Hegemony: Combining Religious Conservatism and Nationalism. *Studies in Indian Politics* 8 (December): 203–213. https://doi.org/10.1177/2321023020963482.

Laclau, Ernesto. 2005. *On Populist Reason*. New York: Verso.

Lerche, Jens. 1999. Politics of the Poor: Agricultural Labourers and Political Transformations in Uttar Pradesh. *The Journal of Peasant Studies* 26 (2–3): 182–241. https://doi.org/10.1080/03066159908438707.

Lindberg, S. 1995. Farmer's Movements and Cultural Nationalism in India: An Ambiguous Relationship. *Theory and Society* 24: 837–868.

Manor, J. 2004. Towel Over Armpit: Small-Time Political 'Fixers'. In *India and the Politics of Developing Countries: Essays in Memory of Myron Wiener*, ed. A. Varshney, 60–85. New Delhi: Sage.

———. 2010. Epilogue: Caste and Politics in Recent Times. In *Caste in Indian Politics*, ed. Rajni Kothari, xi–lxi. Hyderabad: Orient Blackswan.

Michael Kazin. 1995. *The Populist Persuasion: An American History*. 2011 ed., Vol. 15. New York: Basic Books. https://www.cambridge.org/core/article/michael-kazin-the-populist-persuasion-an-american-history-new-york-basic-books-1995-pp-x-381-2400-isbn-0465037933-robert-h-wiebe-selfrule-a-cultural-history-of-american-democracy-chicago-university-of-chicago-press-1995-pp-x-321-2595-isbn-0226895629/8CEB486DA526438F6A0203A7CC62A351.

Narayan, Badri. 2011. *The Making of the Dalit Public in North India: Uttar Pradesh, 1950–Present*. New Delhi: Oxford University Press.

———. 2021. *Republic of Hindutva*. New Delhi: Penguin.

———. 2022. There's a New Addition to BJP's Identity Politics in UP. It's Called Beneficiaries. *ThePrint*, February 4. https://theprint.in/opinion/theres-a-new-addition-to-bjps-identity-politics-in-up-its-called-beneficiaries/820711/.

Nilsen, Alf Gunvald. 2018. *From Inclusive Neoliberalism to Authoritarian Populism: Trajectories of Change in the World's Largest Democracy*. Public Lecture Đ JNU, Delhi, June 2018, June.

Palshikar, Suhas. 2015. The BJP and Hindu Nationalism: Centrist Politics and Majoritarian Impulses. *South Asia: Journal of South Asian Studies* 38 (October): 719–735. https://doi.org/10.1080/00856401.2015.1089460.

Pani, Narendar. 2017. Experiential Regionalism and Political Processes in South India. *India Review* 16 (3): 304–323. https://doi.org/10.1080/1473648 9.2017.1346405.

Parthasarathy, D. 2015. The Poverty of (Marxist) Theory: Peasant Classes, Provincial Capital, and the Critique of Globalization in India. *Journal of Social History* 48 (4): 816–841. https://doi.org/10.1093/jsh/shv044.

Pattenden, J. 2011. Gatekeeping as Accumulation and Domination: Decentralisation and Class Relations in Rural South India. *Journal of Agrarian Change* 11: 164–194.

Philip, Jessy K. 2017. 'Though He Is a Landlord, That Sarpanch Is My Servant!' Caste and Democracy in a Village of South India. *Contemporary South Asia* 25 (3): 270–284. https://doi.org/10.1080/09584935.2017.1353951.

Picherit, David. 2012. Migrant Labourers' Struggles Between Village and Urban Migration Sites: Labour Standards, Rural Development and Politics in South India. *Global Labour Journal* 3 (1): 143–162.

Price, Pamela. 2006. Changing Meanings of Authority in Contemporary Rural India. *Qualitative Sociology* 29 (3): 301–316. https://doi.org/10.1007/s11133-006-9020-2.

Price, P.G., and Srinivas Dusi. 2014. Patronage and Autonomy in India's Deepening Democracy. In *Patronage as Politics in South Asia*, ed. Anastasia Piliavsky, 218–236. London: Cambridge University Press.

Ramakumar, R. 2017. Jats, Khaps and Riots: Communal Politics and the Bharatiya Kisan Union in Northern India. *Journal of Agrarian Change* 17 (1): 22–42. https://doi.org/10.1111/joac.12146.

Rao, Bhaskara. 2017. Reorganisation of Districts in Telangana. *Economic and Political Weekly* 52 (10): 7–8.

Rodrigues, Valerian. 2017. An Expansive Hindutva Agenda? *The Hindu*, March 30.

Ruparelia, Sanjay. 2013. India's New Rights Agenda: Genesis, Promises, Risks. https://papers.ssrn.com/abstract=2807230.

Sauer, Sérgio. 2012. Land and Territory: Meanings of Land Between Modernity and Tradition. *Agrarian South: Journal of Political Economy* 1 (1): 85–107. https://doi.org/10.1177/227797601200100106.

Srikanth, H. 2013. Construction and Consolidation of the Telangana Identity. *Economic and Political Weekly.*

Subramanian, Narendra. 2007. Populism in India. *SAIS Review of International Affairs* 27 (1): 81–91. https://doi.org/10.1353/sais.2007.0019.

Vageeshan, H. 2019. The Enigma of the 2019 Parliamentary Elections in Telangana. *Economic and Political Weekly.*

Wyatt, Andrew. 2013. Combining Clientelist and Programmatic Politics in Tamil Nadu, South India. *Commonwealth & Comparative Politics* 51 (1): 27–55. https://doi.org/10.1080/14662043.2013.749674.

Yadav, Yogendra, and Suhas Palshikar. 2014. Between Fortuna and Virtu. In *Party Competition in Indian States*, ed. K.C. Suhas Palshikar and Yogendra Yadav Suri, 42–99. Oxford University Press. https://doi.org/10.1093/acprof: oso/9780198099178.001.0001.

Yogendra, Yadav. 2010. Representation. In *The Oxford Companion to Politics*, ed. Niraja Gopal Jayal and PratapBhanu Mehta, 347–360. New Delhi: Oxford University Press.

CHAPTER 6

Hindutva and Secularism

Enrico Beltramini

*"India will be a land of many faiths, equally honoured
and respected, but of one national outlook."*
—Jawaharlal Nehru, January 24, 1948 (quoted in: T.N. Madan,
*Locked Minds, Modern Myths: Secularism and Fundamentalism in
India* (Oxford University Press, Delhi 1997), 233.)

INTRODUCTION

The construction of Indian secularism is one of the most precious, celebrated, and fragile fruits of post-Independence India. The edification of
the secular, a space autonomous from confessional religion, was supposed
to be a remedy for the effects of the interreligious tensions, particularly
between Hindu and Muslims. The father of Indian secularism, Jawaharlal
Nehru, with the Congress Party of India, has been celebrated for creating
secular institutions and, most importantly, a climate of tolerance among
members of different faiths. The Constitution of India is adamant that
India is "a sovereign socialist *secular* democratic republic that secures for
all its citizens … liberty of thought, expression, belief, faith and worship"

E. Beltramini (✉)
Notre Dame de Namur University, Belmont, CA, USA

© The Author(s), under exclusive license to Springer Nature
Switzerland AG 2023
B. S. Nayak, D. Chakraborty (eds.), *Interdisciplinary Reflections on
South Asian Transitions*,
https://doi.org/10.1007/978-3-031-36686-4_6

89

(emphasis added).[1] Despite being a nation overwhelmingly Hindu, the Constitution places all religions on the same level and does not give preference to any religion over another. Unity in diversity was the guiding principle of the founding fathers of India. Nehru and his colleagues believed that only a pluralistic democracy could hold the people of different religions together and keep India united. Their project was a form of Indian nationalism, namely, a nation based on the notion of Indianness. Another form of nationalism, however, was challenging Nehru's nationalism: it promoted the idea to convert India into a Hindu state. A Hindu state is built on Hindu culture, which is a distinct culture, and includes all those who were not either Muslims or Christians. At the center of the Hindu nationalist project is the notion of *Hindutva*, one that encompasses all Indians, including those belonging to other religions (with the exception of Muslims and Christians), seen as Hindus. In the words of Veer Savarkar (1883–1966), leader of the *Hindu Mahasabha*, the Hindus "are not only a nation but a Jati (race), a born brotherhood" (Savarkar 1923: 89).[2] The concept of *Hindutva*, in other words, refers to an ethnicized Hindu identity and has been adopted by the Bharatiya Janata Party (BJP) in its 1996 election manifesto in terms of "a unifying principle which alone can preserve the unity and integrity" of India (BJP 1996); it has remained the party's guiding philosophical principle ever since.[3]

Indian secularism has shown itself to have limited and fragile roots in Indian society. Increasingly, the strategy of secular containment, by which Nehru meant that there should be a distance between state and the ubiquitous presence of religion in the public sphere, has been criticized and eventually marginalized. More importantly, the strategy of protecting and nurturing the reality of religious pluralism in the country through the agency of a secular state has lost its verve. The retreat of secularism began in the last decade of the twentieth century, with the famous demolition of the Babri Mosque in Ayodhya in 1992, when the Hindu nationalists pulled down a mosque after a populist campaign because it was assumedly on the same spot as a former temple of a Hindu god. Today, India is ruled by a Hindu nationalist, Prime Minister Narendra Modi. He belongs to a Hindu nationalist political party, the BJP, and he spent his formative years working for a nationalist group called the Rashtriya SwayamSevak Sangh (RSS). He pushes a strategy of homogenization of Indian society centered on the cultural, religious, and political guidance of Hindu identity.

Scholarship on the crisis of Indian secularism and the raise of Hindu nationalism is the result of two strands of debates. The first strand revolves

around the political agenda and the policies advanced by Hindu nationalists. The second strand interprets Hindu nationalism in cultural terms. A
reflection on the destiny of Indian secularism in an era of Hindu nationalism belongs to this second strand. In sum, Hindu nationalism approaches
Indian secularism as a historical product of colonialism that has been in
formation since the nineteenth century, but scholars and defenders of
Indian secularism see it as an ontological reality, an inherent and transhis-
torical component of Indian identity. Before proceeding, however, I need
to define the terms 'secular,' 'secularization,' and 'secularism' and explain
what I mean by 'Hindu nationalism.'

TERMS

A discussion of the secular requires establishment of some basic analytical
distinctions between 'the secular' as a central modern epistemic category,
a synonym, 'secularity,' and two similar terms, 'secularization' and 'secularism.'[4] While the former, 'secularization,' is a genealogical conceptual-
ization of modern world-historical processes, the latter, 'secularism,'
operates as a world-view and historical embodiment of the secular. All
three concepts, 'the secular,' 'secularization,' and 'secularism,' are obviously related but are used to describe three different phenomena operating in three distinct realms of knowledge.

'The secular' is a central modern category to construct, codify, grasp,
and experience a realm or reality differentiated from 'the religious.' One
can explore the different types of 'secularities' as they are codified, institu-
tionalized, and experienced in various modern contexts and the parallel
and correlated transformations of modern 'religiosities' and 'spiritualities.'
In brief, 'the secular' stands for a (ontological) reality. 'Secularization'
refers usually to the genealogy of the secular, that is, the actual empirical-
historical patterns of transformation and differentiation of 'the religious'
(ecclesiastical institutions and churches) and 'the secular' (state, economy,
science, art, entertainment, health and welfare, etc.) institutional spheres
from western early modern to contemporary societies. The thesis of 'the
decline' and 'the privatization' of religion in the modern world have
become central components of the theory of secularization. Both the
decline and the privatization theses, however, have undergone numerous
critiques and revisions in the last 30 years. In sum, 'secularization' is the
genealogy and the theory of secularization; it explains how and why the
modern became secular. 'Secularism' refers more specifically to the kind of

secular world-views (or *Weltanschauungen*), which may be either con-
sciously held and explicitly elaborated or taken for granted. But modern
secularism also comes in multiple historical forms, in terms of different
normative models of legal-constitutional separation of the secular state
and religion, or in terms of the different types of cognitive differentiation
between science, philosophy, and theology, or in terms of the different
models of practical differentiation between law, morality, and religion, etc.
In the end, 'secularism' is both the ideology and the historical incarnation
of the secular; it is the way the secular works.

Finally, I want to frame the borders of what I call 'Hindu nationalism.'
Hindutva—Hindu nationalism, literally 'Hindu essence'—is an ideology
('one culture, one nation, one religion') that aims to create a Hindu *rashtra* (nation) by replacing 'Indianness' on the unique criteria of national
identity, the ultimate goal being to move India toward becoming a Hindu
nation. In the words of Vinayak Domodar Savarkar, who coined the term,
"Hindutva embraces all the departments of thought and activity of the
whole being of our Hindu race." He added that "Hinduism is ... a part of
Hindutva."[5] That said, Hindu nationalism is a political project that
employs religion for political purposes. Additionally, it reinterprets traditional Hindu symbols and practices in a nationalist context. Hindu nationalists challenge both intellectually and practically people of other faiths as
a way to protect themselves from what they consider outside invaders, that
is, Christians and Muslims, even though Christian and Muslim witness has
been circulating in India for centuries.

Hindu nationalism is growing and has been building strength for
decades. It seems now to be working in symbiosis with the ruling Hindu
nationalist party, BJP. Here I do not pay attention to the generic, although
criminal, actions of Hindu fundamentalist organizations such as the RSS,
Vishwa Hindu Parishad (VHP), Bajrang Dal (DB), and Akhil Bharatiya
Janata Party (ABVP), driven by the intent of organized and systematic
persecution against Christians and Muslims and incitement of communal
violence. I instead specifically refer to those government-driven policies, in
place or at least announced, such as (1) the denial of constitutional rights
to practice and propagate one's own religion, (2) the anti-conversion legislation, (3) the revision of the Constitution of India with regard to two
articles of the Constitution that seem to give significant concessions to
minorities or the minority-dominated state, and (4) the ideologizing of
history through rewriting history textbooks within the educational system
(schools, educational institutions, and universities).[6] That said, the list of

governmental policies listed above should be considered prudently. I have no doubt that many BJP politicians would like to revise the Constitution and place restrictions on religious minorities, but I understand that Prime Minister Modi has publicly disavowed any intention to revise the Constitution or introduce federal anti-conversion legislation. Again, I don't doubt a larger agenda at work—but I think that one needs to give the government some credit. To put it differently, I locate 'Hindu nationalism' not at the social, cultural, or eventually broadly political level, but at the level of policy—at the level of the central government of the federal state, which in the mind of Jawaharlal Nehru, the main architect of the relation between the state and religion in India, is ultimately responsible for the secular governance of the public sphere in which secularism as well as religions operate.[7]

Indian Secularism

After the collapse of Mohandas 'Mahatma' Gandhi's plan to promote Hindu-Muslim unity, in 1947 the Indian subcontinent was divided into two states, India and Pakistan. India portrayed itself as a pluralistic nation that welcomes ethnic, religious, and cultural diversity.[8] However, the existence of a weak national identity, the potential for further Hindu-Muslim conflict, and the rise of secessionist and separatist aspirations forced Jawaharlal Nehru (the first Prime Minister of India) to counter the country's ultimate risk of disintegration with the creation of a form of secular nationalism functioning as the ideology of a centralized federal state led by a strong central government. At that time, the main concern of the generation of leaders born out of the fight for independence was the protection of the unity and integrity of the nation.[9] The strategy was to build the post-colonial India around a common Indian identity: Indianness. Indianness was one of the main ideas of the Congress Party during the pre-independence era, and it became a crucial ingredient to helping India remain united: 'unity in diversity.' Indian nationalism, a nation built on the Indian identity, would provide unity to the heterogeneous people of India. On the more practical side, the cornerstone of this strategy was the erection of a state that is officially secular and it is not leaning toward any specific religion. In this way, a modern, secular nationalism would operate as a nation-building force and give foundation to a new, unifying identity for all Indians. It would also contain, regulate, and facilitate the dialogue among the traditional, old-fashioned religious identities.

Nehru understood the dominant role of religion in Indian society. He described the creation of a secular state in a religious society as the biggest problem that he had during his years in power. In 1961, just three years before his death, he wrote: "We talk about a secular state in India. It is perhaps not very easy even to find a good word in Hindi for 'secular'. Some people think it means something opposed to religion. That obviously is not correct … It is a state which honours all faiths equally and gives them equal opportunities."[10] In these words there is, *in nuce*, the character of Indian secularism and the difference between Indian secularism and western secularism.[11] In post-Independence India, religion was not supposed to be limited or privatized. On the contrary, to borrow the words of Gandhi, religion would remain the source of absolute value, the single most important ingredient of social life; the state would support each and every religious community in the celebration of their own myths and rites. Religion would be public as much as politics, because, to mention Gandhi once more, "those who say that religion has nothing to do with politics do not know what religion means."[12] That said, however, the public space hosts both religion(s) and state and is a place of continuous dialogue between religious traditions and between religions and secularism.[13] The public space is, ultimately, a place of dialogue, infused of, and rooted in, the religious, with the state operating as a secular margin, as an agent that is not allied with any particular religion or an instrument of any religious organization.

The generation of a nation-state based on secularism out of a multi-religious reality like India could not come without difficulties. One difficulty is related to the relationship between politics and religion. One simple way to see it is that the public sphere hosts a cohabitation of politics and religions, in which the former is responsible for maintaining the unity and integrity of the nation, guaranteeing the administration of the country, resolving disputes among religions groups, and protecting the constitutional right of religious freedom. The latter conserves its grip on Indian consciousness and remains the metaphysical ground on which individuals and communities stand. A second way to understand the politics-religion relationship is to consider politics and religion distinct from yet entangled with each other. Although in distinct fashions, both politics and religions pursue tolerance, seek justice, and fight hunger, war, and exploitation. In that sense, there is no political factor that is not at the same time a religious factor; there is no religious factor that is not ultimately political. This is Gandhi's view. Politics without religion becomes instrumental and cynical; religion without politics become irrelevant and unswervingly otherworldly.

A second difficulty is concerned with the practical functioning of the secular. The Constitution of India recognized the equal right to freedom of conscience as well as the right freely to profess, practice, and propagate religion (art. 25:1); it also defends the fundamental rights of minority (religious) groups and prohibits the Indian state from discriminating against any citizen on the grounds of religion, race, caste, sex, or place of birth (art. 23:2); finally, it declares that there shall be no official state religion, no religious instruction in state schools, and no taxes to support any particular religion (arts. 25–28). A decisive article of the Constitution permits religious and linguistic minorities to establish and run their own educational institutions (art. 30:1). That said, the Constitution does not define accurately what is meant by a secular Indian state and how politics and religion should be distinct yet entangled. Moreover, the Constitution grants the state the right to regulate "any economic, financial, political or other secular activity which may be associated with religious practice" to provide for social welfare and reform to all sections (art. 25:2).[14] But it does not explain how this right should be exercised in combination with the right to freely profess one's own religion. In general, the Constitution does not give clear directives as to how the pragmatic and diplomatic role of the state is to be implemented with regard to religion and disputes between religious groups; therefore, the remedy for these difficulties is to be found at a more practical level, at the level of the central (federal) government, which has far greater powers than, for example, the central (federal) government of the United States. In the end, how secularism works in India might be found not in the law of the Constituent Assembly but in the praxis of the centralized government.

Crisis of Indian Secularism

In the last few decades, the Indian secularism debate has focused on detecting and analyzing the crisis of secularism in the face of the rising forces of Hindu nationalism.[15] This debate is important because it has contributed to clarification of certain elements of both the nature and the genealogy of Indian secularism. As a matter of fact, some have claimed, with some reason, that the very same notion of 'secularism' in India is ambiguous and that it means different things to different people.[16]

On the one side, there are the critics of Indian secularism who emerged during the time of the struggles for independence, framed by leaders like Gandhi, Nehru, and Ambedkar.[17] Thanks to them, the Constitution of the country remained secular, giving equal regard for all the religions and denying the status of state religion to any one particular religion. In the past two decades, however, Hindu nationalism has labeled secularism assured by the Constitution as 'pseudo secularism' of the minorities in order to propagate their religions. In their view, secularism was imposed by foreign westernized elites onto a profoundly religious Indian population. Revered Indian historian and leading scholar on ancient India Romila Thapar questions whether secularism belongs to Indian civilization.[18] To put it differently, the idea of secularism is an alien import in India and has failed to take root there. Some have chosen a different line of criticism, according to which the main cause of the crisis of the secular is internal to the secular state. In fact, although India has professed to be a 'secular state,' a state which treats all religions impartially, the state has never been completely impartial or detached from religion.[19] On the contrary, the state has regularly intervened to regulate the affairs of some religious communities while leaving others alone (e.g., with regard to temple management and supervision of fairs and pilgrimages).[20] A further line of criticism is articulated by some, who argue that secularism's regulation of religion in Indian society has led to a backlash and radicalization in the form of Hindu nationalism.[21] Regarding this, I mention a book by Elizabeth Shakman Hurd, *Beyond Religious Freedom*; although not focused on India, Hurd offers an illuminating analysis of the unintended consequences of the liberal state's secular regulating instinct toward religion.[22]

In summary, on the one hand, the critics of the *status quo* raise concerns about secularism as a regulatory agent of religion and as being alien to Indian society. On the other hand, the defenders of the *status quo*, namely, the Indian secularism that emerged out of Independence, claim that Indian secularism has its roots in the historical and social realities of India and is quite different from western secularism.[23] Those people argue that a specifically Indian form of secularism has come into being because of the historical conditions under which it emerged.[24] For example, some claim that Indian secularism is distinct from western secularism, for it was transformed in the process of responding to problems like caste discrimination and extreme religious diversity. Gary Jacobsohn calls the result of this process, "the ameliorative model," which "embraces the social reform impulse of Indian nationalism in the context of the nation's deeply rooted religious diversity and stratification."[25] In this context, Rajeev Bhargava asserts that secularism has a clear meaning, that is, "a separation of organized religion from organized political power inspired by a specific set of values." But these elements can be interpreted in several ways. Therefore, secularism has no fixed content but "multiple interpretations which change over time."[26]

What is interesting here is that Hindutva frames Indian secularism as the result of the effects of western secularism in India, effects that should be unveiled and reversed. For Indian nationalism, Indian secularism is only a mythos, a distinct story that transcends reasoning. As such, it cannot be refuted, only out-narrated. And the counter-narrative of Indian nationalists is that Indian secularism is a historical product which has been in construction since the time of British colonialism and that it is too strongly based on a western representation of India as multiethnic and religiously plural. By rejecting secularism, India would be able to return to its roots and recover the ancient tradition of Hindu civilization and its values.

The criticism of secularism and the claim of its apparent failure in the Indian context are known features of the Hindu nationalists. But both criticism and claim do not belong exclusively to them. For several decades now, Indian thinkers of different religious traditions and political orientations such as Ashis Nandy, Triloki Nath Madan, Mushirul Hasan, and Pratap Banu Mehta have been suspicious of secularism as an ontological category and rather interpreted it as a historical process. To borrow a sentence from Grace Davie, "an alternative suggestion is increasingly gaining ground: the possibility that secularization is not a universal process, but belongs instead to a relatively short and particular period of European history which still assumed (amongst other things) that whatever characterized Europe's religious life today would characterize everyone else's tomorrow."[27] An example of this post-secular perspective is the work of Ashis Nandy, who believes that secularism is an unintentional attempt to Christianize India. The entry point of Nandy's argument is that in agreement with Carl Schmitt's political theology, the political history of the West after Hobbes has been at the same time a religious history, in the sense that political concepts are derivatives of theology.[28]

Conclusion

The transplanting of secularism from England to India equates to an importation of Christian concepts. Like Gandhi, Nandy considered the West and India as belonging not to two different histories but to two fundamentally different myths. In his words, Gandhi "rejected history and affirmed the primacy of myths over historical chronicles."[29] The injection of secularism in the veins of Indian society, in Nandy's opinion, is ultimately responsible for Hindu nationalism, Muslim resistance, and Sikh defensiveness in the sense that secularism has artificially attempted to promise what the older religious traditions, primarily Hindu, had guaranteed for centuries before the coming of the Raj, that is, peaceful coexistence in India. Other examples of critics are T.N. Madan and Mushiral Hasan. The former argues that secularism has failed to become part of the shared world-view of regular citizens and for the majority of people in India secularism is "a phantom concept."[30] The latter has observed that "delinking of state and religion remains a distant dream; secularization of state and society an ideal."[31] These and other scholars have raised the fundamental question of whether secularism—a transplanted concept in India of a universal organizational device for the political administration of the religious that supposedly contains within itself a mechanism for mediating cultural difference—has failed. Two misconceptions brought Indian secularism to its demise: first, the Euro/western model of secularization, imagined as an ideological project, is also a historical model; second, the attempt to distance religion from the political and legal processes of a multicultural and religiously pluralist society is foreign to Indian tradition.

The stakes are not just abstractly intellectual; they are also deeply ideological and political. Hindu nationalists add to these highly intellectual criticisms, in fact, the identification of the ultimate cause of this failure, namely, a single religious group that is 'other' to the majority populace and its own religious rites and rights. Nationalism of any kind, Purushottama Bilimoria notes, is constantly desirous of a homogenous nation and reclaims nativism and demands loyalty and allegiance to a single cause.[32] One might add to that that nationalism is permanently committed to condemn those at the margins of difference as basically agents of disorder who are disinterested in conforming. The Indian state instituted a Hindu Code Act regarding a uniform civil code for all 'Hindus' in the nation (including Sikhs), although leaving Muslims to their own Personal Law.[33] This is part of the reason that Hindu nationalists branded Indian secularism in terms of pseudo-secularism. In the form of Bilimoria's rhetorical question, "why should the Hindus alone have to bear the burden of the regulatory and reformative agenda under the watchful eyes of the secular state, bent on secularization every aspect of Hindu faith and life, while the Muslim is exempted and is a willing claimant to the Constitutional license to continue with their own religiously sanctioned social practices, customs, and laws?"[34] The answer, unfortunately, has been raising anti-Muslim rhetoric and mobilization tactics and spreading of communal violence against religious minorities (including Christians).

NOTES

1. The statement is included in the preamble to the Constitution of India. See Sharad D. Abhyankar, "The Constitution of India," in Gisbert H. Flanz (ed.), *Constitutions of the Countries of the World*, Release 97–6 (Dobbs Ferry, NY: Oceana Publications, 1997).
2. Vinayak D. Savarkar, *Hindutva* (Bombay: Veer Savarkar Prakashan, 1923), 89.
3. Bharatiya Janata Party, 'For a Strong and Prosperous India—Election Manifesto 1996' (New Delhi, 1996).
4. This section is both an extract and re-elaboration of José Casanova, *Secular, secularizations, secularisms: The Immanent Frame*, October 25, 2007. At https://tif.ssrc.org/2007/10/25/secular-secularizations-secularisms/.
5. Vinayak Damodar, *Savarkar, Hindutva*; *Who is a Hindu?* (*Bombay: Veer Savarkar Prakashan*, 1969), 3–4.
6. For the revision of the Constitution, the goal of Hindu nationalists is to cancel the articles that permit religious and linguistic minorities to establish and run their own educational institutions and to grant special status to the state of Jammu and Kashmir where Muslims constitute an overwhelming majority. The latter was reached when the Parliament passed a resolution repealing the special status of Jammu and Kashmir under Article 370 of the Constitution, in 2019. With regard to the goal of writing history textbooks, see Robert Eric Frykenberg, 'Hindutva as a Political Religion,' *Dharma Deepika*, July–Dec., 2004, 7–38, 24–5.
7. Madan, *Locked Minds, Modern Myths: Secularism and Fundamentalism in India*, 310.
8. At the time of the partition there were 361 million people living in India; of these people, 315 million were Hindus, 32 million Muslims, 7 million Christians, 6 million Sikhs, 1 million Buddhists, 100,000 Parsians, and a small minority were Jews. Source: Stukenberg Marla, *Der Sikh-Konflikt: Eine Fallstudie zur Politisierung ethnischer Indetität* (Stuttgart: Franz Steiner Verlag, 1995), 1.

9. The statement 'the unity and integrity' is included in the preamble to the Constitution of India. See Abhyankar, 'The Constitution of India.'

10. Nehru. Quoted in Madan *Locked Minds, Modern Myths: Secularism and Fundamentalism in India*, 245–6.

11. Here I quote Professor Neera Chandhoke of National Fellow, Indian Council of Social Science Research: "The first Prime Minister of India, Nehru, identified three features that define secularism. The first two, freedom of religion or irreligion and equality of religious practices, can be protected by democratic rights. The third aspect, that the state should not be aligned to any one religion, is crucial to the principle of equality, even to a weaker form of equality as non-discrimination between groups." Then Professor Neera Chandhoke discusses the risk of an alliance between state and one specific religion: "The overlap between two formidable forms of power poses a distinct threat to freedom of conscience and expression, provides opportunities to a religious group aligned with the state that are unavailable to other groups, and seriously compromises equal citizenship rights as a basic tenet of democracy." He also mentions the question of the protection of minorities: "The task of secularism is to safeguard plurality and ensure equality, and equality has to provide for minority rights—to protect minority communities and promote their cultures. Otherwise minorities will always be at risk in a majoritarian society. This will imperil not only the culture and the practices of the minority community, but also endanger the rights of its members." Neera Chandhoke, "Rethinking Secularism: A View from India," *Global e-Journal*, Vol. 10, Issue 9, February 14, 2017.

12. M. K. Gandhi, *An Autobiography or the Story of My Experiments with Truth* (Ahmedabad: Navajivan Publishing House, 1940), 383. For the sake of this article, it is important to note that Mahatma Gandhi emphasized, at the same time, (1) the inseparability of religion and politics, and (2) the superiority of the former over the latter.

13. Nandy Ashis, Trivedy Shikha, Mayaram Shail, Yagnik Achyut, *Creating a Nationality. The Ramjanmabhumi Movement and Fear of the Self.* 2nd impression (New Delhi: Oxford University Press, 1998), 327.

14. Chatterjee Partha, *A Possible India. Essays in Political Criticism* (New Delhi: Oxford University Press, 1997), 241–2.

15. Madan, *Modern Myths, Locked Minds: Secularism and Fundamentalism in India*; Thomas Pantham, "Indian Secularism and Its Critics: Some Reflections," *The Review of Politics* 59 (1997): 523–40; Rajeev Bhargava (ed.), *Secularism and Its Critics* (Delhi: Oxford University Press, 1998); Sumit Ganguly, "The Crisis of Indian Secularism," *Journal of Democracy*

14 (2003): 11–25; Anuradha Dingwaney Needham and Rajeswari Sunder Rajan, ed., *The Crisis of Secularism in India* (Durham and London: Duke University Press, 2007); S. N. Balagangadhara and Jakob De Roover, "The Secular State and Religious Conflict: Liberal Neutrality and the Indian Case of Pluralism," *Journal of Political Philosophy* 15 (2007): 67–92; Badrinath Rao, "The Variant Meanings of Secularism in India: Notes Toward Conceptual Clarifications," *Journal of Church and State* 48 (2006): 47–81.

16. Madan, *Modern Myths, Locked Minds: Secularism and Fundamentalism in India*, 2, 244; M. M. Sankhdher, "Understanding Secularism," in Sankhdher (ed.), *Secularism in India: Dilemmas and Challenges* (New Delhi: Deep and Deep, 1995), 1–2; H. Srikanth, "Secularism versus Pseudo-Secularism: An Indian Debate," *Social Action* 44 (1994): 39–54.

17. Jakob De Roover, Sarah Claerhout, S. N. Balagangadhara, "*Liberal Political Theory and the Cultural Migration of Ideas: The Case of Secularism in India,*" *Political Theory* 39, no. 5 (September 2011): 571–599.

18. Romila Thapar, "Is secularism alien to Indian civilization?" in Aakash Singh and Silika Mohapatra (eds.), *Indian Political Thought: A Reader* (New York: Routledge, 2010).

19. The Muslims of Kashmir claim that they have not been granted government posts because of their religion, and the same is argued by the Sikhs.

20. Partha Chatterjee, "Secularism and Tolerance," in Rajiv Bhargava (ed.), *Secularism and Its Critics*, 353–66; Rao, "The Variant Meanings of Secularism in India: Notes Toward Conceptual Clarifications," 48–9.

21. T. N. Madan, "Secularism in Its Place," in Rajiv Bhargava (ed.), *Secularism and Its Critics*, 297–320; Ashis Nandy, "An AntiSecularist Manifesto," *Seminar* 314 (1985): 14–24; Ashis Nandy, "The Politics of Secularism and the Recovery of Religious Tolerance," in Rajiv Bhargava (ed.), *Secularism and Its Critics*, 321–44; Ashis Nandy, "Closing the Debate on Secularism: A Personal Statement," in Rajiv Bhargava (ed.), *The Crisis of Secularism in India*, 107–117.

22. Elizabeth Shakman Hurd, *Beyond Religious Freedom: The New Global Politics of Religion* (Princeton, NJ: Princeton University Press, 2015).

23. See, for example, Rajeev Bhargava, "The distinctiveness of Indian secularism," in Aakash Singh & Silika Mohapatra (eds.), *Indian Political Thought: A Reader* (London: Routledge, 2010), 99–119.

24. Neera Chandhoke, *Beyond Secularism: The Rights of Religious Minorities* (Delhi: Oxford University Press, 1999), 42; Pantham, "Indian Secularism and Its Critics: Some Reflections"; Shabnum Tejani, *Indian Secularism: A Social and Intellectual History, 1890–1950* (Bloomington & Indianapolis:

Indiana University Press, 2008), 4–6. To place the evolution of Indian secularism in a global context, see Linell E. Cady and Elizabeth Shakman Hurd (eds.), *Comparative Secularisms in a Global Age* (New York: Palgrave Macmillan, 2010).

25. Gary Jacobsohn, *The Wheel of Law: India's Secularism in Comparative Constitutional Context* (Princeton and Oxford: Princeton University Press, 2003), 49–50.

26. Rajeev Bhargava, "The Distinctiveness of Indian Secularism," in T. N. Srinivasan (ed.), *The Future of Secularism* (New Delhi: Oxford University Press, 2007), 21–2. See also Gurpreet Mahajan, "Secularism as Religious Non-Discrimination: The Universal and the Particular in the Indian Context," *India Review* 1 (2002): 33–51. An interesting addition to the list is Peter Van der Veer's comparative historical sociology study of religion and nationalism in India and China, entitled *The Modern Spirit of Asia*. Although focused on modernity in its multilayered and complex phenomenon, Van der Veer addresses secularism as a constituent element of modernity. He identifies a kind of third pathway between the critics and the defenders of Indian secularism. In his opinion, secularism entered India through the mediation of western imperialism and, as such, it maintains a western origin. He locates the onset of Indian secularism in the nineteenth century: according to Van der Veer, Indian secularism was aligned politically to the emergence of the nation-state, economically to industrialization, and ideologically to an emphasis on progress and liberation. However, the development of secularism in Indian society, in his view, is dependent upon the deep history of such society. In turn, such deep history has resulted in fundamental differences with regard to western secularism. See Peter Van der Veer, *The Modern Spirit of Asia: The Secular and the Spiritual in India and China* (Princeton: Princeton University Press, 2013).

27. Grace Davie, *Religion in Modern Europe: A Memory Mutates* (Oxford, New York: Oxford University Press, 2000), 1.

28. Carl Schmitt, *Political Theology: Four Chapters on the Concept of Sovereignty*, Trans. George Schwab (Cambridge, MA: MIT Press, 1985).

29. Ashis Nandy, *The Intimate Enemy: Loss and Recovery of Self under Colonialism* (Delhi: Oxford University Press, 1983), 55.

30. T.N. Madan, "Secularism in Its Place," *The Journal of Asian Studies* 46, no. 4 (1987), 747–759, 749.

31. Mushiral Hasan, "Minority Identity and Its Discontents: Ayodhya and Its Aftermath," *South Asian Bulletin* 14, no. 2 (1994), 24–40, 26.

32. Purushottama Bilimoria, "The Pseudo-Secularization of Hindutva and its Campaign for Uniform Civil Codes," *Nidan: Journal of the Department of Hindu Studies* 18 (2006), 1–21, 2.
33. Personal laws of Hindus have been largely codified via the so-called Hindu Code Bill (1955–57). The Hindu Marriage Act, 1955, reins in prohibition against the practice of bigamy. Hindu Succession Act gave widows right to absolute maintenance and daughters the right to inherit. The Hindu Code also eased the pressures on divorce and marital difficulties, property rights, and inheritance among Hindus, while it did not reverse the inclinations of caste, patriarchy, and race.
34. Bilimoria, "The Pseudo-Secularization of Hindutva and its Campaign for Uniform Civil Codes," 6.

CHAPTER 7

Understanding the Triumph of Hindutva and Its Social Contract in India

Bhabani Shankar Nayak

INTRODUCTION

The Bhartiya Janta Party (BJP) won absolute majority in 2014 over Hindutva populism, which is more concerned with the struggle for power and pelf and less with religion per se. The enormous growth of Hindutva right-wing politics has both social and economic implications on India's socially and culturally regulated economy. It aims to destroy the organic multicultural fabric of the Indian society and create a majoritarian Hindu state which is antithetical to constitutional ethos. In terms of economy and business, there is a growing consolidation of wealth in the hands of few corporations. Therefore, the rise of Hindutva creates a very unique condition where ethno-nationalism promotes crony capitalism. The rise of Hindutva politics led to the growth of wealth of large businesses and corporations, whereas local businesses declined at the same time in India.

B. S. Nayak (✉)
University for the Creative Arts, Epsom, UK
e-mail: bhabani.nayak@uca.ac.uk

© The Author(s), under exclusive license to Springer Nature
Switzerland AG 2023
B. S. Nayak, D. Chakraborty (eds.), *Interdisciplinary Reflections on South Asian Transitions*,
https://doi.org/10.1007/978-3-031-36686-4_7

The chapter seeks to interrogate the political economy of Hindutva and its global implications. The forward march of neoliberal Hindutva has delegitimised caste and class and gender struggles by branding them as 'anti national' projects hindering the Indian growth story. Such a process seeks to establish unity among the dominant castes and classes. The ruling ideology based on Hindu majoritarianism seeks to forge an overarching religious identity pandering over caste differences for electoral benefits. Needless to mention, the foot soldiers of Hindutva comprise the marginalised communities, the Dalits and Adivasis who are ideologically motivated to engage in violence against the minorities. The political project of Hindutva based on social Darwinism has succeeded in demonising any opposition whether ideological, cultural, religious or even intellectual. It is within this context, the chapter seeks to analyse the linkages between Hindutva nationalism and business entrepreneurship, emergence of crony capitalism and its impact on economic lifeworld.

The Hindutva draws its ideological inspiration from the European fascist organisations like the National Fascist Party/Republican Fascist Party in Italy and the Italian Social Republic under Benito Mussolini, the National Socialist German Workers' Party (Nazi Party) in Nazi Germany under Adolf Hitler, the Fatherland Front in Austria under Engelbert Dollfuss and Kurt Schuschnigg, the National Union in Portugal under António de Oliveira Salazar and Marcelo Caetano, the Falange Española Tradicionalista y de las JONS ('Traditionalist Spanish Phalanx of the Councils of the National Syndicalist Offensive') in Spain under Francisco Franco. European fascism was riddled with many contradictions, but there are no contradictions within Hindutva fascism in India. Ignorance, arrogance, irrationality and unquestionable power bring unity within Hindutva fascism in India. Catholic corporatism has played a major role in sustaining and expanding the plight of people and the power of European fascism. Similarly, the Indian capitalist classes are working as backbone of Hindutva fascism in the country. The Hindutva-led government is working relentlessly for the corporate profit at the cost of Indian citizens. Hindutva fascism is the capitalist predators like their Catholic corporate brethren (Nayak 2017).

The Hindutva onslaught on free press, human rights, minority rights, women's rights, science and reason, militarisation of minds of common people replicate European fascism at work during and after nineteenth century. The attack on Indian constitutional democracy, political opponents, journalists, intellectuals and universities is further step to reinforce

Hindutva fascism in India. Hindutva is the fascist response to normalise inequality, caste, class and gender-based exploitations. The construction of Muslims, Marxists and intellectuals as anti-nationals, criminalisation of dissent and demonisation of political opposition helps in the normalisation of Hindutva fascism. Hindutva constructs external enemies among India's immediate neighbours as well. The creation of internal and external enemies is crucial for Hindutva fascist project to survive (Banaji 2018). The rise of interstate conflicts within India also helps Hindutva politics to thrive.

The Hindutva propaganda on national unity, Gandhian socialism, economic growth and development are false dawns in the national life of India. The Hindutva politics uses propaganda to divert everyday issues of people. Hindutva vigilante-led large-scale and targeted violence and spread of fear are used as twin weapons to normalise faith-based immoral politics for the growth of capitalism (Byler 2022). The Hindutva militias free from judicial prosecutions help in transforming Indian state and democracy that is concomitant with the requirements of Hindutva fascism and capitalism in India. Hindutva fascism enlarges the existing problems in Indian society. It does not have visions and missions to solve any of the problems faced by Indians. There is nothing indigenous about Hindutva fascism in India. These European ideals are implemented in India by Hindutva politics. Hindutva fascism is a project of global and national capitalism in India.

The Hindutva fascism faces the challenges of Indian diversities and its secular constitution. The struggle to protect Indian diversities and secularism is the first step towards the battle against Hindutva. The battle against Hindutva fascism and capitalism is a common battle. The success of such a mass movement can only decide the future of Indians and survival of India.

Hindutva Social Contract

The Hindutva euphoria in legitimising authoritarian state power with the help of electoral democracy is another success story in the history of fascism. The liberal, constitutional and secular democracy is falling apart with the ascendancy of authoritarian waves led by Hindutva politics of hate. The Brahminical social contract based on Hindu caste order, propaganda, populism, relentless indoctrination-led religious polarisation and neoliberal capitalism are five pillars of Hindutva fascism. These five pillars are integral to each other in establishing full-fledged Hindutva fascism and capitalism in India. The evolving neoliberal Hindutva has managed to establish a new form of social contract, which has shifted citizenship to a secondary position to normalise systematic exploitation and subjugation of lower caste, working classes, gender and religious minority communities. The Hindutva populist government led by the BJP is trying to create further centralised and powerful government in Delhi to facilitate crony capitalism (Nayak 2017). The authoritarian model of Hindutva governance promises good days to Indians but failed to deliver the basic health, education, food security and health to its citizens.

The Hindutva fascist forces are reshaping and institutionalising a new form of social contract, which is primarily based on caste-based Brahminical social order (Teltumbde 2020). The Hindutva government is articulating and advancing an ideology of social contract based on othering of religious minorities and marginalised communities in India. The divisive Hindutva social contract is representing bourgeois social contract that articulates and institutionalises medieval ideas of Brahminical social order based on caste and class apartheid. The ascendancy of Brahminical bourgeoisie, the Hindutva social contract is evolving by diminishing secular constitutional democracy in India. The Hindutva social contract is obscuring everyday marginalisation and exploitation in the name of nationalism. The political co-optation of nationalism by the Hindutva regime helps to empower capitalists and marginalises masses (Nayak 2017).

The Hindutva social contract instils fear and perpetuates economic crisis which destroys citizen's confidence in state and government. Such a process of depoliticisation breaks the legal contract between Indian citizens and their state. It weakens all institutions of social welfare and governance. The Hindutva social contract is naturalising crisis and imposing its legitimacy to serve the global and national capitalist classes. Such an organised social, political, cultural and economic engineering create a social structure of conformity that is concomitant with the requirements for the expansion of capitalism and its market society. Modi-led BJP government is creating policies, structures and processes to put the interests of crony capitalists above the interests of Indian masses (Bhattacharya and Thakurta 2020).

The economic policies pursued by the Hindutva fascists reflect the nuances of its social contract that accommodates subordinate and superior caste structure on the basis of consumerism as its operational ideology (Shah 2002). Under such a structure of Hindutva social contract, the state–citizenship relationship is replaced by patron–client relationship.

The hegemony of the Hindutva social contract is subservient to the requirements of the global capitalism in India. The agenda is not hidden anymore. It is clear that the Hindutva fascists are restructuring Indian society, culture and politics to harmonise the primacy of corporates in the everyday lives of people. In pursuit of neoliberal Hindutva social contract, the Modi-led BJP government is subordinating India to imperialist economic structures of global capitalism (Ghosh 2020). Hindutva social contract is corporate social contract.

The Hindutva forces are imposing Hindi, Hindutva and Hindustan to create a monolithic society under a centralised federal state that empowers caste and class elites at the cost of common Indians. The integration and centralisation are twin pillars of neoliberal capitalism (Singh 2008). It thrives under fascism. Hindutva provides perfect conditions to accelerate and accomplish such an objective. Hindutva is an ideology-free zone where corporate profit determines its political future. Hindutva nationalism is a myth that determines the national life in India based on the frameworks of corporate social contract. The essence of Hindutva social contract is to destroy Indian diversity and its federal polity. It does not believe in individual liberty and citizenship rights.

The unbridled growth of Hindutva social contract based on integration and centralisation runs without any risk because of the caste-based Brahminical social order based on hierarchy. It naturalises exploitation, inequality and repression. It demolishes any conditions that challenge such an arrangement between Hindutva and neoliberal capitalism in India. The withering away of secular politics, Indian social, cultural and religious diversity and constitutional state helps in the wholesale privatisation of state-owned resources, liberalisation of economy and laws for the growth of monopoly corporations. The rise of Adanies and Ambanies is part of this project called Hindutva social contract and its strategies. The systematic dismantling of existing constitutional institutions helps in the growth of illiberal Hindutva social contract and its exclusive dominance led by RSS, BJP and all its affiliates. These forces provide oxygen to a dysfunctional capitalist system.

In this way, Hindutva social contract is taking India and Indians in a ruinous path. The forward march of such an agenda needs to be halted at any cost for the unity and integrity of India and for the present and future survival of Indians.

WORKING PATTERNS OF HINDUTVA

In recent years, the Hindutva politics has caused long-term damage to India and Indians. The so-called 56-inch macho PM, the propaganda master manufactures and survives all political crisis including the current mismanagement of the Coronavirus pandemic in India. In spite of deaths and destitutions, the social, cultural, economic and religious base of Hindutva is intact. There are only few scratches in the electoral fortune of the BJP in Kerala and Tamil Nadu. It is time to move away from the analysis based on the personalities of the leaders like Modi and Amit Shah. It is time to blame both the faulty products like Modi and Shah and expose their bigoted manufacturing firm called the RSS. The rule of BJP led by Modi is based on the ideological frameworks of the RSS, developed from 1920s to 2021 provides conclusive proof that the primitive ideology of Hindutva has destroyed the social fabric, economic foundations, religious harmony and multicultural outlooks of India and Indians. During the Modi-led BJP regime, India contributed nearly 60% to the rise of global poverty. It speaks volumes about the failure of BJP government in India. Hindutva politics is neither an option nor an alternative for a modern, progressive, democratic, developed and peaceful India. There is no ambiguity about it.

However, BJP's victory in recently concluded Assam state election, and securing a very large percentage of votes in both Assembly and parliamentary bypolls in different parts of India, is a worrying sign for Indians. The Hindutva politics continue to be a dominant force in Indian politics. Therefore, there are two fundamental questions that need serious discussion: (1) How did Hindutva politics and its myopic leadership managed to convince the electorate to vote for them? (2) How Hindutva works? These two questions need to critically reflect on the core ideological foundations and social base of Hindutva politics.

The riots and assaults on reasons led by Hindutva from Gujarat to New Delhi, ruinous economic and agricultural policies from demonetisation, GST to firm bills, the anti-constitutional citizenship amendment act, the demolition project called 'Central Vista' and the utter failure to manage the Coronavirus crisis are some of the milestones in the Hindutva misgovernance. These avoidable and annihilating crises did not disturb the ideological, social and political base of Hindutva forces in India. The pathology of the toxic Hindutva politics and its violent projects based on illusory capitalist economic growth and development can be defeated only by defeating its reactionary ideological foundations in society, politics, economy and culture. The political oppositions and its fatigue of electoral defeats are only strengthening the Hindutva politics. It is time to change the direction against Hindutva politics and fight its core ideological roots.

The Brahminical social and cultural order, majoritarian dominance, anti-Muslim and religious minorities, anti-Dalit, anti-women cultural propaganda, anti-working-class politics and capitalist corporate command economic system are seven pillars of Hindutva politics in India. The pandemic and all other crises did not disturb these core ideological foundations of Hindutva politics. The struggle for a secular, progressive, egalitarian, liberal and democratic India depends on people's ability to defeat caste, religious bigotry and market fundamentalism promoted by capitalism (Nayak 2017). Hindutva politics works by using these three core value systems which are disastrous for India and Indians. The Hindutva politics is not an illusory project. It is a serious project of national, international and regional capitalist classes.

The Hindutva politics has penetrated into every step of social, cultural, religious, economic and political walks of lives in India with its organisational networks the RSS supported by Indian and global corporates. All constitutional institutions are captured by people with the RSS networks. Most of the schools, colleges, universities, cultural and social organisations are directly or indirectly controlled by the RSS today. The majority of media organisations have surrendered their professional ethics and sold their freedom to the Hindutva advertisement revenue. The power of money, media, political marketing and organisational electoral machine makes Hindutva politics as one of the most formidable and dominant force in India. These combined forces make every Hindutva abnormality and inhuman activities as natural and normal. Social depression, political despondency and acute economic crises are the three net outcomes of Hindutva politics, which create foundation for Hindutva fascism in India. Deaths and destitutions don't disturb Hindutva ideology. Therefore, morality is alien to Hindutva ideology.

In this difficult terrain, India and Indians need radical politics addressing everyday social, cultural, economic and spiritual needs of people. The need-based political struggle intertwined with desires and unwavering commitment to re-establish values enshrined in Indian constitution can revive Indian path to peace and progress by defeating Hindutva core ideology, which is based on caste and capitalism (Desai 2011). The struggle against Hindutva is a struggle against caste and capitalism. It is impossible to defeat Hindutva without defeating caste and capitalism. The caste system and capitalism are twin source of oxygen for Hindutva forces. India needs a radical mass movement to end caste and gender based on economic exploitation, and social, cultural and spiritual oppression.

There is no capitalism, caste and Hindutva with a human face. These forces and their ideology can never be reformed and recycled. The vulgar reality show of Hindutva fascism and its caste-based capitalism is neither conducive for human lives nor for the planet. India and Indians need global support and solidarity movements to re-establish liberal, secular and constitutional democracy in India. The mass movement for social and political transformation is an urgent need of the hour for the survival of India and Indians. The Coronavirus pandemic is an occasion to end the pandemic of Hindutva and all its ideological and institutional infrastructure in India to safeguard its present and future.

Theological Foundations of Hindutva

The Hindu right-wing forces are planning for a while to make the Bhagavad Gita as a national scripture and access to absolute state power is allowing them to fulfil their long-time dream. The decision of the Gujarat government to incorporate the Bhagavad Gita within the school syllabus for Class-6 to Class-12 students from 2022 to 2023 academic year is a dangerous move. This announcement by Gujarat education minister Jitu Vaghani is against the ethos of the Indian constitution. It is an assault on reason, science and education. It is neither helpful for the school children in terms of growth of their critical faculty nor contributes to the creativity power of education in terms of its essentialist and emancipatory roles. These twin roles are central to educational curriculums in its institutional settings. The essentialist role of educational curriculum is to provide skills, tools and methods that increase the employability of students and respond to the immediate needs of society, people and planet. The emancipatory role of education is to discover one's own ignorance and helps in understanding fellow human beings, animals and the planet. Education helps to analyse, understand and explain the conditions that perpetuate servitude.

The essentialist aspect of educational curriculums addresses the immediate needs, whereas the emancipatory aspect of education helps both immediate needs and creates a sustainable foundation for achieving long-term goals of individuals, societies and states. Education emancipates people from their narrow silos of caste, class, gender, sexuality and blind beliefs attached with social, cultural, religious and regional reactionary traditions. Educational curriculums are not designed to score marks and grades to seek a degree/qualification. Educational curriculums are designed to understand and explain the conditions of servitude created by patriarchal, feudal, commercial, industrial and digital capitalist systems that domesticate individuals and their creative abilities and freedoms to serve its purpose. The purpose of capitalist system is to domesticate the labour power of individuals and communities to expand its empire of profit at the cost of people and the planet.

The religious education in all its colours serves capitalism by domesticating individuals, their labour power and their creative abilities. In this way, it creates religious and moral educational foundations where it controls labour, production and consumption—the three pillars of any economic system. The humongous growth of hunger, homelessness, health crisis, economic inequalities and poverty is a direct product of capitalism. These serious issues can't be solved by capitalism as it creates them. As capitalism is facing its worst crisis in its history, it falls back on religious and reactionary forces to implement an educational system which develops compliant culture that never questions the power of capitalism and its fallibilities. The compliant culture is essential for the stability of capitalism in all its forms. The compliant culture also helps in sustaining the reactionary systems based on gender, caste, class, race and sexualities.

This is where the Bhagavad Gita plays a vital role both for the capitalist system and for its religious cronies. The Gujarat education minister Jitu Vaghani said that the aim of his government is to introduce the values and principles enshrined in the Bhagavad Gita in school curriculums. The decision of the Gujarat government is concomitant with the central government led by Mr Narendra Modi, the poster boy of capitalism and Hindutva fundamentalism in India. Modi government's New Education Policy recommends the introduction of religious and traditional scriptures within educational curriculums. Such attempts destroy the very foundation of education in terms of its essentialist and emancipatory objectives. It even destroys the very foundation of Indian knowledge tradition that is based on knowledge that emancipates and enlightens (सा विद्या या विमुक्तये। Sa Vidya Ya Vimuktaye). By incorporating the Bhagavat Gita within the school text, the Hindutva fundamentalists and their governments are destroying the didactically diverse knowledge tradition that challenges the Eurocentric knowledge traditions based on Descartean duality. Therefore, the Hindutva forces have always celebrated Eurocentric philosophers while justifying importance of the Bhagavat Gita. Mr Narendra Modi recalls German philosopher Arthur Schopenhauer to argue the significance of the values of the Bhagavat Gita.

The Bhagavat Gita and its poetic qualities are undeniable truth. It is a beautiful work of mythical literature. People can read it like any other literature and religious mythology. People can use it as their spiritual and religious text and practise it as they wish. But it has no place in the curriculum for school children. The values, principles and philosophies outlined in the Bhagavat Gita help in outsourcing the systematic failures of governments and their crony capitalist systems. It creates a structure of internal causation where nothing is external to individuals and their commitment to work and devotion without expectations. If the Karma theory would be so true, it would not be the TATAs, Ambanies and Adanies of the world to prosper but the women, Dalits, indigenous communities and working classes of the world would be the richest people. The planet would be more egalitarian and harmonious. Therefore, the father of Indian constitution, Dr Bhimrao Ramji Ambedkar was critical of both Hinduism and Bhagavat Gita which perpetuates caste-based Brahminical Hindu social order within its hierarchical structures of power and its underlying justification for inequalities of lives, liberties and properties.

The Bhagavad Gita and its monolithic philosophical outlook domesticate people, their present and future to seek emancipation in next life. Next life is exactly like American dream which lacks any form of material and spiritual foundation in reality. It is like any other advertisement for selling commodities in the market. Good Karma (duty) and Dharma (religion or righteousness) can provide Artha (wealth/power/fame) and be achieved through Bhakti (devotion). These four steps can provide the basis for Gyana/Vidya (knowledge) for the realisation of the 'self' and the 'other' which can lead towards Punarjanma (reincarnation). But the final goal is Moksa (deliverance or salvation) or Nirvana (free from the cyclic process of birth and rebirth. This is the state where human body/life unites/reunites with the supreme soul: the god). The final goal can be achieved by following the steps of Karma, Bhakti and Dharma. Such myopic ideas domesticate people as individuals and communities in such a way that the British colonialism wanted to translate and distribute the Bhagavat Gita among the common masses. The ideals of Bhagavad Gita create a culture of compliant which is concomitant with the requirements of ruling classes and their capitalist cronies. Therefore, the Hindutva fundamentalists are trying to use this pan-Indian text in educational curriculums.

The young minds in the schools and the adult minds in the colleges and universities need the freedom to study whatever they like to understand themselves and realise their goals in life. Freedom to study is central to realise one's own creative potentials. The state and governments have no roles to shape the minds of people in a direction of darkness and unreason. The central logic of the Hindutva politics is to let markets be free but domesticate individuals and govern their minds to comply with the state, government and their capitalist social, political and economic cultures. Let the academicians and researchers shape the educational curriculums within the framework of Indian constitution which promises its citizens right to have scientific and secular education. This is the only way educational curriculums can serve its essentialist and emancipatory roles by fulfilling the needs and desires of people and the planet.

Hindutva and Public Institutions

Public institutions have evolved in post-colonial India in response to crisis created by colonial plunders. Public institutions led by the state and government were shaped by anticolonial struggles in India. In spite of all its limitations, these institutions were designed to ensure and expand democratic and citizenship rights of all Indians irrespective of their caste, class, gender, religion and region. From planning commission to local development and revenue administration, health to education, food security to non-allied foreign policy, public institutions have played a major role in shaping the development trajectory of independent India. These institutions were mandated to develop and implement progressive ideals of public policies to face challenges and address the needs and desires of Indian citizens in the path of peace, progress and prosperity.

Essence and emancipation were twin objectives assigned to the public institutions to govern Indian citizens under a democratic and secular constitution. The essence of human life in terms of quality education, health, housing and food security for a dignified human life was the immediate goal. The emancipation from the conditions of poverty, hunger, inequalities, discrimination and blind beliefs were long-term objectives. The idea of essence and emancipation is interrelated. These ideals are central anchoring point for the vitality and integrity of these public institutions working in the national, regional and local levels. The practice of neoliberal economic policies started by the Congress Party has weakened the public institutions, whereas the Hindutva forces have expanded and consolidated the neoliberal order by destroying the public institutions in India. The neoliberal Hindutva and its exclusionary and ubiquitous governing principles are destroying not only the public institutions but also federal, democratic and constitutional values in India. The erosion of democratic and public institutions helps in the growth of authoritarian governance without accountability. It helps both Hindutva and capitalism to growth together as twins.

The Hindutva forces led by the BJP and shaped by the RSS and its affiliated organisations are restructuring India and Indian society to re-establish privileges and interests of higher castes and capitalist classes. Such a catastrophic reorganisation is based on dominance of Brahminical social order to facilitate capitalist market into every sphere of Indian society, where citizens are going to be converted into customers. This transformation is central to establish the dominance of capitalism in India by removing all institutional regulatory mechanisms and social constraints to this unethical alliance between Hindutva politics and capitalism. Both Vajpayee government then and Modi government now are twin pillars in consolidating capitalism and Brahminical Hindu social order in India.

During the Hindutva rule, it is corporate and crony capitalists who have gained super profit in a massive scale, whereas the poor masses, rural workers, farmers and small businesses have lost income in India. The decline in real income led to the fall of purchasing power of people across the country. The social and economic conditions have deteriorated in a massive scale. Hunger, homelessness, poverty, unemployment and insecurities have accelerated in an unprecedented scale. The poorest of the poor are the biggest loser and gained nothing during the Modi-led Hindutva rule in India.

The timely political reversal of such a scenario is not only necessary but also imperative to the idea of India. It is time to reclaim the public institutions that work for people and not for the capitalist classes. Liberally speaking, empowering of public institutions and increasing public spending on education, health, agriculture and food security are important to restore the Indian confidence on their state. Hindutva mode of governance is no alternative. It has failed to deliver its promises to people but ensure the growth and consolidation of capitalism in India. It is time to reclaim the republic from Hindutva *luteras* and their cronies.

PREDICAMENTS OF HINDUTVA

The BJP and Mr Narendra Modi had promised '*Achhe din*' (good days) and '*Sabka Saath, Sabka Vikas, Sabka Vishwas*' (with all, development for all, faith of all) to capture the political power in Delhi. The majority of corporate media and many liberal intellectuals have projected him as a reformer, popular and experienced leader, who can claim Indian century in the world stage. Instead of delivering economic growth and development, some Hindutva politics and their neoliberal economic policies have ruined the present and destroyed the future potential of India and Indians. The bigoted Hindutva ideology of RSS, reactionary politics of BJP and its crony capitalist policies have increased poverty, inequality and unemployment, jeopardising future development of a prosperous and peaceful India. The Hindutva politics has become a reigning ideology and weapon of the social reactionaries and economic elites. The tyranny of Modi and market is a marriage literarily made in heaven.

Mr Modi-led BJP government has not only emulated the neoliberal economic policies of the Congress Party but also expanded it to every sphere of lives in India. The Hindutva politics has also provided new vistas to neoliberal capitalism. The neoliberal economic policies are based on four pillars, that is (i) liberalisation of rules and regulations that protect labour and natural environment, (ii) privatisation of public resources, (iii) globalisation of market integrations and (iv) withdrawal of state and government from economic and welfare activities but provide security to capital and market. These economic ideals were the foundations of neoliberal capitalism launched by the Congress Party in India during 1991 reforms. These reform policies have consolidated the base of both global and national capitalist classes in the country. Hindutva politics is expanding these reforms to further deepen and consolidate capitalism in India.

The idea of neoliberal capitalism rests on anarchy of deregulations and legal protections for capital mobility to increased market competition. But Hindutva politics has given a new lease of life to neoliberal capitalism by giving absolute freedom to capital to consolidate itself without any competition. The few crony capitalists' friends of BJP have absolute control over Indian economy today. These corporations have grown enormously within and outside India. Hindutva politics has created conditions of capitalist market oligarchy in such a way that killed the idea of freedom and competition. It killed medium and small businesses in India. The oversold ideals neoliberal capitalism found its natural ally in the Hindutva politics of hate. Hindutva neoliberalism in India is capitalism without any form of anxiety of internal conflict, competition or crisis. Hindutva is an organised project of corporate capitalism to govern people and environment to secure long-term social, political and economic stability to capitalist corporates.

The Hindutva politics has transformed Indian state and government as merely a weapon of corporate and capital expansion. It looks as if the state and government are standing behind the capital for its security as people perish in poverty, hunger, homelessness and unemployment. It has destroyed the abilities of Indian state and governmental institutions to govern its citizens. The weakening of the link between the state and citizenship paves the path for the erosion of democracy in India. It shows disastrous consequences for people and country. Such a condition creates fertile ground for the electoral dividends of BJP and Hindutva ideology. It venerates the rich and ruins everything that makes India as a liberal, constitutional and secular democracy. The Hindutva politics continues to grow with the help of corporates. The electoral bonds scheme helps the corporates to control Indian electoral democracy by flowing some of their profit into the political system. The Hindutva politics is the biggest beneficiaries of such a scheme. The BJP and RSS networks are paid, sponsored and sustained by the corporations. In return, the triumph of Hindutva politics solves the moral, intractable material, inherent economic and political nightmares of capitalism in terms of class conflict.

The Hindutva politics has also been successful in creating an environment where party, state and government move together. Any opposition to such a formulation is branded as anti-Indian and anti-national. It is a single-window system to facilitate market forces and control people and their opinion against their will. The society is governed by transactional mass anxiety and fear created by the Hindutva ideology and organisation network of the BJP and RSS. There is no morality in Hindutva ideology and their market forces. The unbridled exploitations of natural resources and working classes are the core of Hindutva capitalism and its neoliberal variant in India. Its frontal attack on 'reason, science, secularism, multiculturalism, social solidarity and liberal democracy' is a systematic design of shock therapy to manufacture crisis.

The global pandemic and the failures of Modi government have created a crack in the political base on Hindutva politics, but its social and ideological base is on solid foundations. There is growing tremor in public opinion against the Modi government, but Hindutva ideological and cultural base continues to be strong due to relentless false propaganda to reinstall Modi as a messiah of Indians. The worshiping of false god in democracy only breeds disasters and Indians have many examples of failures of Modi government from demonetisation to COVID-19 vaccination. Hindutva is project without any principles or coherent convictions. It is a fascist hydra with many faces and constantly changes its forms to survive. The Nagpur project of RSS to convert India into a Hindu state is absence of any reasons. It is a strategy to completely control India and Indian resources with brute force.

The failures of the opposition parties and their abilities in accurately exposing Hindutva politics have led to the strengthening of this reactionary ideology. The worldview of fascist Hindutva and its dogma isn't only posing a serious danger to India but a potential danger to the world peace. It is restructuring Indian society, economy, politics and culture today, but it will have far-reaching consequences on the world tomorrow. In the wake of declining democracy with the rise of Hindutva supremacy led by BJP and RSS is putting our people and planet in peril.

The history of mass movements has swallowed all powerful dictators within its waves and the future of Hindutva will be no different. It is time to have a mass movement against Hindutva fascism and crony capitalism in India. The global solidarity is an inalienable part of this struggle. The struggle against Hindutva fascism and struggle against capitalism is a common struggle. The peace, prosperity and the future of India and Indians depend on the success of this united struggle.

HINDUTVA ROBBERY OF COMMONS

The Indian National Congress under the leadership of Prime Minister Mr Rajiv Gandhi was responsible for the beginning of half-hearted liberalisation policies in the name of economic development and modernisation in India. The half-hearted liberalisation, privatisation and globalisation policies have become the cornerstone of new economic policies launched by the Prime Minister Dr Manmohan Singh. These policies are in full swing under the Hindutva laissez-faire under the leadership of Prime Minister Mr Narendra Modi, whose mantra is based on the idea of 'minimum government and maximum governance'. The market forces and corporates are absolutely free to rob public resources without any form of deterrence.

From river, sand, fishing, water to land, forests, woodlands, play-grounds, mining and minerals are for sale. From defence sectors to bank-ing, postal, railways, health, education, road and transportation sectors are controlled by the market forces. There is nothing in India which can't be sold under the Hindutva government led by Prime Minister Mr Narendra Modi. The Congress Party has laid the foundation of this process of rob-bery and Hindutva forces are accelerating the process and institutionalis-ing it as a norm of everyday lives in India.

The privatisation of public resources is not only about transfer of own-ership and profit to the private corporations. It is a process of privatising profits and socialising risk. The Hindutva theft of the commons is a capi-talist pursuit to dismantle collective foundation of society and public own-ership of resources. It is in a direction of no return where pursuit of profit, atomisation of individual life is central to the growth of market and corpo-rations. The growth of urban monoculture and ghettoisation of lives within housing estates dictate norms of everyday life where individuals mortgage their future and freedom in search of a house in the city. The villages were destroyed by ruining the sources of livelihoods of the villag-ers. The commercialisation and commodification of lives and livelihoods are the only common culture between urban and rural areas in India today.

Hindutva forces are spreading the politics of otherness and hate in everyday life which brings rural and urban areas together against the reli-gious minorities and marginalised communities. The sense of fear and hate are the twin pillars on which urban and rural India is standing to confront a miserable future created by the Hindutva politics. Poverty, unemploy-ment, hunger, homelessness and crime are five net outcomes of Hindutva robbery of India and Indians. The destruction of public resources, public images, public institutions and fellow feelings are central to Hindutva hegemony over society and politics, and crony capitalist control over economy. These processes help in the atomisation project that is concomi-tant with capitalism. Hindutva and capitalism are twin forces that acceler-ate unhitched robbery of life, liberty and livelihoods in India.

Hindutva is a class war and unprecedented class robbery unleashing on Indian masses. Their agricultural land, river, forest, playgrounds, airports, schools, colleges and universities, hospitals are either captured or waiting to be captured by the Hindutva crony capitalist thieves. The cultural, reli-gious and social genocides are conducted by the Hindutva forces in the name of nationalism to control, manage, manipulate, sabotage and dis-mantle any form of unity among working people against this Hindutva robbery to uphold the interests of few corporations in India. The people and their constitutional citizenship rights are disposables.

Hindutva is a collective robbery of public imagination in India. The state power provides legitimacy to such a process that legalised robbery as an art and a beautiful product of previous *Karma*. The unpolluted and simple people were manipulated to vote such a political process that had not expected that '*Achhe din*' (good days) means loss of livelihoods, peace, social solidarity and cultural bond among people. The shared life and resources are ruined in the name of national development, but the reality is different. It is an organised tragedy of all Indians. If you are a Kashmiri, a Muslim, a Dalit, a worker and a tribal, your tragedy is multiplied with every passing seconds. Hindutva generates multiple forms of tragedies in the name of fake nationalism to legitimise robbery. Hindutva destroys a sense of collective belonging to a place and people by dividing people in religious lines. The monolithic and ethnic nationalism of Hindutva is western European in letter and spirit. It is alien to India and Indians.

It is within this context, one needs to understand Hindutva robbery of society, culture, religion, politics, economy and nationalism in India. The very survival of India and Indians depends on the defeat of these forces working overtime and unleashing a terror of the theft of the commons. The alternative narrative needs to be based on the interests of the masses and their control over all public resources in India. To stop the privatisation of India, Indians must stop buying electoral promises from the political market of Hindutva. A collective electoral boycott of Hindutva is the immediate alternative that can halt the forward march of Hindutva robbery in India.

RENT-SEEKING HINDUTVA GOVERNMENT

High inflation, growing unemployment and depreciating rupee are three fundamental issues faced by Indian economy today. The educational and health infrastructure is falling apart. Human development is in the bottom of the nadir. Modi government has no plans to take responsibility to navigate Indian economy away from these crises. It is passing its responsibility on Indian people by reckless hiking of the Goods and Services Tax (GST) on food and other essential items. This nationwide rent-seeking activities in terms of high taxation on goods and services are part of the rent-seeking process. It will have devastating impact on poor and malnourished population, small businesses and rural poor. Such a policy will help corporates and it is going to push poor people into a regime of inescapable hunger, malnutrition and food insecurity. Hindutva is transforming India into a rent-seeking market society, where welfare and social loss are immanent. The GST hike will have negative impact on all Indians and on all sectors of Indian economy. Taxing small producers, businesses and poor consumers is opposed to the idea of economic growth and development as it creates conditions for declining productivity, economic stagnation and inefficiency.

'One Nation, One Tax, One Market' policy slogan by the Prime Minister Narendra Modi has failed to understand the economic diversities in India in terms of its culture of local production and consumption. 'One Nation, One Tax, One Market' policy helps to create conditions, where India becomes increasingly dominated by few crony capitalists affiliated with Hindutva. The international experience of mass rent-seeking economics in developed countries shows that big corporates grab larger share of the wealth without producing any socially meaningful goods and services. The income inequality is a result of rent-seeking market society, where wealthy taxpayers gain. It marginalises the poor masses. The centralised project of Hindutva dominance over politics and corporate dominance over Indian economy will squeeze all creative potentials and labour power of the people in terms of their livelihoods, productive powers, innovation and other income generation abilities. Hindutva is primarily a cultural project to uphold the economic interests of the higher class and higher caste population in India (Nayak 2017).

The Hindutva government led by Mr Narendra Modi and his party BJP cares only for electoral victory to uphold its crony capitalist classes. The BJP government does not care for people and the country. The religious mobilisation of people in the name of cultural nationalism is a political strategy that serves the corporates at the cost of lives and livelihoods of Indians. The market-oriented Hindutva economics creates a tax regime on the masses and a pervasive rent-seeking government and a corporatised security state that destroys welfare state in India. It is a well-known fact that mass rent-seeking society promotes regimes of bribery, corruption, smuggling and black-market. These are foundations for major revenue loss for a developing country like India. A mass rent-seeking state and government led by Hindutva shows that it has failed to create new wealth by generating mass employment or expanding innovation and economic growth. The rent-seeking Hindutva economics is fundamentally inefficient and short-sighted because it reduces productive power of the economy, causes revenue loss and increases economic inequalities.

Hindutva alibi Hindu nationalism, economic growth and development, and India's first projects are steps towards cultural, economic and political genocide of constitutional democracy and citizenship rights in India. The centralisation economic project of Hindutva is the politics of dominance over production and consumption; the hike of GST and other forms of taxation is just a means in this direction. It seeks to transform India into a rent-seeking market society, where strongman economics and vigilante politics is normalised as an integral part of everyday lives. Such a strategy helps both Hindutva and their crony capitalist friends (Nayak 2017).

Hindutva obsession with market-dominated economy for economic growth and its politics of dominance must end for any form of security and sustainability of livelihoods of the marginalised masses in India. The ideas of progress, peace and prosperity are alien to Hindutva politics. Therefore, GST hike on food and other essential commodities and services is neither hurting their human sentiments nor their ideological politics. Their economic policies are directly linked with the immediate gain of their corporate friends, who fund their electoral juggernauts and support the activities of the hate factory called RSS.

The rent-seeking market society dominated by corporate oligarchy in alliance with reactionary Hindutva politics put India and Indians into an indefinite darkness. The securitised corporate states and governments have never worked for the welfare of their citizens. It will not do so in India under Hindutva government. The defeat of Hindutva is central to the peace, prosperity and progress of India and Indians.

HINDUTVA POLITICS OF DECEPTION

Mr Narendra Modi and his RSS brethren are masters of fraudulent claims. There are long lists of lies spread by the RSS, BJP and all their IT cell workers. It is not a personality disorder or lying with fear. Hindutva fascists are trained liars. Modi defended his government's decision on demonetisation by arguing that 'demonetisation' is 'an important step' in his fight against black money and corruption. He appealed Indians emotionally by his make-believe oratory in November 2016. Modi said that 'I have asked the country for just 50 days. If after December 30, there are shortcomings in my work or there are mistakes or a bad intention found in my work, I will be prepared for the punishment that the country decides for me'. Many months and years have passed, demonetisation failed to achieve any of the objectives. Modi has neither taken any moral responsibility nor maintained any political and democratic accountability. The demonetisation decision really destroyed Indian economy. Similar strategy was adopted during the GST bill and it killed small businesses and weakened Indian economy further. The Agricultural Reform policies have further exposed Modi's commitment to his capitalist cronies at the cost of Indian farmers and Indian agricultural economy. His promises of employment to youths, women's empowerment, fellowships to students and increasing farmers income are series of false promises made by Modi. His glaring failures from home to foreign policies and disgraceful management of the Coronavirus crisis reveal his fraudulent claims of good governance and promises of good days for India and Indians.

Governance by lies is a political strategy of Hindutva fascists led by the BJP and trained by the RSS in India. Mr Narendra Modi's inverse relationship with truth should not come as a surprise to anyone. Hindutva fascists have always embraced false narratives to develop their irrational worldviews in the name of 'cultural nationalism' to serve its political project and economic objectives of their capitalist cronies. From the rewriting of Indian history to the Gujarat model of economic development is based on fraudulent narratives. The love for falsehood is not unique to Hindutva fascists. All fascists, anti-democratic, totalitarian and authoritarian leaderships and their ideologies are based on their excellent abilities in mainstreaming falsehoods. The culture of fake news, social media and new information technology is used by the twenty-first-century fascist leaders like Modi to destroy scientific outlooks and reason among masses to control and domesticate people as subservient subjects. The Citizenship (Amendment) Act 2019 passed by the Modi government is not only intended to destroy citizenship rights of the religious minorities but also weaken citizenship rights of all Indians. The Hindutva fascists are against citizenship and democracy. This is why Hindutva fascists are destroying and weakening all institutions of democracy in India.

The followers of Hindutva fascism believe in all hateful falsehood spread by Modi, BJP and RSS. In spite of all crisis, Hindutva fascists have increased their mass based in Indian society and politics. The deception is an inherent political strategy of BJP and integral to RSS ideology. Hindutva fascists capitalise falsehood to capture and uphold power at any cost. The deaths and destitutions do not disturb Hindutva fascists. These forces integrate deception and lies to their everyday practice of governance. It is not populism but a deceptive political culture planted in India by BJP and RSS that weakens Indian state and democracy. The Hindutva fascists use violence and fear as weapons to ensure that people accept their lies as truth. There is growing rape and violence against women and religious minorities in India as Hindutva fascists encourage the fulfilment of their followers' anti-Muslim and bottled-up sexual desires. Hindutva fascists stand with their follower's every destructive action. They have organised public rallies in support of rapists and garlanded leaders of mob lynching. Everyday violence is a governing principle of Hindutva fascists. This is a distinctive process developed and practised by most of the fascists to serve their reactionary political, economic and cultural projects devoid of truth.

Truth is a reflection on realities of life and livelihoods. Hindutva fascists don't reflect on realities. They believe in truth that comes from mythology. They normalise and naturalise their falsehoods as truth with the help of mythology. Therefore, they rewrite Indian history to undermine material and scientific foundations of history and its relevance to people and their everyday life. The rewriting of history is a common project of Hindutva fascists and neoliberal capitalist monsters. Both these forces undermine the material conditions, spiritual harmony and social relationships between human beings and nature. This dehumanising project is fundamental to militarise minds of people to normalise violence and falsehoods spread by Hindutva fascists.

Conclusion

Hindutva fascism isn't a counter-revolutionary movement. It is neither a nationalist nor a cultural movement of transformation of Indian society and politics. It is a revivalist movement established by Brahminical social order to uphold their caste hierarchy and economic interests in the society which is concomitant with neoliberal capitalism. Therefore, Hindutva fascists and neoliberalism capitalism move as twins in India led by Mr Narendra Modi.

There is no economic, social development, health education and foreign policy to guide India today for the future of Indians and their country. The cabinet under Modi is defunct. Everything runs on the basis of Modi's instincts. There is no reason or rhyme in Modi's governance. Lies are the only means to hide all his ignorance and failures. Mr Narendra

Modi blames everyone including his predecessors to ignore and avoid his responsibilities as the PM of India. He demonises Muslims, religious minorities, human rights activists, youth, students and farmers to reject truth and reality. From gas theory to cloud theory, Modi spreads unscientific and irrational outlooks in India which is opposed to the spirit of Indian constitution. Knowledge and science are the enemy of Hindutva fascists and their poster boy, whose classmates and qualifications are unknown. Modi's public conduct encourages fraudulent culture in India. The electoral victory of Hindutva fascists pushes India backwards.

The habitual liars of Hindutva led by Modi put India and Indian in risk. It destroys the present and wipes out everything conditions for a better future of Indians. The revival of India and the future of Indians depend on collective struggles against Hindutva fascism and their irrational, unscientific ideology and deceptive political strategies. In 2021, Indian nationalism and patriotism mean to defeat Hindutva fascism from every sphere of Indian lives. It is a struggle between lies of Hindutva and everyday realities of people in India. The history has witnessed the glorious victories of struggles against colonialism and fascism. Indians have nothing to lose but to defeat Modi and company to fortify the democratic and secular future of India in peace and prosperity.

References

Banaji, S. 2018. Vigilante Publics: Orientalism, Modernity and Hindutva Fascism in India. *Javnost-The Public 25* (4): 333–350.

Bhattacharya, A.K., and Thakurta, P.G. 2020. Contours of Crony Capitalism in the Modi Raj. In *Majoritarian State: How Hindu Nationalism is Changing India*, eds. Angana P. Chatterji, Thomas Blom Hansen, and Christophe Jaffrelot. Oxford Academic, 20 February. Accessed 6 December 2022. https://doi.org/10.1093/oso/9780190078171.003.0011.

Byler, D. 2022. The Social Life of Terror Capitalism Technologies in Northwest China. *Public Culture,* 1 May; 34 (2 (97)): 167–193. https://doi.org/10.1215/08992363-9584694.

Desai, R. 2011. Gujarat's Hindutva of Capitalist Development. *South Asia: Journal of South Asian Studies 34* (3): 354–381.

Ghosh, J. 2020. Hindutva, Economic Neoliberalism and the Abuse of Economic Statistics in India. *South Asia Multidisciplinary Academic Journal* [Online], 24/25 | 2020, Online since 18 November 2020, connection on 06 December 2022. http://journals.openedition.org/samaj/6882; https://doi.org/10.4000/samaj.6882.

Nayak, B.S. 2017. *Hindu Fundamentalism and the Spirit of Global Capitalism in India*. Maryland: Hamilton Books (An imprint of Rowman & Littlefield).

Shah, G. 2002. Caste, Hindutva and Hideousness. *Economic and Political Weekly*: 1391–1393.

Singh, P. 2008. *Federalism, Nationalism and Development: India and the Punjab Economy*. London: Routledge.

Teltumbde, A. 2020. *Hindutva and Dalits: Perspectives for Understanding Communal Praxis*. New Delhi: Sage Publications Pvt. Limited.

CHAPTER 8

Hindu Nationalist Anxiety Around Its Feminine 'Own' and the 'Other'

Dyotana Banerjee and Abhijit Dasgupta

INTRODUCTION

Hijab or headscarf came up at the forefront of the political and popular discourse in India earlier this year (2022) with a viral video capturing a young urban Muslim college-goer, Muskan, being chased by a Hindu mob chanting *Jai Shri Ram* (Hail Ram) inside of her college premises. The college in Karnataka has hundreds of Muslim students who wear hijab regularly to college and Muskan is just one of them. In the video Muskan is seen to enter college in a scooty amidst the protesting Hindu group at the premises with saffron shawl on; she walks past them, and stops, returns the gaze and shouts back *Allah hu Akbar* with her fists up. This image became an instant icon on social media through Kareem Graphy's drawing that displays a woman in burkha standing up against the saffron (Hindu

D. Banerjee (✉)
School of Science and Humanities, Shiv Nadar University, Chennai, India

A. Dasgupta
GITAM School of Humanities and Social Sciences, Gandhi Institute of Technology and Management (GITAM) University, Visakhapatnam, India

B. S. Nayak, D. Chakraborty (eds.), *Interdisciplinary Reflections on South Asian Transitions*,
https://doi.org/10.1007/978-3-031-36686-4_8

right wing) dots (mob) in the background. This particular incident became core concern for the authors to analyse the intersection of Hindu nationalism with the construction of its feminine own and the Muslim other. Such construction of Hindu nationalism of themselves and the other views the country in opposition, mostly in binaries, which often make women a convenient locus of comparison across religions, time and space.

It has been observed lately that Muslim women's issues and their religious-cultural assertion have been the prime site of contestation of the Hindu nationalists against the Muslim 'other'.[1] From criminalisation of triple talaq to crushing of anti-CAA anti-NRC campaigns and protests led by Muslim women across the country, to hijab ban in educational institutions in Karnataka, Muslim women's role in the public sphere has constantly been on headlines for right-wing Hindutva groups and BJP[2]'s engagement with and resistance against them to further Hindutva politics. In what ways does Hindu nationalism engage with the Muslim feminine 'other' in India? How does the Hindu nationalist anxiety manifest in resisting veiling of Muslim women in public? How do veiling and the use of conventional religious codes consolidate Muslim women's presence and agency in the public sphere? We discuss how the Muslim feminine 'other' is selectively included and excluded in the right-wing Hindutva discourses in modern Indian politics to consolidate and further the identity of a Hindu saviour male. The chapter attempts to grapple with these questions as we trace the trajectory of the Hindu nationalist navigation with the Muslim feminine other through an understanding of religious personal law, understanding of dress and the Hindu nationalist demands for Uniform Civil Code (UCC).

Three strands of debates could be identified following the recent hijab controversy in Karnataka. One is about the democratic right of the Muslim citizens within the constitutional boundaries of liberal democracy and the Hindutva forces denying that right to argue religious-cultural symbols must not be worn by Muslims in public places. In their attempt to homogenise attire in favour of a majoritarian Hindu ethos, right-wing Hindu groups build on the narrative of Muslims as defiant nationals in their continued presence in the public space with religious-cultural markers. The second strand, closely aligning with liberal secular view, revolves around the question whether display of religious markers should be allowed as part of the dress code in educational institutions. School uniforms are largely accepted as ways to mask socio-economic distinctions in students to help consolidate the shared identity of the school-goers as students of one institution.

The third strand of the discussion focuses on the right of the Muslim women to decide whether they want to be veiled or not in the different kinds of public spaces. This idea is different from yet closely related to right of the piety foregrounded by Saba Mahmood in her works. Saba Mahmood's analyses on the interaction between feminism and religion bring in the limitation of the secular-liberal politics to understand the potential of the cultural elements to further and strengthen a culture-contingent feminist project. A counter position to this argument could be that while cultural specificity may inform the nature of women's agency and facilitate feminist project, it can also bring about and legitimise the inherent inequalities entrenched within it.

In light of the recent trajectories of Hindu nationalist polity, we notice a pattern of presenting itself predominantly against a Muslim feminine other. Be it the brute force to crush the large protests of Muslim women in the anti-CAA anti-NRC protests across the country or control the mobility of the Hijab-clad college students in Karnataka or ensuring the judicial control by humiliating Zakia Jafri and Bilkis Bano in Gujarat in their continued struggle for justice since 2002 anti-Muslim pogrom, Hindu nationalists are recently repeatedly seen to be against one otherised entity: the Muslim woman. The Muslim women that the Hindu nationalists stand against to communicate their message of othering and control are predominantly women seen to be embracing hijab or other forms of Muslim dress code of the region.

Looking at the historical trajectory of the right-wing discourses, Rashtriya Swayamsevak Sangh (RSS), the social outfit of Hindu nationalism primarily focusses on constructing the identity of a normative Hindu male. It is apparent in its name itself and based on the Hindu male, other identities such as the Hindu female, Muslim male and Muslim female are shaped. Scholar of Hindu nationalism, Bacchetta (2019) argues that although Muslim women do not feature prominently in the formative discourse of Hindu nationalism, for example in the writings of Hedgevar, Golwalkar and Savarkar, identity of Muslim religious female is crucial and indispensable in the furthering of Hindutva agenda. Hindu nationalists have their different strands of portrayal of Muslim women. First, they associate Muslim women with Muslim men as their accomplice in defying the hegemony of the Hindu nationalists. Second is the saviour complex ingrained in Hindu nationalism where they pretend to save Muslim women from Muslim men, their polygamy and Muslim patriarchy. Closely associated to this is the third strand that attempts glossing over Muslim cultural markers with a homogeneous Hindutva project dictating what Muslims should and should not wear and how they take part in public life. Much of these questions of Muslim as 'other' and Hindu nationalists' response to feminine other are foregrounded on the discussion of women's body and what they wear, and various other cultural representation. Often the understanding of respectful female clothing is conceptualised from the upper-caste Hindu male gaze which criminalises or rather vulgarises the clothes of non-Hindu, non-upper-caste women of different social and religious minorities, in this context hijab-wearing Muslim women.

CLOTHING, VEILING AND QUESTIONS OF MODERN MUSLIM WOMEN'S AGENCY

In the context of south Asia, diversity and plurality of everyday life often render dress to occupy a central position in reflecting one's self, virtues, social location, faith and so on. For both men and women, what one wears often become the lens through which he/she is understood. Particularly more so for women, their choice to wear what they deem fit for their self often brings out various complications in social, legal and economic realm. Various images in popular culture reinforce the idea of honourable women, whose clothing represents the honour and respect of the family, kinship and also nation. Often the decision of what a women should wear is regulated and monitored by the patriarchal norms, majoritarian standards and religious authorities. In this context, the politics and pluralism of clothing and 'what one wears' is not an innocent practice; often it explicates various meanings, tensions and hostilities, which make clothing an important area of discussion.

The discussion on clothing and women has been a perennial interest for sociologists and anthropologists. The anthropological scholarship on clothes and identity traverses a lot of interesting themes and questions. For example, according to Roach-Higgins and Eicher (1992: 1), dress of an individual is "an assemblage of modifications of the body and/or supplements to the body". Dress can be thought of as a wide array of body modifications such as "[…] coiffed hair, colored skin, pierced ears, and scented breath", and a long list of different "[…] garments, jewelry, accessories". Alison Lurie (1981: 3) considers dress to be a language which allows one to communicate with each other and express information, function or misinformation about one's standing in the society. Lurie also believes that the language of dress has its special meaning and grammar as she writes, "[…] the vocabulary of dress includes not only items of clothing, but also hair styles, accessories, jewelry, make up and body decoration". Drawing from various scholars such as Spencer and Thorenstein, Carter (2003: 28) understands dress as "[…] a set of rules and regulations governing the relations between the strong and the weak". Deriving also from the works of sociologist and social philosopher such as Georg Simmel, Carter opines dress as a crucial stage of social interaction which ranges from imitation and differentiation, creating both divide and solidarity.

In the context of 'non-western' countries, clothing and colonialism are intertwined, which had even had ramifications post-colonialism in forging a local identity (Chatterjee 1989; Banerjee and Miller 2003; Tarlo 1996; Wickramasinghe 2003). In discussing about colonial women, Chatterjee (1989: 245) opined that clothes acquired an important function in delineating the 'new women of the nationalist ideology'. In the formation of a new woman, *bhadramahila* of the upper-caste Bengali society complimented sari with blouse and petticoat which carved out a substantial difference from *memashibs*, Bengali women from the earlier generations and lower-caste Bengali women. This new kind of sari known as *brahmika* sari not only introduced a culturally superior women but also brought a new subject of nationalist *bhadramahila*, strengthening the link between women, clothes and nationalism. Continuing in the discussion on sari, Banerjee and Miller (2003) bring out sari as an everyday dress, which survived various time periods obtaining a position of respect and raised status. Drawing from narratives across socio-economic backgrounds, often contrasting in many ways, sari emerges as a symbol depicting one's entry to different life cycle rituals, relation with in-laws, shaping one's personality and sexuality. For Banerjee and Miller (2003), the five-metre cloth is associated with respectability. The respect lies in the way one wears, drapes, sits and folds the sari which evokes a particular kind of women whose honour lies not only in what she wears but also in how she wears.

Blending together historical and ethnographic materials, Emma Tarlo (1996: 21) in her fieldwork in Gujarat raises the question "the problem of what to wear". She scrutinises the question and discusses that 'what to wear' is not an innocent question. Rather, it is a political question which throws light on what one is wearing, one's caste, class, rural-urban identity, religious background. Often the question of what to wear is a matter of representation and identity. In her efforts of weaving historical and ethnographic records, Tarlo echoes Lurie's (1981) argument that clothing is a medium of communication which exemplifies various kinds of dichotomies such as graceful/disgraceful, manliness/effeminate, native/non-native. The various divisions and differentiations in the society across gender, religion, caste, class are often implicated in the question "what to wear". Thus, for Tarlo (1996), clothing, identity and representation are in a continual negotiation bringing into various facets of clothes and its meaning in contemporary Indian society. Historian Nira Wickramasinghe (2003) in the context of Sri Lanka draws interesting connection between the past and the present, focusing on the relationship between colonialism, nationalism and clothing. Tracing the formation and evolution of clothes from Sri Lankan colonial past, she examines changes at the material level, representing 'authenticity' and identity through the advent of sewing machine, colonial records and official costumes. In the context of colonial Sri Lanka, she argues that clothing is a social, economic and political acts, enabling clothing to be a powerful medium which allows one to put across one's voice. However, she also admits that clothing as a voice lacks stability and often conveys misleading information.

A whole new interesting perspective on cloth, identity and representation is perhaps best identified in the writings of Saba Mahmood (2005). Let us elaborate on the writings of Mahmood as her discussion and analysis of the Muslim women's movement in Cairo, Egypt, suit our context. Mahmood (2005: 2) conducted two years of fieldwork with Muslim women from several socio-economic backgrounds who participated in the revival mosque movement in Cairo to understand the ways "teaching and studying of Islamic scriptures, social practices, and form of bodily comportment considered germane to the cultivation of the ideal virtuous self". The discussion of bodily comportment, reading of Quran, *hadith* with each other in and beyond the mosque and most importantly wearing of veil (*hijab*) as an expression of their piety, often allows them to critique many of the Islamic as well as liberal secular practices.

Through the ethnographic accounts of the Muslim women's participation in the mosque movement, Mahmood tries to move away the binary framework of resistance of subordination associated with secular-liberal framework of freedom and autonomy. Through the lifeworlds of the Muslim women, Mahmood opens the discussion of agency from any predeterministic frameworks (see Bautista 2008). Rather she allows us to develop theories particularly from the experiences these women had with their faith in the movement, which often rendered topsy turvy to many liberal's notion of Muslim women. In opening up the discussion on agency, Mahmood propounded that the discussion of agency is embodied as it denotes their moral values by virtue of enacting corresponding bodily techniques (Dasgupta 2021).

Mahmood (2001, 2005) critiques the discussion of freedom and the liberal secular definition of 'victim' and 'subjugation', 'virtues and values' associated with the way Muslim women are identified in contemporary society. Instead of working with a universal definition of agency, she looks into the particular definition of piety and female agency which is grounded in norms and the kind of personhood or self they aspire to be by being loyal to the commands of God such as doctrines, scriptures and sermons. Deriving her argument from the Muslim women's negotiation with the Islamic practices, agency can be defined as 'subject's capacity for action'. This capacity of skill allows them to traverse the moral subjectivities which are often experienced through embodied practices. Extending her argument of embodied agency, Mahmood goes beyond the discussion of veiling from patriarchal practices or as a means to assert one's Muslim identity; rather, she conceptualises veiling as a "conscious act of self cultivation" where body plays an important role in forming and moulding one's piety[3](Mahmood 2005). Considering veiling as an important part of examining one's piety, Mahmood (2001) refers to various scholars in the context of "modern Egyptian women" and their relation to veil (el-Guindi 1981; Hoffman-Ladd 1987; Zuhur 1992). Interrogating with these scholars, she identifies veiling to perform multiple purposes; for example functionalist approaches explain women's veil as an armour which provides them safety from sexual harassments on public spaces and low cost of attire. While some identifies veiling as a symbol of resistance against the way popular media represents women's bodies.

While these studies are exciting and have produced interesting observations, there remains a gap in the way veiling is associated with female modesty or piety as Islamic virtues. Mahmood's (2005) discussion on piety is "not intentionality of the actor"; rather, the relationships are articulated "between words, concepts and practices that constitute a particular discursive tradition". In looking for piety in words, concepts and practices, Mahmood (2001) embraces piety in a way one conduct herself dependent on the body, speech and a way of being in order to "attain a certain kind of state of happiness, purity, wisdom, perfection or immortality" (Foucault 1997: 24 cited in Mahmood 2001: 210). According to Mahmood (2005), embodied agency indicates the way the bodily techniques play a role in disciplining the pious Muslim women to encode her moral behaviour, values and virtues. She also adds that often in the secular-liberal framework, these virtues are seen as inactive, submissive and lacking a kind of individual autonomy. Building on her definition of agency and piety as embedded in virtues like humility, docility and shyness, Mahmood (2001, 2005) argues that these virtues and values are often communicated through veiling and the way it acquires a disciplinary practice which defines the bodily deportment. Thus, for Mahmood, veiling is not merely a means of 'gender inequality'; rather, it is the way of cultivating and developing a particular way of living.

Considering veil as a disciplinary apparatus as well as a signifier of deportment, veiling contributes in "being and becoming a certain kind of a person" (Mahmood 2001: 215). In forming a particular kind of personhood, veiling and virtues like shyness and patience often get interlinked, which is not necessarily a regulation of a feminine body but also disciplining of mind and body. Through her interesting accounts of Muslim Egyptian women, she presents us Nadia's relationship with *sabr* (patience), which allows her to endure suffering as per the norms of the tradition of Islam. This Islamic notion of *sabr* creates a new personhood who is a *sabira* (the one who exercises *sabr*). Similarly, for the Egyptian Muslim women, the virtue such as shyness (*al haya*) is not a matter of choice but is a collection of 'good deeds' that one must develop first, if lacking. For the women, shyness is often understood in relation to veil. Just as one feel embarrassed in the beginning to wear a veil due to many personal and societal reasons, but later lack of a veil induces shyness. It feels one is disobeying God's command which is not prescribed in creating a virtuous ethical self. Thus, one notices that body, virtues and self-cultivation are closely linked to each other (Mahmood 2001). What one can observe and affirm for the Egyptian Muslim women of Cairo is that veiling is considered an 'essential practice' and not a practice which is not loosely based on patriarchal norms; in fact, it is through veiling that mind and body are disciplined to become a kind of specific Islamic self.

Deriving from Foucault, Butler and Mauss, Mahmood (2005) operates in the terrain where body informs one's ethical practice as well as becomes an apparatus for emancipation. The practice of veiling is not to be understood in the framework of subordination or oppression; rather, the pietistic woman through 'technologies of self' indicates that external actions and internal self are connected in such a way which tends towards a relationship with God. What Mahmood does interestingly, tries to locate her subjects not in the liberal feminism idea of agency and protest nor does she support the resurgence of Islamic forms as an agency directed against the 'failed' modernising projects. Transcending this binary, Mahmood (2001, 2005) focuses on the everyday lives of the Muslim to tease out the way clothing performs an important task to delineate agency, which is embodied in nature. This agency does not arise from meta-narratives; it is rooted in the little things of everyday life such as clothes which one wears in the specific social, political and historical context.

Coming back to the questions of Muslim women in hijab in public sphere in India and the Hindutva groups' anxieties around it, one must interrogate how Muslim woman is perceived in the Hindu nationalist discourse and how different trajectories and strands of Hindu nationalist politics engage with the Muslim women 'other'. Moreover, it is crucial to understand what role does Hindu nationalism and the right-wing politics play in constituting the Muslim public selves through their resistance against constitutional measures such as religious personal law and their demand for Uniform Civil Code (UCC). By enforcing the demand to have UCC, questions on plurality of everyday lives where clothing is an important factor get compromised to suit the majoritarian interest of what and who should be called an Indian.

Religious Personal Law and the Consolidation of Identities

The search and codification of personal law in colonial times gave rise to a number of paradoxical trends. As the British colonialism began in India in 1757, some subjects like inheritance, marriage, caste and religious usages were chosen under the scope of personal law following the contemporary British classification in matters pertaining to testament and property distribution, religious worship, marriage and divorce. Ecclesiastical law and its keepers, called Bishop's court, paved the way for Brahmins and Maulavis to be the custodians of personal law despite the impossibility of representation of all sects and variety of religious groups with a particular religion. But making of categories called for dependence on the Shastris for obtaining the 'authentic' and 'authoritative' versions of Hindu law and also the need for compiling a written, codified version so that it became a practical handbook for British administrators to deal with personal matters. In a way, the British themselves became the patrons of Shastra and there was hardly anything 'authentic' about the colonial construction of the laws.

The search for the one uniform Hindu law however made the colonisers suspicious about the 'corruption' due to the multiplicity of texts and lack of system in regulating Hindu personal laws. While the caste to caste or family to family variation among the Hindus was too complicated to handle, the attempt to compile Muslim laws was even more challenging given the complexity of translation from Arabic to English. However, Shariat Application Act was enacted in 1937.

The search and codification of personal laws unleashed a new process of identity making and breaking. One paradox is that if the process of codifying personal laws was meant to provide freedom to religious communities in terms of their own religious practices, in practice, it actually helped colonisers exercise more control over the colonial subjects as the conformity towards separate community laws meant conforming to the watertight religious categories made by the British at the altar of multiple other identities. Hindus and Muslims were now defined by law.

The freedom to exercise flexibility and variety across caste and region was getting lost. The space to celebrate cultural pluralism was actually shrinking. For example, the "scriptural tradition of upper-caste Brahmins, hitherto applicable only to the twice born castes became the basis of law for all colonial subjects designated as Hindu, overruling customary practices, regional variations, and differences of class and caste affiliation" (Mukhopadhyay 1994: 112). This gave rise to another paradoxical trend. The gender ideology within patriarchy became stricter. Control of women's sexuality had now become legitimised through Brahminical traditions which began to be adopted by lower castes. Following the new Brahminical trend, women from lower castes were no longer permitted to remarry or initiate divorce or work outside home. Polyandry and levirate, hitherto a common practice among many tribes and lower caste peasant groups, began to be condemned by Brahminical morality. Being 'pativrata' and 'secluded' was now valorised as an upper-caste practice, and these now became crucial to the 'Hindu' way of being.

The state's apparent claim to 'stand above society' by 'dividing' the law pertaining to public matters and that of the private in reality created massive turmoil within and between communities. The official rhetoric of 'non-interference' of colonial state was not able to hide how 'colonial' the reinterpretation and rewriting of religious texts actually became. The liminal religious and occupational practices among the Hindus and Muslims of the lower strata were vanishing and an ideological justification for reinforcement of community identity was being shaped.

UCC AND THE HINDU NATIONALIST PROJECTION OF PRO-MUSLIM WOMEN IMAGE

Hindu nationalists and feminists broadly support Uniform Civil Code (UCC) in India, which calls for one set of laws to be followed by all religious groups. But they support it for different reasons. While feminists do not want women to be oppressed by the patriarchal practices of religious laws, Hindu nationalists want a uniform code so that minority religious groups cannot be entitled to any freedom in regard to their own religious practices.

The debate in contemporary India over the UCC reflects the conflict between two concepts of rights in the Part three of the Fundamental Rights of the constitution. Individual's right to equality and freedom is ensured by the Articles 14–24 of the constitution, and the religious freedom and the cultural and educational rights of the minorities are covered by Articles 25–30 from which the religious communities derive the right to exercise their own personal laws. Since personal laws covering subjects like marriage, property inheritance and guardianship of children discriminate against women, Part three of the constitution presents a contradiction between a woman's right as an individual citizen and a religious group's right as a collective body to be protected by democracy. The demand for the UCC by the Hindu nationalists reflects an attempt of homogenisation in favour of the majority community. Hindu nationalists advocate UCC for various reasons.

First, they argue that 'non-interference' of the state in the domestic and religious affairs of the minority subjects means giving too much freedom away to minority religious groups which deserve to inhabit India only by accepting the superiority of Hindus as a majority community. Second, they oppose the construction of a minority identity, especially a 'Muslim identity' which they believe would be solidified if the state allows the codification of community doctrines. Hindu nationalism is not ready to accept any form of acknowledgement offered to religious minority; to them, personal laws are symbolic. It implies the reaffirmation from the government that minority religious communities do exist and they need not fall under a broad, enforced, homogenised version of law, but they are allowed to celebrate their cultural specificity being completely protected yet not interfered by the state. Third, Hindu nationalists call those political parties and groups who oppose the idea of UCC 'pseudo-secular' and even 'antinationalist'. Hindu nationalists construct their own definition of secularism by arguing that all religious groups should conform to whatever is good according to the majority religious community of India. They resent the fact that Hindu personal law has been 'reformed' by the state intervention, yet Muslim personal law has been left 'untouched'.

Fourth, a very popular rhetoric to strengthen the Hindu nationalist argument has been that BJP and other Hindu nationalist groups are 'pro-women' and their opponents are 'communal' and 'anti-women'. Their stance is to convince voters by arguing that those who are for personal laws are trying to reinforce religious and 'communal' identity. They themselves are the 'true seculars' as they talk about Uniform Civil Code that would apply to everybody irrespective of religion.

Women's rights issues have been intertwined with the debates of UCC since mid-1980s as feminist groups started talking about eradication of oppression of women by different personal laws. The question of women's protection against personal laws became a central point of debate in Shah Bano's case when Rajiv Gandhi, as a Prime Minister, ignored Supreme Court's judgement that asked Bano's husband to pay maintenance to his divorced wife, as she had no other means of support. The governmental stance to encourage the Muslim personal law to limit the liability of the husband to support the wife by playing the card of iddat period which, according to Muslim personal law, does not support a destitute.

Personal laws often are oppressive and exclusionary towards women. They are indeed the mechanisms to perpetuate and strengthen patriarchal control. But the homogenising thrust of the UCC, the construction of nation through only the dominant voice of the majority, and the exclusion and marginalisation of multiple identities and interest are equally dangerous and oppressive in a democracy. The claim that Hindu personal law was reformed while 'other' communities were 'allowed' to cling to regressive anti-women laws is itself ambiguous. As Menon (2004) argues, Hindu personal laws were merely codified under strong resistance from traditionalists within Congress. In the fear of losing votes on the first general election, the proposed Bill to remodel marriage and inheritance laws was dropped until it was pushed through by Nehru during 1955–1956 as several Acts regarding marriage, succession, adoption and maintenance. The

Acts were not unqualified in their approach towards women's rights though. Upper-caste North Indian religious practices were forced upon bypassing vast heterogeneous and even more liberal customary provisions by codification as mentioned earlier in the chapter.

One should not overlook the fact that there are progressive features in Muslim personal law which benefit women more than Hindu personal law. One example being the right of mehr that gives Muslim marriage the status of a civil contract, is an exclusive property of the bride. The pro-UCC groups often talk about integrating the 'positive aspects' of all personal laws, but one must understand that it is not realistic; for instance, the introduction of mehr in Hindu marriage is not possible and the marriage in this case is sacramental and cannot be transformed into a contract. Uniform Civil Code would be an ideal alternative to the gender oppressive personal laws as the Civil Code of Goa, which BJP often attempts to sell countrywide, shows us how non 'uniform' and gendered it is. Marriage, by this Code, can be annulled by Church if any one of the parties insists. Also, 'limited' polygamy and bigamy have been allowed to Hindus and rights of 'illegitimate' children are limited and caste hierarchies are legitimised by oath-taking ceremonies in court. We would not deny that there are positive aspects as well. For example, each spouse is entitled to 50 per cent of all assets of owner and one needs spouse's permission before disposing the assets. But the code has not considered the unequal power relations in a marriage and the issue of domestic violence (Menon 2014).

One may argue that there needs to be initiative within communities to generate reforms so that individual rights do not cause fear in minority communities that reforming their personal laws is merely a pretext to erase their identity. A number of Islamic states have managed to come up with gender just laws. If the state helps the minority communities to feel safe and confident, attempts of self-criticism within communities would follow. To us, common gender just, egalitarian codes matter; talking about 'uniformity' coupled with abstract and hollow ideas of citizenship which is unfair towards minorities and women make no sense. Questions of gender justice need to be taken into account both in case of personal and secular laws. Imposition of a uniform law on heterogeneous groups need not necessarily be egalitarian.

One needs to challenge some of the common sources of inequality in all personal laws. One of them being the assumed heterosexual structure of family in personal laws. Inclusion of homosexual family and live-in couples should be incorporated in all personal laws. The popular rhetoric of

UCC about 'rescuing' Muslim women from 'polygamous' Muslim men consolidated right-wing base in demonising Muslim men. Instead of valorising monogamy, it is important to protect individuals by reconceptualising all relationships in contractual terms so that partners in bigamous marriages as well as outside formal wedlock become liable to take responsibility of the other person in the relationship if needed.

It is not personal laws which are always the evil; nor does Uniform Civil Code always demand pro-majority stances. Establishing long-term comprehensive gender just and egalitarian framework of rights for individuals needs to come not only through the reform of personal laws from within but also through the reform of 'secular' laws so that benefits like equal wages, maternity and paternity benefits are available and accessible to all individuals. Also, the overemphasis on individual might reveal a complete political picture in recent debates over land acquisition by Indian states. A school of feminist scholarship (Haksar 1999) has critiqued the individual rights to property and the granting of property rights to Hindu women to be a strategic move by the state as encroachment of common or public land by state becomes more difficult if it is a collective ownership. Negotiating with and pressurising an individual is a lot easier. So it is not just a question of individual's right but a need to evolve and develop more egalitarian customs within communities (e.g. tribal communities) as well. Merely focusing on individual members (women, in these communities) and attempts to getting them land would not generate egalitarian, gender just outcomes.

CONCLUSION

By bringing together the recent discussion of the hijab controversy, the ongoing attack of Hindu nationalism on minorities, and the debate on personal law and Uniform Civil Code, the chapter lays bare the various ways Hindu nationalism problematised the position and status of the Muslim women both within their society and also within the larger Indian community. The conflation of religion and culture and understanding of the Indian society from the lens, tropes and examples of Hinduism, particularly an 'upper caste', 'book view' Hinduism, is often manifested through the everyday understanding of clothing explains that Muslim women hardly appear in the imagination of India as a country. It is often Hindu nationalism which pits Hindu women against Muslim women. While a particular construction of Hindu women is seen as an epitome of civilised, feminine Indian women, on the other hand, Muslim women are always seen as oppressed victims who need to be saved by Hindu men. The manufacturing of these kinds of contrasting women by Hindu nationalists keeps women as the prime site and victim of imagination of nation, which fails to celebrate India's democratic and plural character.

NOTES

1. The basis of Hindu nationalist mass mobilisation is the creation of an 'enemy' or 'other' and a Hindu 'self'. Hindu nationalism presupposes the superiority of Hindus and believes in creating India as a Hindu nation. According to this school of thought, only religions that have their holy places of worship within the geographical boundary of India could be incorporated into the Hindu fold (Jaffrelot 1999).
2. Bharatiya Janata Party, a Hindu nationalist political party was formed in 1980 in India. BJP's political project of Hindutva envisions India to be a Hindu Rashtra where Hindus are entitled to greater privilege for being the majority population than the non-Hindu religious minorities. See M.S. Golwalkar, *We or Our Nationhood Defined and a Bunch of Thoughts* for details about the political philosophy of Hindutva.
3. The literature on veiling is wide and detailed. Apart from Mahmood's work on Egypt, other work includes Sharma's (1978) study of ghunghat (veiling) in the context of Ghanyari, a north Indian Himalayan village in India; Abu-Lughod's (1986) analysis in Bedoiun society; Alvi in the context of Pakistani Punjab; Abraham (2010: 203) in the context of Bikaner, Rajasthan, analyses veiling through the practice of ghunghat. The caste Hindu married women use the end of the sari (pallu) to cover the head. The practice of the ghunghat is generally performed by the married women in front of her in-laws and older kin. She argues that ghunghat not only covers one's head, but it also to a certain extent acts as an attitude of submission of women in the larger society. Abraham's (2010: 203) study of gender and neighbourhood in the context of Bikaner, Rajasthan, discusses the practices of veiling and *purdah*, which are often applied in the context of veiling of eyes and voice, like *ankhe ka pardah* (veiling of the eyes) and *awaz ka purdah* (veiling of the voice).

REFERENCES

Abraham, Janaki. 2010. Veiling and the Production of Gender and Space in a Town in North India: A Critique of the Public/Private Dichotomy. *Indian Journal of Gender Studies* 17 (2): 191–222.

Abu-Lughod, Lila J. 1986. *Veiled Sentiments: Honour and Poetry in a Bedouin Society*. California and London: University of California Press.

Bacchetta, P. 2019. Communal Property/Sexual Property: On Representations of Muslim Women in a Hindu Nationalist Discourse 1. In *Forging Identities*, 188–225. Routledge.

Banerjee, Mukulika, and Daniel Miller. 2003. *The Sari.* New Delhi: Roli Books.

Bautista, Julius. 2008. The Meta-theory of Piety: Reflections on the Work of Saba Mahmood. *Contemporary Islam* 2: 75–83.

Carter, M. 2003. *Fashion Classics from Carlyle to Barthes.* Oxford, GB: Berg.

Chatterjee, Partha. 1989. The Nationalist Resolution of the Women's Question. In *Recasting Women: Essays in Colonial History*, ed. Kumkum Sangari and Sudesh Vaid, 233–253. New Delhi: Kali for Women.

Dasgupta, Abhijit. 2021. Everyday Christianity in a Kolkata Neighbourhood: A Sociological Study. PhD Thesis Submitted to Department of Humanities and Social Sciences, Indian Institute of Technology, Bombay.

el-Guindi, Fadwa. 1981. Veiling Infitah with Muslim Ethic: Egypt's Contemporary Islamic Movement. *Social Problems* 28: 465–483.

Haksar, N. 1999. Human Rights Layering: A Feminist Perspective. In *Engendering Law. Essays in Honour of Lotika Sarkar*, ed. Amita Dhanda and Archana Parasher. Lucknow: Eastern Book Company.

Higgins-Roach, Ellen Mary, and Joanne B. Eicher. 1992. Dress and Identity. *Clothing and Textiles Research Journal* 10 (4): 1–8.

Hoffman-Ladd, Valerie. 1987. Polemics on the Modesty and Segregation of Women in Contemporary Egypt. *International Journal of Middle East Studies* 19: 23–50.

Jaffrelot, C. 1999. *The Hindu Nationalist Movement and Indian Politics: 1925 to the 1990s: Strategies of Identity-building, Implantation and Mobilisation (with Special Reference to Central India).* Penguin Books India.

Lurie, Alison. 1981. *The Language of Clothes.* New York: Random House.

Mahmood, Saba. 2001. Feminist Theory, Embodiment, and the Docile Agent: Some Reflection on the Egyptian Revival Movement. *Cultural Anthropology.* 16 (2): 202–236.

———. 2005. *Politics of the Piety: The Islamic Revival and the Feminist Subject.* Princeton and Oxford: Princeton University Press.

Menon, N. 2004. *Recovering Subversion: Feminist Politics Beyond the Law.* University of Illinois Press.

———. 2014. Uniform Civil Code: The Women's Movement Perspective, Kafila. October1.http://kafila.org/2014/10/01/uniform-civil-code-state-of-the-debate-in-2014/

Mukhopadhyay, M. 1994. Between Community and State: The Question of Women's Rights and Personal Laws. In *Forging Identities: Gender, Communities and the State*, ed. Zoya Hasan, 108–129. New Delhi: Kali for Women.

Sharma, Ursula M. 1978. Women and Their Affines: The Veil as a Symbol of Separation. *Man* 13 (2): 218–233.

Tarlo, Emma. 1996. *Clothing Matters: Dress and Identity in India. C.* London: Hurst and Company.

Wickramasinghe, Nira. 2003. *Dressing the Colonised Body: Politics, Clothing and Identity in Colonial Sri Lanka.* New Delhi: Orient Blackswan.

Zuhur, Sherifa. 1992. *Revealing Reveiling: Islamist Gender Ideology in Contemporary Egypt.* Albany: State University of New York Press.

CHAPTER 9

Dominance of Exploitative Relations in the Matrix of Class Struggle in Bangladesh

Farooque Chowdhury

Introduction

Right shouldn't be defined in narrow sense. Moreover, the term Right is widely used in a loosely defined way. With a lot of variants and sub-variants in countries over a long period of time since the French Revolution, the term Right sometimes creates confusion among a group of scholars and analysts. Right-wing covers variants in terms of approaches, *modus operandi*, extent, root/source, force, thrusts that ultimately stand for the exploiting classes, *status quo*, class-divided society, exploitative relations and private property. Market's dominance, sectarianism, supremacist and racist concepts, retrogressive ideas, and similar concepts/ideas/approaches belong to the Right. All Right variants and sub-variants explicitly or implicitly deny class struggle and class contradiction, historical and dialectical process, and scientific approach to questions related to society and the exploited masses of people. Instead, the Right stands on idealism that appears noble-minded but anchored in the depth of securing exploitation

F. Chowdhury (✉)
Dhaka, Bangladesh

© The Author(s), under exclusive license to Springer Nature
Switzerland AG 2023
B. S. Nayak, D. Chakraborty (eds.), *Interdisciplinary Reflections on
South Asian Transitions*,
https://doi.org/10.1007/978-3-031-36686-4_9

based on private property. No variant of the Right goes for abolition of private property, although it's difficult to find the mainstream discourse on this aspect while discussing the issue.

The Right's variants, depending on time and space, functionally and ultimately stand for a society operating with exploitative relations in the spheres of production and distribution. The variants include the hated Nazis, Fascists, nationalists and ultra-nationalists, market-mongers, proponents of *laissez-faire*, deregulation, privatization, de-centralized economy, limited role of government, strong state, social Catholic Rightists, Christian Democrats, classical liberals, neo-liberals, hate-mongers, liberal/social/fiscal conservatives, neo-conservatives, and opponents of egalitarianism and all forms of liberalism. It not only considers socialism and communism as its arch-enemy but also opposes that form of social democracy, which is fundamentally different from the ideology and politics of socialism, a system led by the exploited. The Right stands for class compromise by the exploited and with the exploiters—an approach that bribes a section of the exploited/gives something to the exploited in exchange of ensuring class domination of the exploiting classes.

The Right camp includes followers of authoritarianism, retrogressive ideas and upper-class interests. The trend/stream takes appearance/shape of Radical Right, right populism and even anti-capitalism and anti-individualism with certain characteristics. Once, in countries, it took shape collectivist movement. The Right, at times and in countries/societies, appears as Right-wing libertarianism/libertarian conservatism/conservative libertarianism. It, at times, fought a section of the rich/exploiters. Its position, at times, goes against industrialization. It is, at times, identified as Reactionary Right, Radical Right, Moderate Right, Extreme Right and New Right. There're Right Populists and its sub-variants. A part of the Right sometimes goes for extending popular measures that include health and education facilities for the commoners. Even, in the Left camp, the Right sometimes appears as Right Opportunism.[1]

The Right never talks about/goes for [1] class struggle leading to the radical change/triumph of the exploited, [2] abolishing of exploitative production relations/tools of exploitation/private property/inequality cropping out of exploitation, and [3] democracy for/of/by the exploited. The Right stands for democracy of exploiting capital/classes.

This wide area of the Right is sometimes missed by some analysts, leading to [1] confuse with the Left, [2] having a narrow approach like identifying the Right only as a certain political party (PP)/an alliance of political parties, [3] missing the Right ideology/politics, [4] reformist measures/initiatives as pro-people/poor, [5] capital's source/role/character/regeneration/accumulation.

The term Right has been used in this chapter as the ideology, politics and economy standing for/operating with exploitative relations, which manifest in state machine; in policies, principles and proclamations; in education, culture and propaganda; in legislation, taxation and fiscal measures; in handling of market(s); in class struggle.

THE POINT OF DEPARTURE IN BANGLADESH

The origin of the Bangladesh state lies in the period of the glorious War for Liberation, the valiant armed struggle waged by the people of the land in 1971. Ignoring this phase creates confusion in comprehending following political developments and classes/sections related to these and the class character of dominance. The Proclamation of Independence reflects two aspects of that time:

[1] Aspiration of the people waging the armed struggle for liberation from all forms of exploitation and
[2] the class power dominating the struggle.

Just before beginning of the armed struggle for liberation, the War for Liberation, the people were moving forward after completing a phase of mass upsurge that

[1] challenged the neo-colonial state of Pakistan and compelled the state to retreat from a few of its long-held positions;
[2] subdued and overthrew a dictatorial rule, the Ayub regime;
[3] overthrew rural allies of the regime, Basic Democrats at rural level and
[4] established universal franchise.[2]

These developments were significant in terms of class, class power and class alignments. The mass upsurge, unprecedented in Bangladesh, spread and popularized pro-people/progressive, democratic, secular ideas and demands for economic and political programs that articulated aspiration of the people, which got reflected in following political demands, acts and developments. The Proclamation of Independence, a fundamental political document, reflects the reality of that time—demands, aspirations and, in essence, the dominating class power.

The mass upsurge of 1969 was a watershed moment in the political history of Bangladesh, then East Pakistan, the eastern province of Pakistan. The upsurge sweeping the entire land uprooted the Pakistan state's ideological basis and its class power in the political sphere in Bangladesh, then the eastern wing of Pakistan. In all real senses, Rightist politics, which was dominating the land since mid-August of 1947, lost all its steam, power and influence since the near-about half-a-year-long 1968–1969 upsurge. The Rightist political organizations of/connected to the dominating classes/interests, though super-active to regain lost ground, were appearing lame in influencing and impacting the vast swath of politics, which was overwhelmed with pro-people, anti-Right, secular, progressive organizations, politics, programs, ideas, concepts and slogans. The Rightist politics had no trace in the rural areas.[3]

Since March 25, 1971, the Pakistan state began a genocidal campaign as a way to keep the Baangaalee people subdued forever and unleashed its army on the task of genocide, that took toll—three million people killed in a span of nine months, an unimaginable figure in terms of the time— nine months:

[I]n March 1971 [...] the [...] Pakistani military launched an all-out war [...] in East Pakistan, forcing the region to declare itself an independent People's Republic of Bangladesh.[4]

The genocidal military campaign impacted psychology, stand and actions of the people of the land. Moreover, along with unrestrained exploitation of the people and land by the ruling elites of the Pakistan, there was their hatred to the Baangaalee people: "[T]he vengeance, pride and venom with which West Pakistani military officers carried out the carnage in East Bengal after March 25, 1971" is reflected in "the remarks of a Major Kamal who told an American construction worker, interviewed on *CBS* television, that after the West Pakistanis had conquered East Bengal, each of his soldiers would have a Bengali mistress and that no dogs and Bengalis would be allowed in the exclusive Chittagong Club. As a member of the West Pakistani 'educated class' I [Feroz Ahmed] can testify that this is by no means an isolated case. [...] Instead East Bengal has become a theater of the most gruesome drama of death and destruction since Auschwitz. [...] [T]he massacre of hundreds of thousands of innocent civilians, the burning and strafing of thousands of towns and villages and the exodus of millions of refugees, has qualitatively changed the nature of the struggle in Bangladesh [...]."[5]

The Bangladesh people's glorious War for Liberation was full of people's active participation, political/armed activism and organization, control over wide areas of rural life, subduing of the Rightist elements in rural areas, wiping out of ideology and concepts, essentially Rightist, the Pakistan ruling elements and their state machine upheld and implemented. In numerical term, absolute overwhelming majority of the military force that was waging the people's war was from the poor, landless, near-landless, lower- and middle-class peasantry while the minor sections/classes, the rich farmers, big landholders, moneylenders were defending the neo-colonial state. That was a change of class power in the rural Bangladesh, and at that time, Bangladesh was overwhelmingly rural, agricultural, and the urban and industrial centers were a few in the entire land, the industrial capital virtually turned inoperative during the entire period of the War for Liberation (March 1971 to December 1971).[6]

The Bangladesh War for Liberation had two trends:

[1] the dominating trend of the Mukti Bahini, Freedom Fighters, led by the Awami League and
[2] the leftist-led armed struggle.

The Mukti Bahini, under the leadership of the exiled Bangladesh Government, conducted guerrilla war and was super-active and in the offensive throughout the land. It was the biggest armed force in the land, with thousands and thousands of fighters, having support of the entire Baangaalee people. The Mukti Bahini had liberated zones in different regions of the country. The Pakistan army could not step into those liberated zones. People living in these liberated zones carried on their economic activities—agricultural production, localized commerce and artisanal industry that mainly included manufacturing of farm implements and household items by potters, carpenters, ironsmiths, weavers.

The leftists, fragmented and factionalized, and a part disoriented in terms of strategy, tactics/military line, conducted guerrilla war in a number of areas of the country. The leftist-led guerrilla forces, smaller in size, also liberated areas, a few in number. They could retain a few of those liberated areas, actually pockets of guerrilla activities/guerrilla zones/base areas, all through the period of the War for Liberation, while the rest were lost at different times of the war. It was not the dominating trend in the war.[7] Many non-Communist reporters have carried stories concerning E.P.C.P.'s [East Pakistan Communist Party] encounters with the Pakistan Army and cooperation with Mukti Bahini [the Force of Freedom Fighters under the leadership of the Provisional Government of Bangladesh] at the local level.[8]

With these two trends the dominating politics and political leadership was of the exiled Bangladesh Government, and of the Awami League, as the Awami League was the party having absolute majority of the people's representatives elected through the elections conducted in 1970, and they formed the constituent assembly. In physical terms, the Awami League was organizing, supervising and carrying on most of the work related to the War for Liberation that included youth camps, recruitment centers of the Mukti Bahini, guerrilla training camps, relief work among the populace, about 10 million, which left the country following the Pakistan army's genocidal campaign throughout the country.[9]

But, neither the exiled Bangladesh Government nor the Awami League leadership was in control of the economy, as the reality of that time was the limit. The same was with the small and weak leftist camp. The mode of production in the land remained as it was before March 1971, although the pro-Pakistan Rightist camp lost political ground.

In politics of the country, the entire environment was full of a progressive program. The slogans for an exploitation-free society, nationalization of major parts of the economy, fair distribution of resources, realization of rights of the labor and poor peasantry were fully accepted by the entire people. This political environment couldn't be ignored by the leadership of the War for Liberation, consequently of which the leadership had to proclaim that socialism was one of four principles of the Bangladesh state. The rest of the principles were democracy, secularism and nationalism. The principles demand a discussion, even if in brief, as there're confusions regarding the principles. The first point: Democracy, irrespective of bourgeois or proletarian, is not devoid of secularism. Bourgeois democracy emerged along with separation church from state, although the bourgeoisie in countries have compromised this position of separation at later stage and even fed and fanned the opposite approach, utilized the power of church, etc., for self-interest which was separated from state. The second point: Socialism isn't devoid of democracy. The breed of democracy that socialism practices is by, of and for the exploited, the majority of a given society in a given time, which in turn is dictatorship on the exploiting classes, the minority part of that society in that time. Very often socialism is compared as opposite to democracy, which is based on incomplete and confused assumption about socialism. The third point: With socialism, nationalism stands on internationalism; it's neither like bourgeois nationalism nor ultra-nationalism.

The Bangladesh principles stated were reflected in actions at that time. The War for Liberation was going on the basis of those principles—no effort was there to practice/uphold/secure communal, sectarian politics—and there was no scope for securing exploitative relations, as all the efforts and work were concentrated on two areas: organizing and carrying on the war, and securing people's lives within and outside of the country. There was no scope by the exiled Bangladesh Government and the political forces leading the War for Liberation to handle any industrial or commercial enterprise, land tenure system, trade, taxation, distribution of property during that phase of war. [The Bangladesh Government issued a number of directives related to trade, levy/tax, etc.] At that time, the Rightist politics had no space to operate within the Bangladesh-wide surging wave of War for Liberation. No program and directive of the exiled Bangladesh Government told about the Rightist politics or economy. So, for the Rightist politics in Bangladesh, the table was turned by the people at that time.

Bangladesh Thrusts Ahead

On December 16, 1971, the occupying Pakistan army surrendered to the allied force consisting with the Bangladesh Mukti Bahini and the Indian Army. From that day, the Pakistan state lost all authority and control over Bangladesh. It was in economy and politics, in the areas of legislation, judiciary, ideology, culture and education.

After the liberation of Bangladesh in 1971, Awami League, the political party leading the War for Liberation, formed the government as it was the absolute majority party in the *Jatio Sangsad* (JS) legislative assembly (the first parliamentary elections were held on March 7, 1973); the party remained loyal to the election manifesto it announced for the election held in 1970; consequently, the Constitution that was framed in 1972 declared the four basic state principles: democracy, nationalism, secularism and socialism.

The new state—Bangladesh—had to come into connection to and handle the existing property relation, in the areas of industries and agriculture.

Major property and property relations were in two areas: industry and agriculture. Most of the industries were nationalized as the owners were mostly pro-Pakistan state, and they left the country abandoning those industries. Banks met the same fortune. In the area of agriculture, fully rural, the pre-Liberation War relations, transactions, classes and their holds remained as there was no nationalization/confiscation/transfer/redistribution of land property or land/agricultural reform. Neither the dominant political force nor the government had any such program to break up/uproot/cancel existing property relation in the area of land ownership/tenure system. The industries that were nationalized were operated under state's directive with state-appointed administrators as head of the enterprises. The state that was organized was not going for radical change in property relations. The legal mechanism—laws, regulations, courts of law, etc.—the state wielded was fundamentally based on exploitative property relations. The same was with the administrative system and arrangement, and the local government. The Constitution, however, proclaimed, in its preamble, a few principles, which were pro-people, not entirely Rightist, and reflected the aspiration and mood of the masses of people prevailing at that time.

The situation consisting with mechanism and declarations was of contradictions that reflected compromise between powers of opposite classes/sections, which with the gradual passing of time took a definite shape. This "gradual passing of time" was actually a time of concentration and consolidation of capital and state machine in the newly independent country. The state machine that was in the country was essentially the old machine that was operating before December 16, 1971. Other than occasional utterances—announcements, declarations and promises—the machine was basically the same: Working for securing the exploitative property relations. The announcements, declarations and promises were made not only verbally; written—documents—promises are also there. But no document went for terminating exploitative relations or, even, initiating measures that can facilitate a radical change in the exploitative relations, tear out links of exploitation, strengthen role of socio-political forces in the area of politics and political power so that the forces can initiate radical change. The pronouncements, principles, policies, whatever was made/declared/enshrined, sounded/appeared lofty; but, in reality, in functional term or in term of execution and/or operation none not even went to the level of breaking the base/shackles of exploitation or making a challenge to the relations of exploitation.

Economy: The economy tells the dominance—who dominates or whose dominance.

The economy that now dominates the Bangladesh society is exploitative. In agriculture, industry, domestic and external trade, in budgetary measures and allocations, in fiscal and taxation arrangements, the exploitative relation persists. There's no scope to identify these as non-Rightist.

The "Preamble" of state's Constitution pledges:

"The high ideals of nationalism, socialism, democracy and secularism" [...] "shall be the fundamental principles of the Constitution."

The Constitution's part on "Fundamental Principles of State Policy" declares:

The people shall own or control the instruments and means of production and distribution, and with this end in view ownership shall assume the following forms—

(a) state ownership, that is ownership by the State on behalf of the people through the creation of an efficient and dynamic nationalised public sector embracing the key sectors of the economy;

(b) co operative ownership, that is ownership by co operatives on behalf of their members within such limits as may be prescribed by law; and

(c) private ownership, that is ownership by individuals within such limits as may be prescribed by law.

And,

It shall be a fundamental responsibility of the State to emancipate the toiling masses the peasants and workers and backward sections of the people from all forms of exploitation.

And,

The State shall endeavour to ensure equality of opportunity to all citizens.

And,

The State shall adopt effective measures to remove social and economic inequality between man and man and to ensure the equitable distribution of wealth among citizens, and of opportunities in order to attain a uniform level of economic development throughout the Republic.

And,

The State Shall endeavour to ensure equality of opportunity and participation of women in all spheres of national life.

And,

Work is a right, a duty and a matter of honour for every citizen who is capable of working, and everyone shall be paid for his work on the basis of the principle "from each according to his abilities, to each according to his work".

And,

The State shall endeavour to create conditions in which, as a general principle, persons shall not be able to enjoy unearned incomes, and in which human labour in every form, intellectual and physical, shall become a fuller expression of creative endeavour and of the human personality.

But there's difference between proclaiming certain principles/policies/ goals and force of its execution/implementation, which is a completely legal question. Moreover, there're issues of power, sharing of power, arrangements of using/handling of power, which are connected to fundamental issues of economy and politics including ruling machine, where interests play role/influence.

The National Budget and Five-Year Plans/other planning documents, similarly, proclaim or talk about poverty alleviation, etc., but do not challenge the exploitative relations nor empower the exploited masses of people nor provide them space and tools for challenging the exploitative relations. It's not that challenging exploitative relations are expected from these documents. This can't be expected as long as these are in the hands/ manufactured by the power that doesn't go for challenging the exploitative relations. But it's a confirmation of the power of the class forces that dominates; and these class forces are not Left, so the Right, with variants with color and shade.[10]

The economy finds dominant operation of new-liberal/market-oriented policies and domination of the private capital. Since 1975, the state followed policies/suggestions of the World Bank and the International Monetary Fund, which was lessened later in areas of the economy. But the dominant part of the economy stood on exploitative relations.

Politics and ruling machine: Politics covers all areas concerning life of people, rulers, production and distribution, institutions, organizations, arrangements and processes that are organized/activated with these, although, at times, a section of scholars consider the issue in a narrow sense, and they concentrate on areas with a compartmentalized approach. This chapter looks at the issue in actual sense—the whole people's life that includes struggles at class and production levels, political parties, ideologies, ruling machine, economic, social, cultural, political programs, measures at/by institutions and organizations.

The sequence of politics has been described by many scholars/a lot of literature.[11] Instead of repeating of those descriptions, presenting the pattern of political developments is useful for further analysis and drawing conclusion.

The dominant sections of the Bangladesh society are well organized and hyper-active in political parties. Factions of the dominant sections have respective political parties. These political parties' ideologies and programs related to politics, economy, society, culture, environment, constitution, legislation, administration, local government, rural development, agriculture, industry, youth, women, public instruction, science, foreign policy, etc., are basically pro-*status quo*. None of these programs challenge the exploitative relations. The stand is Rightist.

Secularism as a principle is announced by one of the mainstream major political parties (PP) while the rest don't go for that. However, the PP announcing secularism as one of its principles took contradictory stand in the JS while it made an amendment (15th Amendment) to the Constitution. The amendment restored secularism as a guiding principle of state but retained Islam as the state religion of Bangladesh. It should be noted that the state religion was introduced to the Constitution in 1988 by a military ruler—Lieutenant-General Ershad.

However, on the question of religious extremism, there's a major difference between the major PPs. While Awami League takes strong stand against religious extremism, other major PPs use religion directly or indirectly.

The political map showing the dominant parties' position related to the PP and major public political activities of the major PPs finds the following:

\# Adherence to capitalist economy, and no challenge to the exploitative relations in economy. Whatever difference was there between the major PPs on the question of economy that has narrowed down, and none of the PPs oppose market-oriented economic policies; the ideological divide between the major PPs on economic policies disappeared.

Immediately after the emergence of Bangladesh, there were many PPs; then, a single PP was organized; then, again many PPs emerged; and, consequently, two PPs dominate the political scene. The trajectory shows factions within ruling interests.

Mainstream academic political literature talks about "state-sponsored" PPs/organizing of PP by using state machine including intelligence organization, and through distribution of state resources, once. The move also shows state and capacity/incapacity of a certain section(s) of the dominating interests.

Once, PPs adhering to sectarian politics were banned, followed by withdrawal of the ban, and later, again imposition of the ban. It's a show of in-fighting within the dominating interests.

Use of religion in politics and discarding of it are found in the dominating politics.

It's also found that secularism is pronounced as one of the party principles by a major PP although the PP, at times, takes contradictory stand on the issue. It shows the play of a certain ideology in the dominating politics.

At times, PPs usually identified as right and left entered into political/electoral alliance(s).

At times, major PPs boycotted election and at times participated election. Thus, participation in and boycott of election appear as tactics of major PPs. The same goes with parliament: participation, boycott, resignation from parliament by one major PP or the other. It shows the state and method of factional fight within the camp of dominating interests.

All the time, one or the other major PPs raise allegation of fraudulent parliamentary election.

Elections at local government level saw both non-PP and PP-based elections. It's a maneuver of dominance.

The politics/state experienced the following trajectory: civilian rule (CR) to military rule (MR) to CR to MR to CR to MR to CR, which was interspersed by two referendums in 1977 and in 1985.

The dominating interests had to resort to, out of factional fight, the following approach for securing governance: Non-party Caretaker Government (NCG) for conducting national election to discarding of the NCG-system. (The NCG was first introduced in 1990. The

Caretaker Government Act was passed by the 6th Parliament as the 13th amendment to the Constitution on May 25, 1996; and the NCG held the elections of 1996, 2001 and 2008.) It shows [1] state of factional fight within the camp of dominating interests; [2] unstable condition of the governing system; and [3] problem of credibility and acceptability of the governing system within the camp of the dominating interests.

\# Involvement of imperialist countries and other countries in the governing process/electoral system/governance is found in the political sphere of the dominating interests. These include involvement/interference of diplomats and organizations. It shows the state/condition of the dominating interests.

A part of the mainstream academia alleges:

\# A few PPs have lost ideology/a decline in the PPs' ideology.
\# Money and muscle power in politics.
\# "Businessmen remained heavy contributors to party funds. They invested in particular politicians who could then work as their business intermediaries and even as partners."
\# The rich persons' increased role and influence in major PPs. Domination of persons "from upper socio-economic status background in the leadership of the parties". "[M]any politicians have [...] transformed themselves as businessmen [...]." "[M]en with money became more influential in party politics. For many people, politics became a business investment which then had to be recouped with manifold returns."
\# Increased trend of criminalization of politics.
\# Bureaucracy was involved in political movement.
\# Involvement of the so-called civil society.
\# Street protest, agitation, general strike.
\# "Political violence has become an integral part of politics in Bangladesh."

But the fact is state never sponsored political parties, as state is not any human entity; rather, state, as a machine, moves/acts according to the human entities, actually class(es)/section(s)/faction(s) of class(es) that operate the machine. Persons in charge of state machine, acting on behalf of a certain class, organized political parties, used power derived from their control over state machine and apparatus.

A section of scholars allege that a number of political parties have given up their ideology. But the allegation is not true. All the political parties have ideology, and that ideology is according to their interests, and that is reflected in/realized through the way the political parties act/behave. Even, there may be difference between factions of/within political parties. That difference doesn't tell that a certain faction has given up its ideology while another is upholding that. Rather, the difference shows difference in approach/area of thrust or interest/method the factions consider appropriate for realizing interest or the factions' failure to resolve contradiction between them/problem in sharing gain/handling of competition—a failure in distribution of gains reflecting limitation/inefficiency of the system. The higher the failure/problem the acute/intense is the contradiction/outburst of contention. This failure/problem is sometimes suggested by a group of scholars as decay of certain political parties.

The basic element missed by these scholars is scientific approach, which are [1] cause(s) is/are not searched, and [2] basis of the development is not enquired. Questioning the following would have led the mainstream scholars to find real reason of the PPs' role/behavior pattern: [1] Why is this happening? [2] What's the source of this? [3] Why this has not happened in an earlier/another time/period? Even, the incidents/developments they identify as "a new development" or "something degeneration" are also found in other societies with advanced/backward economy and political arrangement for rule with name of "democracy", etc. Their approach or finding, thus, stands as [1] narrow, [2] mechanical, [3] superficial, (without substantive facts, information and argument) and [4] erroneous, which leads, in actual terms, to nowhere though at first sight those look serious/deep/meaningful. It's a void in the mainstream scholarship. They know, but they forget that even in advanced bourgeois democracies/republics, there are [1] factions and factional fight, deeply divided factions and intense factional fights within the ruling classes/dominating political parties, [2] use of force/violence in different forms, and there're other forms of exerting force where violence is visibly absent, [3] street demonstrations/mobilization of masses to advance dominating interests/pressure by contending faction, [4] use of money in politics, [5] use of state machine in furthering political moves or pressing down political opponent, even within self-camp, etc. They, these scholars, deny comparing this reality and consequently fail to or deny to find out the real problem, the meaning of the manifestation—violence, money, etc., although these signify state of politics of the dominating/exploiting classes; but, finding out the state of politics, source, etc., would have provided rationale for radical change.

The administrative and local government system and arrangement stand for *status quo*. In no doubt, the system serves the existing ruling system. The arrangement that has come out through colonized and neo-colonized period was initiated and organized by the British colonial masters with the sole purpose of securing their rule. In areas, the local government began as "Ferry Fund", "Road Committee", "Local Committee", by the colonial British imperialists under acts like the Bengal Act VIII of 1851, Chowkidari Act of 1870, District Road Cess Act of 1871, Bengal Local Self-government Act of 1885 and Village Self-government Act of 1919. Then it evolved with gradual expansion and tightening of colonial grip and exploitation, with furthering capacity of its faithful orderlies at local level, followed by further developments in the neo-colonial period of Pakistan, which was developed further since the emergence of Bangladesh. No system at local level challenges and breaks down the exploitative system or dis-empowers the exploiters.[12]

The legal system that operates is fundamentally inherited from the British colonized days flowing through the neo-colonized Pakistan days; and it's based on property relations, as happens in all class-based societies. The laws related to property, capitals and labor fully favor and secure capital, stand for exploitative relations and operate as a tool for controlling labor/keeping labor in chains of capital. The same goes with the related arrangements and tools.[13] It should be noted that Oliver Goldsmith, an eighteenth-century poet, declared: "Laws grind the poor and rich men rule the law."[14] Another writer from the late-nineteenth century said: "The great lesson we learn [from seven centuries of English Parliaments] is that legislation with regard to labor has almost always been class-legislation. It is the effort of some dominant body to keep down a lower class, which had begun to show inconvenient aspirations."[15]

Democracy: Democracy, one of the most discussed and debated issues in Bangladesh, with its type, forms and *modus operandi*, is being practiced. It has been amended/modified/reshaped. To a section, it's democracy, whereas to another, it's autocracy or illiberal democracy or authoritarianism. Even, factions of the ruling classes have taken contradictory positions on the issue at times.[16]

Ideology, culture and science: The ideology, culture and science that dominate the Bangladesh life uphold exploitative relations. In no way it engages, and instructs to engage with, with the following tasks: Question—questioning of all sorts of [1] authority beginning from the area of knowledge and the practice of pursuance of knowledge, [2] arguments presented by the forces of *status quo*, [3] whatever is presented as self-evident, truth and fact, and as evidence of anything claiming to be truth and factual, [4] logic and arguments presented as infallible and unfaultable, [5] connection between elements forming founding blocks in economy, politics, society, history and philosophy.[17]

Media and propaganda: The media and propaganda that the exploitative system owns and operates dominate the entire socio-political-ideological scene. The media's ownership, its extent and reach, the messages, ideas and concepts it carries/conveys/transmits are fully based on exploitative property relations. Extent of propaganda of the mainstream political parties, capital marketing commodities, and finance/bank capital stands as evidence of the dominance. Ideological propaganda carried on in different popular forms show the extent of its reach and its influence on the masses of people. The well-designed, customized propaganda, in the shape of many forms and tools, are ever-present everywhere, every day, every corner, from urban and industrial areas to the far-flung rural areas, villages in deep interior, even in small, poor communities that reside seasonally in river shoals. The messages, targeted to different age, professional and earning groups, are so craftily designed that these appear as road/tool to emancipation/peace/achievement/success/everything and ultimate destination of life while hiding exploitation/exploitative relations/commodities' command and control over life/brutalities of market.[18]

Non-governmental organizations: Non-governmental organizations (NGO), international, regional, local or big, medium and small, and donor-NGOs and fund and directive-recipient NGOs occupy a large swath of the Bangladesh society. It begins from economy and reaches to the area of politics. Microcredit/microfinance/microenterprise is a major area of operation by the NGOs. The activity named "micro" is not micro although almost all discussions tout, consider and analyze it as micro—an act of deception and a convenient approach to propaganda. The microcredit activity, even, pushes the poor to the market for engaging with a duel with barbarous market, although, in this duel, the poor isn't a trained and efficient market-fighter.

These organizations' other areas of operation include farming, trade, artisanal manufacturing unit, education and politics. Not all NGO are directly involved with politics. In the area of politics, these organizations act according to their donors—a long hand of the states that donate money in different ways, which are universal, practiced in many countries, and well-known today. A lot of socio-political spaces that the NGOs occupy today were vacuums, consequences of absence/lack of or abandoned by the pro-people/progressive/Left political forces; and donors of the NGOs directed these organizations to the vacuums.[19]

In no term these organizations talk about/analyze/preach exploitative relations, class struggle and trajectory of class struggle, and organizations, forms and modes of class struggle to be carried on by politically aware exploited masses of people. Whatever the NGOs preach/analyze/suggest/advise/organize is entirely reformative, extending reach of dominating capital and its ruling machine. All their flounces with signboards inscribed with the terms "poverty alleviation", "empowerment", "rights", "having credit is the poor's right", "democracy", "transparency", "awareness build up", "education", "group cohesion", etc., are in ultimate analysis for [1] *status quo* including existing exploitative relations; [2] dominating capital/international finance capital; [3] containing (i) contradictions between classes, (ii) labor/reserve army of labor and (iii) discontent with existing structure, which are a form of class truce; [4] regeneration of capital; [5] organizing/expanding market of certain commodities; [6] imperialism.

Imperialism: The socio-economic-political-ideological-cultural life in today's world, irrespective of the North and South spheres, is not free from imperialism. No analysis, finding out alignment and power, role, influence and impact of opposing class forces, is possible without finding out coordinate of imperialism in the society being looked into.[20]

In Bangladesh, imperialism takes active role and interferes in the area of politics. [Its interference in the area of economy is another area of discussion, which is not the present chapter's area of coverage.] The brand/type/character of politics and ruling mechanism that it tries to infuse/impose/implement is old and well-known—imperialist, subjugationist, making part of imperialist geo-strategy and tactics. It's well exposed, as much of its activities aren't carried in dark, rather openly/publicly. The forces it backs include Rightist, retrogressive elements. None will claim that the imperialist plan/design/agenda/activities/the brand of democracy it markets is non-Rightist. At times, imperialism plays important role in politics, a role not minor at all, with the activities of its operatives/

diplomats/organizations, diplomatic and non-diplomatic/ideas/plans. The fund allocated for implementing its brand of democracy is not negligible in term of Bangladesh; and imperialism fuels the Right.[21]

CLASS STRUGGLES

Class and class struggle are essential issues to look into if political map and questions related to politics, that is, rise/dominance of the Right, are searched for analysis/dissection of politics or class politics. One of Lenin's statements on class is the following:

> Classes are large groups of people differing from each other by the place they occupy in a historically determined system of social production, by their relation (in most cases fixed and formulated in law) to the means of production, by their role in the social organization of labor, and, consequently, by the dimensions of the share of social wealth of which they dispose and the mode of acquiring it. Classes are groups of people one of which can appropriate the labor of another owing to the different places they occupy in a definite system of social economy.[22]

The class struggle that goes on in Bangladesh society is the same like in all class-divided societies, as quoting from Marx and his closest comrade Engels:

> "The history of all hitherto existing society is the history of class struggles."
> "[O]ppressor and oppressed, stood in constant opposition to one another, carried on an uninterrupted, now hidden, now open fight, [...]."[23]

The opposing classes with incompatible interests and contradictions between them are always in the opposite moves within the antagonistic mode of production and manifested in economic, political and cultural forms.

With enlargement of capitals through primitive accumulation and higher accumulation of capital through appropriation of surplus value, the capitals in Bangladesh have secured stronger position. This empowerment has widened and strengthened its position in all areas of life—in society and politics; in ideology, education and propaganda. The capitals in manufacturing, finance, construction, trading, farming, etc., have strengthened self-positions that have enabled these to carry on offensive in its class war against the labor, and against the exploited masses of people, against the entire society. Domestic markets, markets in Bangladesh, of its products and services are an indicator of the capitals' expanse and power. Other than the domestic markets, a part of the capitals operate in markets abroad. At the beginning, 1972, the size of capitals in the economy was incomparably smaller than today's. Today, the capitals are engaged with bigger ventures in manufacturing, construction, processing, finance, servicing. Consequently, its power has increased. This power is mirrored in areas of politics and rule. Over the decades, its experience has widened. Similarly, the size of labor chained by capitals stands as another indicator of the capitals' expanded power. The size of labor today is much bigger than its size in 1972. This is another aspect of the capitals—the power to exploit such a big size of labor, which means its appropriation and accumulation is incomparably bigger than 1972. Moreover, the labor has gone through phases of demobilization, fracturing and inactivating of its organizations, and absence of class awareness and experience, class politics, literature and leadership. In addition, a significant portion of the labor is younger in age in terms of its interaction with/selling self to capital.[24]

This reality tells of nothing but capitals' uncontrolled, unhindered, unobstructed charge on labor, and broader society. It's a reality of class war that goes on today. In this reality, powerful position of the Right, capitals' ideological/political manifestation, is ensured. This reality is reflected in all related areas including the area of discourse. This state of class struggle has enabled capital to dominate with the Right—Rightist ideology, idea, politics, and programs and measures that hoodwink capital's exploitation, ensure capital's unhindered accumulation, activate class truce, and ideologically and politically disarm labor. In other words, it's the Right's domination, domination of exploitative relations. In this class struggle, the class approaches to assessment of social reality, with its contradictions, is different—the dominating and the dominated classes have respective approaches. The approach by the dominating classes manifests in the Right's program—economic, social, political, ideological, cultural and organizational. Even, the content and aims of class struggle of the opposing classes are opposite. These are reflected in politics, policies and programs of respective classes. The capitals' dominant position is ensuring the Right's dominance; and a few features of the on-going class struggle are manifested in the Right camp's factional fight.

The dominant discourse: The dominant discourse, one indicator of state, extent and intensity of class war by the dominating class(es)/section(s) against the dominated, is centered on many issues, from ocean to sky, from earthly "worthlessness" of life to eternal peace, but radical change of the existing exploitative relations. Exposing the source of suffering, class power, arrangements for domination by the dominating interests, the illogic, irrationality and inefficiency of the exploitative system, the system's stalling capacity in delivering emancipation, and finding out alternatives or allowing space to the dominated discourse does never come, as it's designed and operated to secure the exploitative relations—reverberating the reality: Right's dominance.

The elegant appearing pattern of dominating discussions on related issues, dominant or alternative, bear a similarity: Descriptions and a few comments, sporadic and isolated, on questions of politics, avoiding searching source of problems, trends, practices. A lot of literature on politics/political questions is available with a same style: Description of

[1] political incidents/events/developments, but absence of analysis and finding out connections/relations and source, be it property/capital/trade interest or imperialism.
[2] a few leaders' pronouncements/moves, but absence of source and class basis of those pronouncements/moves.
[3] absence of finding out class connections/interests and role of class struggle.
[4] unquestioned acceptance of definitions related to economy and politics dominating capital/its ideology uses.

The same goes on the questions of economy/political economy, philosophy and history, and even, science. Be it stock market or labor market, consumption or productivity or labor "welfare", health care or education or curricula in the area of formal education or environment, the dominant ideas, concepts, definitions, explanations, rationale, way of looking at facts prevail. In some areas, it's far-Right while in other areas, it's the Right without the forcefulness and ruthlessness of the far-Right. The difference in deepness of the color Right doesn't take out the reality of Right's domination, which is often missed by a section of the mainstream scholars/analysts. This section considers only the far-Right as the Right, which is confusing and erroneous; and it's a tact to hide the fundamental question—exploitative relations dominating the life of the masses, the reality that creates the rationale for radical change in the relationships between human and human, human and life and nature, an essential for a humane, dignified, peaceful, prosperous society, as the exploitative relation destroys everything that's humane.

Notes

1. *Encyclopaedia Britannica, Encyclopedia of Democratic Thought*, Routledge, 2001, *English Oxford Dictionaries, The Concise Oxford Dictionary of Politics*, 2009, *Encyclopedia of Politics: The Left and the Right*, SAGE, 2005, T Ball and R Bellamy (eds.), *The Cambridge History of Twentieth-Century Political Thought, Populism: a Very Short Introduction*, OUP, 2017, Paul Johnson, *A Politics Glossary*, Auburn University website, Ian Adams, *Political Ideology Today*, Manchester University Press, 2001, Hans-Georg Betz, *Radical Right-Wing Populism in Western Europe*, Palgrave Macmillan, 1994.
2. Literature on the mass upsurge of 1969 that includes works by Badruddin Umar, Haider Akbar Khan Rono, Lenin Azad, Mohammad Farhad, Tariq Ali; press reports that include reports by leading Baanglaa and English dailies from Dhaka, and reports by *Ganashakti* [*People Power*], legal weekly of the pro-Mao East Pakistan Communist Party (Marxist-Leninist) [EPCP (M-L)]; *11-point Program* of the students' alliance.
3. *ibid.*
4. Feroz Ahmed, "The struggle in Bangladesh", *Bulletin of Concerned Asian Scholars*, 4:1, 1972, https://doi.org/10.1080/14672715.1972.1040627 1, Published online: July 5, 2019.
5. *ibid.*
6. Works on the War for Liberation by A K Khandakar, Badruddin Umar, Kader Siddique and many commanders/persons at leading position of the armed struggle and by Freedom Fighters; reports on the war, many of which are available in Government of Bangladesh (GOB), *Bangladesher Shaadheenataa Joodha Dalilpatra* [*Documents of the Bangladesh War for Independence*], vols. IX, X and XI, Dhaka, Bangladesh, 1982; press reports; works on the war by Farooque Chowdhury.
7. Haider Akbar Khan Rono (ed.), *Mookteejooddhe Baampantheeraa* [*The Lefts in the War for Liberation*], Tarafdar Prokashoni, Dhaka, December 2018; works on the war by Haider Akbar Khan Rono, Noor Mohammad, Ranajit Chakrabarty and Farooque Chowdhury; reports on the war, conducted by the EPCP (M-L), by Gani, Indra and Raghu in *Janajooddha* [*People's War*], the underground monthly of the EPCP (M-L); and report by Shamsur Rahman Kebal, in *Bichitra*, now-defunct, Baanglaa weekly from Dhaka, Bangladesh.

8. *Far Eastern Economic Review*, April 4, 1971, and *Economist*, July 10, 1971, cited in Feroz Ahmed, *op. cit.*
9. GOB, *Bangladesher Shaadheenataa Joodha Dalilpatra*, vols. III and IV.
10. GOB, National Budget and Five-Year Plan documents.
11. Sources of this section of the chapter, and its later parts, until other sources are mentioned, include the following: GOB, *Constitution of the People's Republic of Bangladesh*; works on Bangladesh politics by Abul Fazl Huq, Ahmed Shafiqul Huque, A F Huq, A M A Muhith, B K Jahangir, Craig Baxter, Franda Marcus, Golam Hossain, G W Choudhury, Habib Zafarullah, Hamza Alavi, Lawrence Lifschultz, Lawrence Ziring, Moudud Ahmed, M. Moniruzzaman, M Rafiqul Islam, M Rasheduzzaman, M A Halim, Md. Abdul Wadud Bhuiyan, Md. Imdadul Haque, Md. Nurul Amin, Meghna Guhathakurta, Mohammad Eisa Ruhullah, Mohammad Mozahidul Islam, Muhammad A. Hakim, M Y Akhter Nizam Ahmed, Peter J. Bertocci, Rafiuddin Ahmed, Rehman Sobhan, Ridwanul Hoque, Rounaq Jahan, S Aminul Islam, S I Khan, S S Islam, Stanley A. Kochanek, Syed Serajul Islam, Talukder Maniruzzaman, Tareq Shamsur Rehman, Titin Purwaningsih, Willem van Schendel, Zillur Rahman Khan; autobiographies/biographies/memoirs by a number of former high-ranking civil and military officers.
12. GOB, *Bangladesh District Gazetteers* of different districts of Bangladesh, Bangladesh Government Press, Dhaka (at that time Dacca), Bangladesh, 1975, 1977, 1979, etc.
13. M Jafar Ullah Talukder and M Jashim Ali Chowdhury, "Determining the Province of Judicial Review: A Re-evaluation of 'Basic Structure' of the Constitution of Bangladesh", *Metropolitan University Journal* 2 (2), 2008; M H Rahman, "Our Experience with Constitutionalism", *Bangladesh Journal of Law* 2, 1998; Ridwanul Hoque, *Judicial Activism in Bangladesh: A Golden Mean Approach.*, Newcastle-upon-Tyne, Cambridge Scholars Publishing, 2011, "Taking Justice Seriously: Judicial Public Interest and Constitutional Activism in Bangladesh", *Contemporary South Asia*, 15, 2006, "The Recent Emergency and the Politics of the Judiciary in Bangladesh." *National University of Juridical Science Law Review*, 2(2), 2009, "Constitutionalism and the Judiciary in Bangladesh", in Sunil Khilnani, Vikram Raghavan and Arun K Thiruvengadam (eds.), *Comparative Constitutionalism in South Asia*, New Delhi: Oxford University Press, 2013; M A Halim, *Constitutional Law and Politics: Bangladesh Perspective*, Rico printers, 1998; Nizam Ahmed, *The Parliament of Bangladesh*, 2002; M Y Akhter, *Electoral Corruption in Bangladesh*, 2001; The Constitution of the country, Bangladesh Code, and laws related to property, capital, company, commodity, contract, tax, labor, union.

14. Cited in Roger Cotterrell, *The Sociology of Law: An Introduction*, Oxford University Press, New Delhi, India, 2007.
15. *ibid.*
16. Note no. 11.
17. Personal observation for years using a number of indicators that include [1] information and entertainment and its media, [2] formal and informal education, [3] propaganda, [4] political literature, etc.
18. Scanning of media, advertisement of a number of commodities, marketing strategies/tactics/market war of/by a number of multinational and national companies, entertainment, political incidents and events, mainstream discussions and debates, mainstream research.
19. Literature/reports on microcredit that include data from and reports by Credit Development Forum (CDF) and major microcreditors in Bangladesh, the World Bank, Aminur Rahman, Atiur Rahman, Farooque Chowdhury, Lamia Karim, Milford Batman.
20. Reports of major NGOs, organizations/structures that identify those as "civil society organizations", press reports, and Sarah C. White, "NGOs, Civil Society, and the State in Bangladesh: The Politics of Representing the Poor", December 16, 2002, IISS, The Hague, https://doi. org/10.1111/1467-7660.00119; Rehman Sobhan, "Identity and Inclusion in the Construction of a Democratic Society in Bangladesh", *Journal of the Asiatic Society of Bangladesh* (Humanities), vol. 51, no. 2, December 2006, and "Civil society, policy dialogue and democratic change in Bangladesh", in G S Cheema & V Popovski (eds.) *Engaging civil society: Emerging trends in democratic governance*, UN University Press, Tokyo, 2009; Harry Blair, "Civil society and pro-poor initiatives in rural Bangladesh: finding a workable strategy", *World Development*, https:// doi.org/10.1016/j.worlddev.2004.09.011, 33, 6, 2005; M Rezaul Islam, "Non-governmental organizations and community development in Bangladesh, International Social Work", https://doi.org/10.1177/00208 72815574133, 60, 2, 2016; Fahim Quadir, *Civil Society in Asia: In Search of Democracy and Development in Bangladesh*, 2015; David Lewis, "Organising and Representing the Poor in a Clientelistic Democracy: the Decline of Radical NGOs in Bangladesh", *The Journal of Development Studies*, https://doi.org/10.1080/00220388.2017.1279732, 53, 10, 2017; David Lewis, "On the difficulty of studying 'civil society': Reflections on NGOs, state and democracy in Bangladesh", contributions to *Indian Sociology*, https://doi.org/10.1177/006996670403800301, 38, 3, 2016, Sujay Ghosh, "NGOs as Political Institutions", *Journal of Asian and African Studies*, https://doi.org/10.1177/0021909609340063, 44, 5, 2009; Farhat Tasnim, "Civil Society and Political Structures in Bangladesh, Civil Society in Bangladesh", https://doi.org/10.1007/978-981-33-

4404-4_4, 2021; Farhat Tasnim, "Politicized Civil Society, Civil Society in Bangladesh", https://doi.org/10.1007/978-981-33-4404-4_6, 2021; Jasmin Lorch, "State Weakness and Civil Society in Bangladesh, Civil Society and Mirror Images of Weak States", https://doi.org/10.1057/978-1-137-55462-8, 2017; Palash Kamruzzaman, "Civil society or 'comprador class', participation or parroting?", *Progress in Development Studies*, https://doi.org/10.1177/146499341201300103, 13, 1, 2012; Abu Elias Sarker, Mohammad Habibur Rahman, "The Role of Social Accountability in Poverty Alleviation Programs in Developing Countries: An Analysis with Reference to Bangladesh", *Public Organization Review*, https://doi.org/10.1007/s11115-014-0275-x, 15, 2, 2014; Kasia Paprocki, "'Selling Our Own Skin:' Social dispossession through microcredit in rural Bangladesh", *Geoforum*, https://doi.org/10.1016/j.geoforum.2016.05.008, 74, 2016; and Abu Ahasan, Katy Gardner," Dispossession by 'Development': Corporations, Elites and NGOs in Bangladesh", *South Asia Multidisciplinary Academic Journal*, https://doi.org/10.4000/samaj.4136, 13, 2016.

21. Works on imperialism by Harry Magdoff, John Smith, Lenin, Paul M Sweezy.

22. Works/reports on "assistance for democracy" by the US; works by Badruddin Umar, Farooque Chowdhury.

23. Lenin, "A great beginning", *Collected Works*, vol. XXIX, Progress Publishers, Moscow, erstwhile USSR, 1977.

24. *Communist Manifesto, Collected Works*, vol. VI, Progress Publishers, Moscow, erstwhile USSR, 1976; GOB, census/survey documents on population, labor force, manufacturing/industrial units/enterprises; reports by Bangladesh Bank, and by other banks/financial organization; reports on branches of the economy; reports of/on major companies, markets of different/major commodities; literature/reports of/by associations of industrialists and traders; press reports on loan default, forgery, money laundering; *Panama Papers*; reports/literature on/of unions/labor; works of union activists/leaders; works by Abul Barkat, B K Jahangir, Habibul Haque Khondker, Hamza Alavi, Kamal Siddiqui *et al.*, Lipon Kumar Mondal, M Husain, Peter J Bertocci, Stanley A Kochanek.

CHAPTER 10

Biopolitics, Nostalgia and the Making of Nations: Exploring the Nexus Between Race, Citizenship and Gender in India Following Covid-19

Debadrita Chakraborty

INTRODUCTION

Writing about the structural and political state of affairs in India post the lockdown that was replete with chaos, injustices and inequalities, author Arundhati Roy concluded her article in the *Financial Times* with the hope that like previous pandemics, covid-19 too will "force humans to break with the past and imagine their world anew" (2020). Like the rest of the world, India too awaited for its transition into a new order—its population having retreated from mobile realities into small pockets of isolation limited to "immediate family" units and individual dwelling spaces. However, what gripped India during this waiting period were socio-political and

D. Chakraborty (✉)
University of Petroleum and Energy Studies, Dehradun, India

© The Author(s), under exclusive license to Springer Nature
Switzerland AG 2023
B. S. Nayak, D. Chakraborty (eds.), *Interdisciplinary Reflections on South Asian Transitions*,
https://doi.org/10.1007/978-3-031-36686-4_10

economic uncertainties as opposed to the onset of new possibilities in a post-pandemic order (Chakraborty 2020).

With centuries of patriarchy, hierarchy and prejudices embedded within India's psyche that constantly overpowered and invisibilised subalterns, the liminal stage (that in-between phase of "what was" and "what will be"—that which transforms and readies you for a new experience) was ineffective for India's marginalised, and a privilege and an escape point for urban India's upper and middle caste-classes (Chakraborty 2020). Despite thinkers like Jean-Luc Nancy labelling the pandemic as a universal equaliser due to its global effect—a "communovirus" that "brought [the world] together in the need to make a common stand"—the reality was far from Nancy's imagination and Roy's utopia of a world free from the "carcasses of prejudice and hatred" (Nancy 2020; Roy 2020).

In India the worst affected by the pandemic were those doubly and triply marginalised by caste, class and religious oppressions further widening socio-cultural, economic and political inequalities. To this divisive politics should be added the gender gap that became ever-widening with daily reports of domestic violence and abuse of women irrespective of caste, class, ethnicity and religion. Incidents of everyday forms of injustices, violence, discriminations and disparities during the covid-19 pandemic led to dramatic reconsiderations of relationships among citizens and between them and the state (Maduro and Kahn 2020). Acts of national re-imagination by citizens and the state were also circumscribed by the quarantine that forged new forms of isolation and social segregation. Further, the continuous spread of the contagion in different parts of the country also marked a resurrection of the nation state as the dominant actor in an age of fear and lockdowns as it terminated economic activity, endorsed state racism and employed necropolitical mechanisms to "let live" those who followed state instructions of social distancing and hygiene whilst eliminating the lower castes-classes (marginalised section of the population) made redundant due to the economic lockdown.

Against the closure of the borders, the rise of state power through constant surveillance of its citizens, socio-economic dysfunction and precarity engendered by one of twenty-first-century's deadliest planetary catastrophe, this chapter proposes a "decolonial cosmopolitan turn" that India's political and cultural counter-resistance movement could progress towards, in a post-covid-19 era as an opposition to majoritarianism. The chapter is divided into three sections, with the first section briefly examining India's "unequal" transition to the post-covid-19 world order by addressing the surge of class-, caste-, religion- and gender-based inequalities, violence and injustices from a biopolitical-necropolitical lens. In particular, the chapter will address the triple contagions of gender violence, class/caste-based stigmatisation and Islamophobia that adversely affected/subalternised women, lower classes and castes and Muslim minorities in India. I aim to portray these contagions as biopolitical/necropolitical strategies used by the nation state to repress the liable category of the population—those who no longer remain "instruments of labour" for the capitalist state. The second section will discuss the post-lockdown situation in India that witnessed the Hindu nation state at large and the Modi administration in particular who, having segregated the population using the dual technologies of biopolitics and necropolitics, heralds a new Hindutva world order by laying foundation to the Ram Mandir (temple) on a site which was home to a 450-year-old mosque until its demolition in 1992. I will also discuss the controversial Modal Farming Acts effected in September 2020, which I will argue is the state's biopolitical mechanism of controlling agricultural economy and is akin to the Citizenship (Amendment) Act of 2019 that aimed to biopolitically control citizenship entitlements of India's largest minority population. In this section, using the concept of "restorative nostalgia" I will discuss how the Hindutva think tank and its political leaders view this new order as an alternative to western modernity, addressing this nostalgic rooting/routing for/towards the past as India's "decolonial turn". In the final section, I will discuss the theoretical framework of decoloniality, comparing it with the Hindu state's formulation of the decolonial concept. Finally, I will conclude the chapter by deliberating on the concept of cosmopolitics, particularly the notions of cosmopolitan empathy and cultural ambidexterity as a decolonial method against brahmanical hegemony and its construction of systematic and systemic caste, class, ethnic hierarchies and homogeneity through my study of cultural counter-resistance movements both during and post-covid-19 lockdown. The rationale behind the chapter is to respond to the questions: Are there possibilities of a decolonial future? Will a new future dehierarchise and decolonise brahmanical power systems in India?

THE COVID-19 CONTAGION VERSUS INDIA'S TRIPLE CONTAGION: SOCIO-ECONOMIC AND POLITICAL OPPRESSION DURING THE LOCKDOWN

The first case of covid-19 in India was identified on 30th January 2020, the very day when the World Health Organization (WHO) declared the contagion a global public health emergency. However, in March 2020, India reported not only its first covid-19-related death but also an increase in the number of coronavirus cases which stood at 1000 by 29th March and spiked to 247,195 by early June (Worldometer 2020). To contain the spread of the virus, India implemented surveillance in mid-January, followed by a series of travel advisories and restrictions, and efforts to repatriate and quarantine Indian nationals arriving from abroad (Bharali et al. 2020). In order to respond to the public health emergency presented by the covid-19 pandemic, the government further invoked the Epidemic Diseases Act. However, the Act which was enforced through an ordinance in April is in reality a century old and was established in India during colonial rule at the time of the bubonic plague outbreak in 1896. As Banerjee points out,

"The Act was an emergency measure that further extended its already authoritarian power in the colony. Cities were put under martial rule and military patrols conducted house searches, forcibly evacuating the infected to quarantined hospitals. Driven by public-health beliefs that the disease was a product of native "filth" and "darkness"—rather than zoonotic bacterial origin—they hosed down neighbourhoods with disinfectants, confiscated possessions, and tore apart walls and roofs to literally bring light into the huts of the diseased poor. Sometimes, they razed entire huts to the ground" (2020).

The invocation of this Act following the Janata Curfew and a hasty 21 days lockdown from 25th March 2020 is a reminder of how coloniality's civilising mission to generate a homogeneous, hierarchical, capitalist, socio-cultural and political system in India was replicated and extended in post-independent modern India through the sustenance of British colonialism's biopolitical form of governance in order to "control", "classify" and "oppose" social, cultural and political lives of sections of India's population. The act which emphasised the power of the state and central government in implementing measures to contain the spread of the disease, penalties for violation of the measures and legal protection to the implementing officers without taking into consideration citizen's rights, increased urbanisation, labour migration, globalisation and most importantly human rights (Arunachalam and Halwai 2020: 484) was nothing short of a biopolitical strategy where the "biological" is captured by the "political" that renders certain lives more disposable and expendable than others by virtue of "laws, policies, sets of rules, techniques and procedures, public-health mechanisms, technologies, and bureaucracies" (Taşkale and Banalopoulou 2020: 146). Thus, what the pandemic exacerbated was India's democratic leadership which was already under the scanner (prior to the pandemic) due to state racism that consisted of systematically differentiating and discriminating ethnic, religious, class, caste and gender minorities to the point of their elimination (necropolitics).

The public sphere under the Hindutva government posited a repressive, high-caste, chauvinist version of Hinduism and endorsed a bigoted and divisive narrative of good citizen/bad citizen[1] that recognised the interests of the educated upper castes whilst ostracising Adivasis, Muslims, Christians and atheists who are seen as outsiders and a threat to the nation and citizens only in a "minority" sense (Banaji 2018: 344). Such a narrative (before the pandemic) was responsible for incidents of everyday violence undertaken by upper-caste Hindu vigilante groups against lower-caste and religious minorities in India, including lynching, extra-judicial killings, molestation, rape and pogroms built upon caste and communal prejudices (Mander 2015). The dominant Hindu nationalist ideology's anti-secularism principles, endorsement of upper-caste supremacy, and opposition of pluralism, diversity and socio-economic equality resulted in a situation during the pandemic where the governing capacity of the nation state became unresponsive to the aspirations of the well-being of the citizenry, "rejecting an inclusive and ecumenical conception of the common good" (Walker 2020: 24).

Fearing exposure of their limited capacity to address the pandemic in terms of advocating social policy and public health measures, governments both democratic and authoritarian across the globe introduced a quasi-curfew, a lockdown of movements and activities. Following a Janata Curfew (public curfew) announced on 22nd March 2020, India entered a 21-day national lockdown from 24th March until 14th April 2020, which was further extended until the end of May 2020, introducing a set of social disciplines. Some of the measures included stay-at-home policy except for essential journeys, obligatory observation of social distancing in public and prohibition of non-home-based work or public gathering for the purposes of shopping and leisure and isolation and quarantining for those infected. Whilst critics and thinkers have read citizen participation in these measures as a collective action of the ruler (government) and the ruled (citizen) against the pandemic, an opportunity to mobilise a national effort that is broadly inclusive and egalitarian since the measures adopted by the democratic authority were for the collective good, the Indian government's efforts to contain the virus and ensure public health safety measures were far from effective. Elected on a populist mandate, the government's biopolitical governance that segregated the population on account of "who gets to live" and "who must die" (Foucault 2008) was hardly able to sustain the required level of social discipline and retain trust in its socio-political and economic competence. Following the lockdown and declaration of the pandemic containment measures, India witnessed instances wherein populations were hierarchised, differentiated and marginalised on the race, class and sometimes citizenship status and also by access to healthcare services (Taşkale and Banalopoulou 2020: 146) whilst the upper and middle caste-classes continued to receive privileged treatment and to free ride on the contribution of the labour caste-classes who were rendered permanently disposable.

Although the Indian government continued to reassure the public creating the perception of infection risk minimisation through the imposition of restriction on modes and places of transmission such as domestic and international travel and public gatherings, a glaring blind spot existed amidst these measures in the form of socio-economic equities. According to Bhalotia et al., "covid-19 exacerbated pre-existing inequities in urban India and those at the lower end of incomes suffered the most" (2020: 3). Unlike Europe which had an economic buffer capacity and finances available to mitigate the worst impacts of the pandemic, in Africa and Asia, about half a billion of the population were pushed to poverty with decrease in income by 20 per cent that severely affected lower castes and classes.

Within days of announcing a nationwide lockdown as a way of containing covid-19 infection, the state's repressive and inefficient response to the crisis was revealed in its management of India's working classes, especially the urban migrant poor, causing economists to define the state's assault on the poor as a humanitarian crisis parallel to the pandemic situation. One of the ways in which the state regulates life biopolitically is through "political-economic considerations, where the power of capitalism and capital-labour relations intervenes directly to regulate life itself." This means that while the biopolitical function of the state is directed towards optimising the life of the population through economic activity including circulation of goods, capital and building urban infrastructures, it also aims to prioritise profit over people exploiting human capital for financial accumulation (bio-necropower of capital). With the economy having come to a grinding halt with the lockdown, the government did not have the opportunity to elect capital over population. In such a situation, the state which already had been following a racialised biopolitical discourse hierarchising population, marking certain lives inferior and some superior, undertook a politics of life that ultimately generated massive death (both metaphorical and literal). According to the likes of Timothy Campbell, under a neoliberal governmentality there is little distinction between necropolitical "letting die" of liberal biopolitics and the "making die" of a totalitarian rule (2006). For Achille Mbembe contemporary biopolitics that endorses capital as a prerequisite for human life is concerned with "the subjugation of life to the power of death" (2003: 39). This differential vulnerability was tragically illustrated by the trajectory of the urban labour classes—one of the invisible victims of the socio, political, economic and pathological implications of the coronavirus.

The national lockdown and the subsequent economic standstill revealed that the city would only be hospitable to the working classes (the underbelly of India's development model, those that drive India's capitalist development) as long as they were "a living machine of variable capital supplementing the dead machine of constant capital" (Chakrabarti and Dhar 2020: 105). Millions of migrant labourers who lured by income/employment and the glitter of a "free life" in the cities working in manufacturing and construction sectors were left stranded on the city streets post the lockdown without jobs, homes and lack of transports that would have helped them travel back to their rural homes. Majority of workers in these sectors are often temporary, with employers bearing minimum liability towards their welfare or social security. A report by the Stranded Workers Action Network (Swan) stated that 89 per cent of the daily wage and casual workers had not been paid wages that pushed them to the brink of starvation, rendered them homeless and vulnerable to the contagion. Further, sociologists have affirmed that 38.4 per cent among these urban labourers belong to the Dalit, indigenous community or are members of Other Backward classes (OBCs), thereby manifesting how the condition of the working class in India is thus tied in a mutually constitutive relation with the condition of the working castes.

Although India's caste or varna system, a four-fold categorical hierarchy of the Hindu religion known to govern every realm of Indian life including economic, legal, social, religious and cultural, was theoretical that existed in Hindu texts in the pre-colonial era, the system was reinforced in the British era. In their attempt to homogenise and simplify the hierarchies of the caste system, the colonisers translated and sealed diverse myths, beliefs, polytheistic religious practices and laws into systematic caste hierarchies suppressing Hinduism's divergent syncretic oral and performative traditions and polytheistic worshipping practices. Elevating selected and convenient Brahman-Sanskrit texts like the Manusmriti to canonical status, the British institutionalised the four-fold caste system so that the native's social identity no longer remained malleable as in the pre-colonial times. It is this Oriental notion of Hinduism that has been taken up strategically by members of the Indian upper caste and disseminated as if "uncontested and arising from a primordial past" (Banaji 2018: 344).

The Orientalist desire to establish a single high-caste version of Hinduism also known as brahmanical Hinduism began to be realised by high-caste Hindu vigilantes as they ostracised tribals, lower-caste Hindus, Muslims and atheists from the public sphere, labelling them as threat to the nation and the state. Even as the new constitution banned the practice of ostracisation and untouchability of the lower castes in post-independent India, the tenacity and pervasiveness of caste-based atrocities continue to permeate everyday life. The Dalits became the worst sufferers of this arrangement. Known to exist outside the Hindu caste hierarchy and traditionally regarded as untouchables, the Dalits, who officially in India are known as Scheduled Caste communities, continue to suffer at the hands of the upper castes who, in their bid to sustain their privileges, threaten and force members of this marginalised group to performing tasks that are deemed ritually polluting which include leatherwork, disposing dead animals and manual scavenging. Members of the lower castes not only suffer economic and social subjugation but also are bodily marginalised and stigmatised—their bodies considered to be polluted (given their menial occupation) whilst those higher up in the caste-based hierarchy are regarded as pure. During the pandemic such atrocities became several-fold as the state's brahmanical necropolitical forces violated the lower castes to the point of their elimination (death).

The inherited legacies of the colonial encounter that have shaped the socio-political fabric of the nation and institutional and cultural hierarchies were further deepened during the pandemic crises by governmentality that combined biopolitical and necropolitical logics to establish social, political and physical borders that classify and stratify populations using symbolic and material markers of caste and class. State institutions that are designed to provide a modicum of protection for workers, the poor and the vulnerable section of the population, isolated them into "camps" akin to the concentration camp system of the totalitarian state. According to Agamben, the "camp" is put to function when the state of exception becomes the rule. Agamben defines the "state of exception" as a condition wherein governments have the right to legally justify limits on personal and constitutional freedoms. Within a "state of exception" juridical law is suspended due to an emergency or a serious crisis threatening the state. However, within modern liberal democracy, the state of exception, once a temporary suspension of law, became a stable, generalised condition: "the declaration of the state of exception has gradually been replaced by an unprecedented generalization of the paradigm of security as the normal technique of government" (2005: 14). This tendency provided the totalitarian states which emerged in the twentieth century with the framework by which rule by a permanent state of emergency was possible (*ibid.*: 2).

Following neoliberalism's draconian policies that aim to keep alive those within the circuits of the global capital (i.e. the upper and middle classes) and let go off those sections who have been made redundant from these circuits (i.e. the working/labour classes), the state during the lockdown established a "state of exception" to eliminate the poorer section of the population who became a burden due to their poverty and susceptibility to the contagion. Thus, even though the escalation and risk of the contagion emerged from the upper caste-classes of India, including the privileged cosmocrats and foreign nationals who have access to multiple continents and time-zones, it was the lower caste-classes comprising daily wage labourers who were forced to live in make-shift camps in city sidewalks during the lockdown without provision for basic amenities like sanitation, ration and adequate space for social distancing. Such repressive necropolitical technologies manifested by the state in its attempt to eliminate the poorer section of the population breached the right to equality under Article 14 of the Indian Constitution. The state's repressive apparatus that functions on violence and anomie further stripped this section of the population of political and legal attributes, culminating in what Agamben calls a "bare life"—"a legally unnamable and unclassifiable being" (Agamben 2013: 134)—when state authorities subjected them to extreme humiliation by treating their bodies with disinfectants upon their return to their home states. The states and the central government on their part did little to arrange transportation for the migrant labourers to help them reach their homes in rural India. Such forms of state violence that include experiences of oppression, indignity and exclusion were not practised in airports when the government brought back thousands of stranded Indians from different parts of the world, which speaks volume about cultural hierarchisation and neoliberal segregationism in India (Chakraborty 2020).

Further, the media captured how state forces perpetrated everyday forms of humiliation on the working classes with police officers wielding their batons on migrant labourers for travelling back to their rural homes during the lockdown and reportedly overturning fruits and vegetable vendor's carts who already were suffering from economic loss due to the lockdown. The necropolitical praxis of the state forces were further evident when the prime minister addressed the quarantined upper and middle classes restricted to their private spaces in his speeches, boosting their morale with campaigns like "taali-thali" (clapping for health workers) and lighting diyas (to preserve hope and optimism against death and disease), whilst ignoring the plights and predicament of the home-bound migrant labourers and failing to provide them with relief packages, thus leaving the labourers and their family famished, vulnerable to the contagion and on the edge of death.

The biopolitical/necropolitical state mechanism of "who may live and who must die" does not rest on the sovereign state solely and is expanded through a variety of social actors (especially those sections of the population favoured by the state) who are given a free reign to control, confine and potentially exterminate the "liable"/weaker section of the population (Chakraborty 2020: 4). The biopolitical state's incarceration, infantilisation and demonisation of the migrant labourer as "bad citizens" who are "dangerous" and potential "virus spreaders" because they are "unhygienic" and "illiterate" (Jain 2020), were practised at the societal level especially by urban upper caste-classes. Having been assured financial security, thanks to work from home opportunities and physical protection within the confines of their homes, the casteist upper classes of the metropolises reproached lower caste, especially Dalit, labourers for breaking lockdown rules and vilifying their bodies which for centuries have been perceived as pollutants for the upper castes, as fraught with disease and carrier of the coronavirus.

Although the return of the urban working caste-classes to their rural homeland was welcomed by Marxists sociologists and economics who predicted a rural reconstruction of sorts where Dalits and the tribals would be in control of the farming process in areas where they own lands as opposed to their exploitation in the metropolises, the reality was far from such utopia. Prioritising profit over people, the state lifted the lockdown on 31st May 2020 just two months post its announcement in late March 2020. The rationale was to acquire herd immunity—a long-term strategy to deal with the contagion that involves the population being infected with the virus until they acquired collective immunity against it. The reason behind such a risky approach as most political theorists have noted is thanatopolitics, that is the politics of death, "the resistant and rhetorical counterpart to the dialectics and reductive ontologies of biopolitical life" (Murray 2018: 718). Since the utter and abject disposability of human life is the enduringly manifest result of capital accumulation, herd immunity exemplifies a thanatopolitical economy that consumes the future in the present. That is, a thanatopolitical economy needs endless reproduction and circulation to remain "healthy". As a consequence, life is rendered disposable, expendable and sacrificial to the neoliberal capital. The Indian government, after two months of lockdown, decided to put in place a corona stimulus package, perhaps to mitigate the rising anger of the migrants, of additional Rs. 40,000 crore ($3.08 billion) for the Mahatma Gandhi National Rural Employment Guarantee Act (MGNREGA). To what extent this rescue package was able to mitigate the vast income and employment problem remains unclear.

While the working-class population were stripped of their legal status, transformed into a bare life without rights in the public sphere, the lockdown policies negatively affected women irrespective of class and caste, locked within the private sphere of their homes. Despite escaping the casteist and classist discrimination inflicted on their lower caste-class counterparts, urban women had to bear the burden of unpaid work, grappling with their new-born identity as full-time care-givers, cooks, house-helps, cleaners, teachers and work-at-home professionals during the lockdown. Owing to the sexual division of labour, and gendered roles and social norms of performing domestic and care work in a household, the burden of unpaid work fell disproportionately on women during the lockdown, leaving little or no time for them to undertake productive activities like education or employment, or leisure (Chauhan 2021: 2). Despite their participation in the public sphere as wage earners, women have time and again been forced to undertake their primary responsibility as homemakers with little help from their male partners and husbands—a norm enforced by the Indian patriarchal ethos. Largely undervalued and subjugated within the domestic spaces, urban women as per the National Commission of Women suffered physical, emotional and psychological abuse at the hands of their male partners who themselves emasculated by the uncertainties post the lockdown, lack of social life, physical and social restrictions, and rising stress due to the impending economic crisis (Chakraborty 2020: 4).

Despite having claimed their emancipation, autonomy and agency within the public sphere, urban women received little support from the state that overlooked their trauma by not prioritising intimate partner violence in their public policy responses to the Covid-19 pandemic, thereby driving a huge section of the urban female population at the "edge of life" and metaphorical death. Thus, the private sphere during the lockdown proved itself far from a dwelling place, conveying "simple pleasures, familial togetherness, privacy and freedom, a sense of belonging, of security, a place to escape from but also to return to, a secure memory, an ideal" (Dixit and Chavan 2020: 13). On its part, the state as a sovereign power did little to ameliorate urban women's predicament by introducing humanitarian measures and schemes that takes into account women's physical, mental and financial security, healthcare and nutrition during the lockdown. While the state power disregarded urban women's co-existence with everyday forms of violence within the private sphere of their homes, the corporate sector in order to derive maximum profit employed a necrocapitalist[2] (capitalism's structural violence in society) [Banerjee 2008] mechanism exposing urban women employees to irregular work schedules and increasing workload along with threats of redundancy (metaphorical death) of those considered disposable by the authorities in favour of productive functioning of the industry.

Despite being disregarded by the state and exploited by necrocapitalist market forces, urban women from upper- and middle-class households were not bound by caste, class, cultural and religious oppressions unlike women of lower castes, classes, and religious and ethnic minorities. As noted earlier, the market forces in collusion with the government that forced working classes out of labour, having exploited them with low wages and precarious, unhygienic living conditions, equally impacted female factory labourers and construction site workers. Further, reliance on single income where the male member is the only earning member of the working-class family also drove women and their children at the "edge of life" with some of them having lost their husbands to the covid-19 infection. Moreover, women's health and nutrition schemes were suspended during the lockdown period. Under the Integrated Child Development Scheme (ICDS), the country's 1.3 million Anganwadi centres that provide critical nutrition counselling and supplementary food to pregnant and lactating mothers were closed due to the lockdown (Asadullah and Raghunathan 2020).

Asadullah et al. further noted how the return of the urban labour classes to their rural hometowns resulted in reduction in economic opportunities for rural women including both private agricultural jobs and social protection schemes such as the Mahatma Gandhi National Rural Employment Guarantee Act (MGNREGA). The loss of economic and food security not only pushed them at the bottom-most position in the necropolitical hierarchy but also drove them to their metaphorical deaths as they confronted domestic violence and abuse at the hands of their migrant labourer husbands. According to Plummer (1984), for the working classes, the sense of masculinity is associated with hard labour along with distance from femininity. The loss of employment and confinement with their female counterpart during the lockdown initiated a crisis in the working-class men's masculine sense of self leading to violent oppression of women, placing them in constant risk of losing their lives as they become raw material for necropolitical production (Martínez-Guzmán 2019: 302). On the other hand, within the urban sector, the rhetoric of pandemic-driven ostracism disseminated by state discourses and by the upper caste-classes of the metropolises took an economic toll on female domestic workers in the cities who were laid off by their upper- and middle-class employers without pay or even a month's ration. Many of these women were either wives of migrant labourers or single parents who have had to manage to keep their children alive in times of shortage and the lockdown-induced destitution (Chakraborty 2020: 7). Besides their physical confinement within crammed spaces, lower-class and -caste women have been subject to invisible confinements/death worlds by the state, denying them basic hygiene products such as menstrual pads, especially in the rural areas, and contraceptives, leading to unwanted pregnancies and sexually transmitted diseases post the lockdown.

According to Butalia, "Reproductive and sexual health services did not come within the ambit of essential services, so women had no access to abortions (a right Indian women have had since 1971). Those ready to give birth often had to go from hospital to hospital seeking a bed and medical attention. SAMA, a Delhi-based women's organisation, was forced to file a petition in the courts demanding that pregnant women be given the right to have an ambulance carry them to the hospital" (2020). State, societal and masculine necropolitics have not only led women to lose control of their bodies but also of the younger generation of women the right to education, especially in poverty-stricken urban and rural areas where young girls, burdened by domesticity and lacking necessary electronics and digital tools for online education (in rural India only 14.9 per cent had access to the internet with males being the primary users), will have to favour home-making and child rearing, burying their dream of an upwardly mobile life. Moreover, as an oppressed gender living under the shadows of patriarchy, women in India, according to patriarchal cultural dictates, are made to consume nutrient-rich foods less frequently than men. Such traditions have worsened during the lockdown due to the economic crisis being faced by the working classes. Malnutrition borne of the current economic crisis could lead to permanent exclusion from the labour market and government workfare schemes, contributing to a new cycle of poverty among working-class women (Chakraborty 2020: 7).

The Rise of a New Order Post-pandemic: Hindutva and the Decolonial Turn

If history is any indication, pandemics in different eras have engendered deep-rooted socio-cultural prejudices globally. Be it the witch-hunt for the typhoid "super-spreader" Mary Mallon who was accused and vilified for carrying the bacterium causing typhoid and quarantined on an island for 26 years or the plague epidemic in Bombay in 1896 when the state acquired special legal and judicial powers to prevent the spread of epidemic which later became the model for subsequent governments to use disease or epidemics to justify authoritarian measures.[3] However, the post-lockdown scenario proved different for the nation state. On the one side, it was predicted that despite the ravages of the pandemic, India would accelerate the post-pandemic transition to more sustainable and resilient societies—to undertake short- and long-term measures to improve the long-term productivity and resilience in the region. On the other side, the state used both biopower and nostalgic memory to construct a Hindu nation state that entails its personal and collective sacrifice, traditional femininity and masculinity, orthodox religion as a basis for patriotism.

Taking cue from the lockdown when nostalgia was used as a political tool to divert populace from India's socio-political and economic crisis through nostalgic pop cultural events and uploading social media content of a romanticised past, the government too employs nostalgia narratives that look back and promise to rediscover "the good old days". Such nostalgic narratives revolved around the loss of tradition, a mythical integrity, an eviscerated global status and a romanticised past. To the public nostalgia or the longing for the past mattered especially post-lockdown as a result of the socio-economic crisis faced by the nation during the pandemic. As Flinders observes, "nostalgia provided a barrier or buffer against further change. It is not about going back but stopping a process of rapid socio-political change in which large sections of society really do feel left behind. Nostalgia provides a link to a 'deep story', to use Hochschild's term, which is in itself a powerful form of emotional anchorage" (2018).

In an effort to build a community founded on the desire for homogeneous, less diverse communities, the government tried to imagine a "Hindu Rashtra" (Hindu nation) through the liberation of Ram's birthplace. The campaign for a "bhavya" (grand) Ram temple in Ayodhya three decades ago (a populist platform that catapulted the right-wing party from two parliamentary seats in the 1980s to political dominance) witnessed foundation post the lockdown as the government used a silver brick to lay the foundation stone of the Ram Mandir on 5 August 2020. The Ram temple was to be built on a site which was home to a 450-year-old mosque until its demolition in 1992. The government not only resorted to an awareness campaign which ironically doubled up as a fundraising campaign in a midst of a crisis.

Almost immediately after the covid-19 lockdown was announced, Indian classic television shows like *Ramayan* and *Mahabharat,* that shaped the childhood of many desi millennials, made a comeback on Doordarshan. Unlike the internet, where the nostalgia-driven subculture seems to be an organic progression, here it was a conscious decision. By constructing what is known as "historical nostalgia" or a longing for the bygone days within the population, the state through broadcasting media regulates people's lives by producing narratives that translate into a discourse of patriotism and national prosperity—a powerful way to clock Hindutva hegemony and racialisation of the ethnic and religious minors in India. The Ayodhya dispute that was long used by the Hindu nationalist party to gain political power was employed once again, this time in the form of the foundation of the Ram Mandir, thus fulfilling the wishes of millions of

Hindus who had been waiting to commemorate the birthplace of Ram following the demolition of the Babri Masjid—a sixteenth-century Mughal-era mosque—in 1992. Awareness campaigns on the foundation of the Ram Mandir that doubled up as a fundraising campaign in a midst of the pandemic entrapped citizens in a false nostalgia of a mythic Vedic "golden age" that existed prior to the Mughal Empire and the British Raj, Hindutva attempts to write a historiographical account that contradicts the "shame" of foreign invasion. For populist governments across the world nostalgia has always been exploited as a way to refer to the glorious past of their countries that has been lost today. The pandemic that left many socio-economically aggrieved was a perfect opportunity to stir up among them a wish for the restoration of a Hindu Rashtra.[4]

According to Byom, restorative nostalgia has two core elements: the restoration of origins and the conspiracy theory about how home or values were lost (2002). Much of the rhetoric of populist parties conforms strongly to this restorative form, premised on an idealised memory of the "past" and/or of "home", and a conspiratorial narrative about the role of external forces in threatening this vision. Considering the receptiveness of citizens to such messages, there appears to be a particular affinity between those experiencing social pessimism and populism parties. Populists "provide a clear vision of how society should change, namely returning to how it used to be before the social changes that have occurred in recent decades" (2016). Taggart has written extensively about the role that the "heartland", a romanticised physical, emotional and temporal place, has played in the formation of populist narratives (2000). Inglehart and Norris emphasise that populism captures "a mythical golden past" for a time when society was less diverse, the nation wielded greater global influence and traditional gender roles offered natural status and agency (2016).

In fact, many of the slogans of the ruling party's campaigns emphasise, as Roy points out, a nostalgia desire for a mythic, national past—fantasising about a super pure, racial superman and the restoration of national vitality. Restorative nostalgia does not consistently conjure a historically accurate recollection of past events, is rather prone to inaccuracy and centres on emotion rather than the details of what happened. At a societal level, this means that nostalgic discourses have a strongly idealised and utopian streak, which eradicates the negatives of the historical past and develops a "longing for a home that no longer exists or has never existed" (Boym 2002).

Specifically, populists use nostalgia to create borders between the authentic us and the immoral them in order to generate an intergroup cleavage between the people and the elites. As Boym explains, when one nostalgises about "the way the country was", one may express conservative attitudes towards migrants or minorities; conversely, when one nostalgises about social protest, civil rights movements or tradition of tolerance, one may express more liberal attitudes towards immigrants or minorities (2002). This is a result of the conspiracy theories embedded in the concept of restorative nostalgia that describes how the past ("home") has found itself under siege or has been lost. This, according to Boym, is constructed through a narrative that is "based on a single trans-historical plot, a Manichean battle of good and evil, and the inevitable scapegoating of the mythical enemy" (2002).

In India the ethnic minorities have found themselves constructed as the principal obstacle or threat in such a conception along with other enemies during the pandemic. Thus, what started as the good citizen/bad citizen narrative (whereby those following covid rules were granted lives whilst the socio-economically downtrodden were thrown into [metaphoric] death camps) later translated into us/them narrative where the "them" are the religious and ethnic minorities of India.

Taking a Decolonial Turn with Cosmopolitan Memory

The populist campaign for a Hindu nation as an alternative to western modernity was able to influence many from the majority religion since individuals are clearly capable of construing memory in accordance with their own subjective beliefs and desires, choosing to ignore information that may contradict their previous views, and construing the memory vector solely through the prism of their own viewpoints and preconceived ideas. On the flip side, however, individual memory would also mean that it demonstrates the primordiality of the maintenance of an authentic memory to individual identity, for it is clear that even with the spectre of severe repression, the individual does not interiorise the dominant memory but instead formulates his or her own judgements on public memory discourse and even strives to express his or her repressed memory (Ryan 2014).

With citizens acting in accordance with their individual memories, national memory has morphed into an unstable, unpredictable site of dispute, acutely susceptible to subversion of the accepted version of events, a fact which leads to the continuing narrative reconfiguration of those same events. As an opposition to majoritarianism including the nation state's tactics of using biopolitics/necropolitics as a way of containing brahmanical homogeneous hierarchies, and promoting militant nationalism as a rhetoric of decolonisation, citizen (individual and collective memory) in India can take a "decolonial cosmopolitan turn". This would entail "learning from injustices suffered in the past in order to struggle against those committed in the present and separating oneself from the 'I' to move towards the other" (Todorov 1992).

Conclusion

Drawing on the logic of cosmopolitanism, people remember what happened to foreign others as members of humanity, but they also invite those others to contribute to shaping the content of collective memory. Cosmopolitanism thus allows people to extend identifications beyond national borders and engage in transformative dialogues with "ethnic" others, steering their collective autobiographies away from the logic of nationalism. Cosmopolitan memory thereby enriches rather than diminishes the national memory culture by causing it to incorporate a previously absent ethical dimension that supersedes corrosive national memory conflicts. It is the practice of cosmopolitan memory borne of the loss of lives and socio-economic freedom of most section of India's population alone that can bring about cultural and religious syncretism in a post-pandemic India.

Notes

1. Such a discourse bears strong semblance with the "good Muslim"/"bad Muslim" narrative initiated by western political discourses in the aftermath of 9/11. The purpose was to privilege those that bore their allegiance to western secularism and eliminate those that resisted the western world's vilification of Muslims as prone to affiliation with politicised and radicalised form of Islam.
2. A term coined by Subhabrata Bobby Banerjee, necrocapitalism is a form of capitalism where a country"s trade and industry are founded on, linked to

and dependent directly or indirectly on death and the profits accruing from it.

3. The Epidemic Diseases Act gave the colonial government the right to inspect and isolate anyone suspected of being infected with plague, in public places, trains, ships and inside their homes. It simultaneously protected the state or the government officials from any legal action while acting under the act. Colonial authorities [had] almost unrestricted power to restrict the movements of the poor, migrant workers and Muslim pilgrims. [Such measures] continued to be the mainstay of the colonial state"s anti-plague campaign well into the first part of the twentieth century.

4. Rashtra in Hindutva similarly connotes a sacred nation emerging from indigenous Hindu claims to a bounded geography.

REFERENCES

Agamben, G. 2005. *State of Exception*. Translated by Kevin Attell. Chicago: University of Chicago Press.

———. 2013. *The Highest Poverty: Monastic Rules and Form-of-Life*. Translated by Adam Kotsko. Stanford: Stanford University Press.

Arunachalam, M.A., and A. Halwai. 2020. An Analysis of the Ethics of Lockdown in India. *Asian Bioethics Review* 12: 481–489.

Asadullah, M.N., and K. Raghunathan. 2020. *Tackling India's Deepening Gender Inequality during COVID-19. South Asia @ LSE*. Blog Entry.

Banaji, S. 2018. Vigilante Publics: Orientalism, Modernity and Hindutva Fascism in India. *Javnost—The Public* 25 (4): 333–350.

Banerjee, S.B. 2008. Corporate Social Responsibility: The Good, the Bad and the Ugly. *Critical Sociology* 34 (1): 51–79.

Banerjee, D. 2020. *Fantasies of Control: The Colonial Character of the Modi Government's Actions during the Pandemic*. Accessed June 30, 2020. https://caravanmagazine.in/perspectives/colonial-character-of-the-modi-governments-actions-during-the-pandemic.

Bhalotia, S., S. Dhingra, and F. Kondirolli. 2020. City of Dreams No More: The Impact of Covid-19 on Urban Workers in India. *A CEP Covid-19 Analysis*. Accessed April 8, 2022. https://cep.lse.ac.uk/pubs/download/cepcovid-19-008.pdf.

Bharali, I., P. Kumar, and S. Selvaraj. 2020. *How Well Is India Responding to COVID-19?* Accessed August 4, 2022. https://centerforpolicyimpact.org/2020/07/28/how-well-is-india-responding-to-covid-19/.

Boym, S. 2002. *The Future of Nostalgia*. Basic Books.

Butalia, U. 2020. How Has the Pandemic Changed Work and Life for Women in Publishing (and for Feminist Publishers). Accessed July 12, 2022. https://scroll.in/article/967706/how-has-the-pandemic-changed-work-and-life-for-women-in-publishing-andfor-feminist-publishersUrvashi.

Campbell, T. 2006. Bíos, Immunity, Life: The Thought of Roberto Esposito. *Diacritics* 36 (2): 2–22.

Chakrabarti, A., and A. Dhar. 2020. Non-violent Socialism: Marx and Gandhi in Dialogue. In *'Capital' in the East: Reflections on Marx.* Singapore: Springer Nature.

Chakraborty, D. 2020. *India's Post-coronavirus Transition Won't Be Easy. Here's Why.* Accessed January 9, 2023. https://politicalquarterly.blog/2020/05/27/indias-post-coronavirus-transition-wont-be-easy-heres-why.

Chauhan, P. 2021. Gendering COVID-19: Impact of the Pandemic on Women's Burden of Unpaid Work in India. *Gender Issues* 38 (4): 395–419.

Dixit, M., and Chavan, D. 2020. Gendering the COVID-19 Pandemic: Women Locked and Down. *Economic and Political Weekly* 55: 17. Accessed April 14, 2022. https://www.epw.in/journal/2020/17/commentary/gendering-covid-19-pandemic.html.

Flinders, M. 2018. The Politics and Power of Nostalgia. In *Oxford University Press's Academic Insights for the Thinking World.* Blog Entry.

Foucault, M. 2008. *The Birth of Biopolitics. Lectures at the Collège de France, 1978–1979.* New York, NY: Picador.

Guzmán, A.M. 2019. Masculine Subjectivities and Necropolitics: Precarization and Violence at the Mexican Margins. *Subjectivity* 12: 288–308.

Inglehart, R., and Pippa Norris. 2016. Trump, Brexit, and the rise of Populism. Paper presented at 2016 meeting of the *American Political Science Association.*

Jain, T. 2020. *COVID-19, Necropolitics and The Migrant.* Accessed August 10, 2022. https://sabrangindia.in/article/covid-19-necropolitics-and-migrant.

Maduro, M.P., and P.W. Kahn. 2020. *Democracy in Times of Pandemic Different Futures Imagined.* Cambridge: Cambridge University Press.

Mander, H. 2015. *Looking Away: Inequality, Prejudice and Indifference.* New Delhi: Speaking Tiger.

Mbembe, A. 2003. Necropolitics. *Public Culture* 15 (1): 11–40.

Murray, S.J. 2018. Thanatopolitics. In *Bloomsbury Handbook to Literary and Cultural Theory,* ed. J.R. Di Leo. London: Bloomsbury.

Nancy, J.-L. 2020. *Communovirus.* Accessed November 24, 2022. https://www.versobooks.com/blogs/4626-communovirus.

Roy, A. 2020. Arundhati Roy: *The Pandemic Is a Portal.* Accessed December 8, 2022. https://www.ft.com/content/10d8f5e8-74eb-11ea-95fe-fcd274e920ca.

Ryan, L. 2014. Cosmopolitan Memory and National Memory Conflicts: On the Dynamics of Their Interaction. *Journal of Sociology* 50 (4): 501–514. https://doi.org/10.1177/1440783312467097.

Taggart, P. 2000. *Populism.* Philadelphia: Open University Press.

Taşkale, A.R., and C. Banalopoulou. 2020. The Biopolitics of the Coronavirus Pandemic: Herd Immunity, Thanatopolitics, Acts of Heroism. In *A Rethinking Marxism Dossier: Pandemic and the Crisis of Capitalism*. Brighton: ReMarx Books.

Todorov, T. 1992. *The Conquest of America: The Question of the Other*. Perennial.

Walker, N. 2020. The Crisis of Democracy in a Time of Crisis. University of Edinburgh School of Law Research Paper Series. Accessed February 7, 2022. https://papers.ssrn.com/sol3/papers.cfm?abstract_id=3642537.

Worldometer. 2020. Accessed November 24, 2022. https://www.worldometers.info/coronavirus/.

CHAPTER 11

The Hajj in Communist Eyes: Abdullah Malik's Hajj as an Islamic Dystopia

Raza Naeem

INTRODUCTION

On the morning of 27 December 1972, leading Pakistani communist intellectual and activist Abdullah Malik departed from his home in Lahore towards Mecca for his Hajj pilgrimage. *Hadees-e-Dil: Aik Kammunist ka Roznamcha-e-Hajj* (Hadith of the Heart: A Communist's Hajj Diary) is a record of that almost 7-week journey. Certainly, the Hajj narrative is not merely a twentieth-century phenomenon; Muslims from the Indian subcontinent have been going for Hajj since the heyday of the Mughal Empire. In the twentieth century, radical Muslim intellectuals such as the African-American Malcolm X and the Iranians Jalal Al-e Ahmad and Ali Shariati went and published widely publicized Hajj journeys, in their *Autobiography of Malcom X, Lost in the Crowd* and *Hajj*, respectively.

However, there is hardly a text which documents the Hajj pilgrimage by an avowed Marxist or communist across the length and breadth of the

R. Naeem (✉)
Lahore, Pakistan

© The Author(s), under exclusive license to Springer Nature Switzerland AG 2023
B. S. Nayak, D. Chakraborty (eds.), *Interdisciplinary Reflections on South Asian Transitions*,
https://doi.org/10.1007/978-3-031-36686-4_11

Muslim world from South, South-east and Central Asia to the Middle East and North Africa, as well the growing pockets of Muslims in Europe and North America. In translating this text for the first time into English, almost 50 years after the journey itself was undertaken, my understanding is that this particular Hajj text signals newly available—and newly transnational—political and ethical imaginaries and sets of practices grapple with the gains, losses and remaining struggles of the nationalizing anticolonial era. Nearly two decades after the historic Bandung Conference, more than a decade after the success of the Cuban Revolution, just a year after the brutal break up of Pakistan that led to the creation of independent Muslim Bangladesh and in the midst of Zulfikar Ali Bhutto's nationalist reforms in Pakistan, Malik set off for a journey in which he searched for idioms beyond political discourses with which he—and most twentieth-century radical politics—was so prominently associated. In Malik's case, the Pakistani left was increasingly divided between pro-Moscow and pro-Peking camps, and even more so in the brutal aftermath of the 1971 division of the country, allowing the nationalist Bhutto an opportunity to rise to power in Pakistan.

With this context as a backdrop, *Hadees-e-Dil* should also be read as Malik's search for a means to articulate his worldly concerns. Unlike Al-e Ahmad and Malcolm's Hajj travelogues, Malik's life was marked by both a consistent profession to communist and physical longevity. So his work does not resist any categorization. In addition, unlike the sudden deaths of the two writers mentioned above, Malik's long life and service to communist politics are usually seen as a footnote in the onrush of Islamic fundamentalism in Pakistan, following the overthrow of Bhutto and subsequent rise of the dictatorial Zia-ul-Haq regime. So the reception to his work has been very divergent by subsequent readers.

In this text, Malik responds to the crisis of nationalism, socialism and communism not by settling on a holistic and totalizing Islamist ideology—as many of his erstwhile comrades contended—but he turns of Hajj through a rejection of metaphysics and an engagement with the ethics of experience on the Hajj. In fact, at the end of his long preface to the work he admits, 'You will find a strange hotch-potch of "reason and unreason" in these pages and this is very much called the hadith of the heart.'

ABDULLAH MALIK'S HAJJ

Malik is significantly lesser known among non-Indian, non-Urdu speaking readers than among Pakistanis and Urdu-speakers across south Asia. He is arguably one of the most important nonclerical Pakistani intellectuals. All his life he remained a communist and never broke from the Communist Party. Later in life, he travelled incessantly and reported from across the communist world, including the Soviet Union, Central Asia, Eastern Europe, Cuba and China. He faced a great deal of criticism, especially from his fellow-dissident communists who unlike him broke away from communism after the dissolution of the Soviet Union in 1991 and from his Islamist opponents who even brought him on trial during the Zia-ul-Haq dictatorship. Interestingly, there has been very little scholarly interest in his *Hadees-e-Dil*; most scholars, if at all, prefer to look more closely at his copious Urdu journalism, memoirs and histories of political movements in Punjab and his trilogy on the Pakistani military. As a corrective to this approach, I argue for *Hadees-e-Dil* as a text to be studied and translated in its own right. Indeed, there is an exciting tension within the communist pilgrim, as well as between his ideology and praxis reflected in the subtitle of the book. Malik also takes a few specifically political stances: he is part-reporter and part-participant but also occasionally the polemicist we find in his other works.

As Malik's first-ever text to be translated into English on the occasion of his birth centenary (2020–2021), this work also provides us with necessary insight into its author living and travelling as he did in the hurly-burly of the early 1970s, with the great Arab leader Gamal Abdel Nasser dead just a couple of years earlier and Saudi's rising role in Arab and Muslim politics rapidly rising, to be consolidated just 8 months after Malik concluded his Hajj in the form of the 1973 oil embargo following the Yom Kippur War. Thus, this text gestures towards an ethics that remains in fluid conversation with the leading ideologies, politics and philosophical movements of their day.

MALIK'S HAJJ DIARY

To read and translate this text in the twenty-first century is to understand Islam as a set of practices that have the potential to produce new (progressive and emancipatory) politics and social relations. The proposed translation of Malik's Hajj diary comes at a time of renewed scrutiny over Saudi

Arabia following its role in the continuing war in Yemen, as well as the brutal murder of Saudi journalist Jamal Khashoggi in Istanbul, and the complicity of Saudi Crown Prince Mohammad bin Salman in these events, as well as the increasingly focus on the Hajj itself following the limited number of Hajis allowed in this year due to the COVID-19 pandemic. Like the earlier Hajj travelogues of Malcolm X, Al-e Ahmad and Shariati, Malik's travelogue not only has the potential to internationalize the Hajj as a travel experience not just limited to the Muslim community but also speaks to anticolonial and Southern concerns regarding justice and exploitation that have taken on a new resonance with the onset of globalization. Thus, at a time of renewed spotlight on the Muslim world, the English translation of Malik's work will not only resonate with Muslims in south Asia but also the global Muslim community across the world, as well as introducing both sceptical and well-meaning Western citizens that there are many different ways to be a Muslim, as Malik pleads in his book as well.

These are first-time original translations of extracts from *Hadees-e-Dil.*

30 December

It is that same time of morning, I am seated in the sacred Sanctuary watching the scenes of humans. I have offered the Tahajjud in this very place. A very refreshing cool wind is blowing and the faithful are circumambulating the Kaaba. Their affection during the circumambulation is true in its place but behind it the feeling of persuasion and worship of an unseen God and Prophet (PBUH) is at work. But I think that these thousands, millions of people are circumambulating here, praying. This is very much being bound by a blind faith behind which centuries of sanctity and the civilization of dozens of generations is present; but when men bearing advanced and scientific ideas visit the tombs of their leaders and when governments and nations weave a halo of sanctity around their leaders, there is preaching day and night about their ideologies, philosophy and ideas. Or when Soviet citizens go visit the mausoleum of Lenin or communists like us living outside sing about its greatness, then too there is the feeling of a slight worship at work. When we had called out to Stalin by proclaiming him the Great Father or pay obeisance to Mao Zedong then what is it? Basically where men's helplessness and control of nature is still wanting, this is very much its expression. These are the various manifestations of the feeling of insecurity of Man. These manifestations together provoke Man to worship some individual. When we worship God, pray, circumambulate the Kaaba, plead by begging with tears, ask for recovery of the sick, ask for employment; want salvation from poverty even then and when we sing songs for Marx, Engels, Lenin, Stalin, Mao and communist leaders, behind it is this very idea that they are better and greater humans than us; the way they told will take us to that destination where our wishes will be fulfilled. The struggle for communism too is a struggle against helplessness but there is a basic difference as well in that that communism and its ideas determine the mode of struggle against Man's helplessness, show the way and move the people for struggle; but on the other hand, a metamorphosis is attempted by means of prayers whose result is not visible in the daily life of people. Compared to this when communists struggle under the leadership of communist parties, they organize workers, move peasants; then in this duration they cut down the chains of human helplessness and during this process they make man face a new faith and fervour, after which these formal prayers do not influence him much and I think that I, who is racking his brain today over these prayers, is the reason by any chance that the struggle and action which had made me a communist, has that struggle become extinct, has my relation with it been cut by any chance. Since at one time there as a discussion that could anybody be a true communist without being a party worker; so the result was that party membership is compulsory ad unavoidable for becoming a communist. Actually what does the party membership mean; it means participating in struggle and the restraint of discipline and control because by this very process does change take place and he becomes a better communist. And perhaps I, who is going round in the circles of 'Why' and 'What', so behind it too is the absence of the Communist Party of our country and disconnection in this practical struggle which despite all my broadmindedness has trapped me in a blind faith. Since the truth is that Marxism—if it is the science of the laws for social change—then a person who does not participate in making this change appear, how can he be called a Marxist.

If one looks at the changes happening in socialist states on these bases, then the situation becomes somewhat obvious. Since in socialist countries comparatively, security is to be had; illness is treated; freedom from unemployment and starvation is obtained that is why the feeling of prayer assumes a somewhat different shape there and reason and perception is fully at work in these prayers. But as far as underdeveloped and backward countries are concerned, where not only feudal but in certain conditions tribal relations are still present, even to accept the unity of God with a true heart and to believe upon it is a very progressive step but the human here in fact mostly does worship an unseen God verbally but in his heart he bows his head before the greatness of some individual. He lowers the picture of this individual within his chest and actually worships it unconsciously; and like worship of the unseen God is imagined to be a higher destination of human progress and to reach this far, Man struggled for thousands, millions of years; he turned away from so many goddesses and gods; worshipped so many natural elements and then conquered them and then repented of worshipping them. He chiselled idols for thousands of years and bowed his head in prayer before them. To the end that he subjugated all the elements of nature, kicked away the gods and goddesses, demolished idols and lowered an unseen God within the heart, bowed his head in prayer before them. He refused all other gods; belief in one god stood to be the manifestation of human reason and perception; it was deemed to be the higher and exalted destination of human progress, and who knows that hundred and thousands years from today refusal of the existence of God be deemed an even higher and exalted destination and perhaps this is why this process is happening in the socialist countries; but with us too are a thousand, lac problems in the path of the worship of an unseen god and admitting his oneness. And millions of humans even after verbally blabbering of his oneness and greatness, place him alongside various people on the throne of greatness. For example when we form pirs and saints in our hearts despite all their being elected (by God), actually we are satisfying a passion of worship for individuals; after all what else is it but denying the greatness of God by weeping over them even by forming them in the imagination? Does Man by any chance slightly enjoy submission of Man by Man, worshipping him, praying to him? Do we by any chance want to sing the praises of the unseen god by shaping all his powers and glories in the form of some Man? Do we not want to vanquish ourselves before him? Or to submit to him?

When some person takes a step against human worship then it takes Man further towards the destination and obviously the group forbidding human worship will be in a minority. This is the very reason that within Islam the Hanbalis and the Ahl-e-Hadith are in a minority and those who forbid the worship of both Man and God will be even more of a minority. But despite this, they will definitely preserve Lenin's corpse. If this is not the satisfaction of a passion of worship by Man of a man like himself then what is!

Yes the number in which women are enamoured of and possessed by religion, too proves the point to some extent that more than God they accept prophet, pirs and saints. When they call husbands a metaphorical god, then what is it than the satisfaction of a passion for shaping God and worshipping Man? If the number of women coming for Hajj here is not greater than men, it is not fewer as well, but why? Around the world women worship religion more, the reason for it too being that the passion for human-worship is boundlessly greater within them. Here poor, indigent, aged, young are present in such numbers that it cannot be said. Women are much more insecure than men in the world. Whoever will be more insecure will be more religious.

Now is the time for the Asr prayer and we are sitting on the roof above after the prayer. Today all day accounts weighed heavy on the nerves. The house rent and the expenses for Medina and Arafat amounting to 1700 Rials have to be paid to the Muallim. We have received 2350 Rials in all. Now we have to spend a period of more than a month within the remaining 700 Rials. We have to visit Medina and more important than everything, we have to make the sacrificial offering from it. What we are thinking now, the same will apply to others on a greater level. Whether there is a contradiction between these thoughts and the focus of prayer or not; in any case we are amusing ourselves by comforting one another.

After the Asr prayer, we left the sacred Sanctuary intending to buy vegetables from the bazar to cook at home and will make do with it for one or two days because now the only saving to be made was with food and anyways the food available in the bazar is very bad and bad-tasting to the extent of meat and curry. One night we bought half a plate of meat and peas for a Rial but returned after just a morsel. Yesterday we ate lunch at a Malabari hotel. What did we eat, the same two plates of dal and two puffed-up chapatis like we make them here. For two Rials and a one and a half more.

By the way there are many Pakistanis and Indians present here who know Arabic really well and they have mixed. Perhaps the process of immigration has carried on here since centuries. Ulema and other people have been residing here from our side too since centuries; one class is very much the ulema who came to reside here and systematically started the work of teaching and learning here and made a name for themselves too in it; the respected Maulana Gangohi, Ubaidullah Sindhi and the recently-deceased Hafiz Habibullah son of Maulana Ahmed Ali. I had a desire for a long time to come meet him here; since I have had very old friendly and brotherly relations with him and I always remembered him but when I had the opportunity to come here he passed away in the very same year. (Verily we belong to Allah, and verily to Him do we return.

We bought vegetables after leaving the sacred Sanctuary but when we reached home Ayesha's condition was a bit slack and she was tired. Actually she had become exhausted by circumambulations and repeated walking, which also led to her becoming sleepy. So after that we offered prayers very much at home and slept after eating dried fruit.

Hajj Politics: How Pakistan Politics Brought Fascism Even to Mecca

Every impartial observer of our national history will deem the Maududi party a traitor to the ideology of Pakistan and the Muslim masses. This terrorist fascist organization has apparently clad itself in the clothing of peace and anti-communism, but behind the scenes its actual principle is to provide a justification for imperialism, capitalism and feudalism in the sacred name of Islam.

When doors for independent political process are closed in any country or society, these types of mischiefs begin to spread like the cactus plant and leprosy, and a time comes that the political leadership comes into the hands of traitors. How the so-called democratic parties have continued to dance to the tunes of Maududism within the recent popular movement is not a thing of the past. Those who until yesterday did not have the courage to come before the Pakistani people owing to their opposition to the ideology of Pakistan are being presented today as the guardians of the ideology of Pakistan. The Maududi party indeed treated the Muslim peoples of the subcontinent like Mir Jafars in the national war of 1947, but all those people who are promoting this party today too will be deemed as criminals in the court of the people.

At such a moment when those who claim to lead the people, have become bent to sell the people to such an anti-people party which has opposed the Pakistan Movement, the jihad in Kashmir and the movement for equality, there is a dire need for a voice of truth to be raised from somewhere which can unveil this impure conspiracy by warning the people.

One such voice of truth is provided from the pages of our history by the distinguished Pakistani communist journalist, writer and activist Abdullah Malik (1920–2003), the centenary year of whose birth was celebrated in 2020 and who wrote an unposted letter to the founder and leader of the Jamaat-e-Islami, Maulana Maududi, during the former's pilgrimage to Mecca in the winter of 1973. This unposted letter forms a small part of Malik's Hajj travelogue titled *Hadees-e-Dil* (Hadith of the Heart), which I am translating into English at the moment. It is recorded by Malik under the heading 'A Letter Which Was Not Posted' and gives a revealing expose of the Jamaat's politics of surveillance and spying against its opponents even during a holy occasion as the Hajj at the height of the Cold War and worldwide anti-communist hysteria.

The letter itself is preceded by Malik's journal entry on 29 January, as well as another preamble to the letter giving a context of why he chose to write the letter and is being presented here in print for the very first time in the original English translation given that the first post-COVID Hajj is currently underway in Mecca, in the hope that readers of this valuable letter will be grateful to Malik for peeling off the veil from the face of national hypocrites at a critical turn in our national history.

29 January

I went down to find our Muallim (government-appointed guide for pilgrims) *Abdullah Attas sitting on a raised platform at the shop of the owner of our rented house. We exchanged salutations and I too sat near him. He told me that do tell me about yourself in that why are Jamaat-e-Islami folks so much after you and then Abdullah told me the doings of the people of Jamaat-e-Islami about me in detail which include everyone including Khalil Hamidi, etc. These things really upset me and I began to think that these 'religious' and lovers of Islam are involved in politics even after arriving here. I was extremely anguished …*

We went into the Haram and I wrote a letter to Maulana Maudidi sitting there, narrating the full incidents. I am thinking to send this detailed letter to Maulana Maudidi and have its copy sent for publication and run a whole campaign on this, otherwise they will try to use the ceremonies of the whole Hajj gradually through the government of Saudi Arabia for their own ends. Now I feel that the rumours about Pakistan which begin to go round here daily, one sees the hand of these agents of this very Jamaat-e-Islami behind them. Their enmity of Bhutto can take them to any limit. I don't know I have written somewhere before or not that despite serious disagreements with Jamaat-e-Islam I always had a continuous conjecture about the people of this party; but the events of 1970 and 1971, for example, the burning of the Koran, the attempt to have individual journalists fired from jobs and then at the very end, when a case was brought against me for making a speech in favour of Bangladesh and against the army action during Martial Law, the workers of Jamaat-e-Islami and their student supporters firmly gave evidence from the side of the police. At that time I felt that No, this is a very inferior sort of party and Maulana Maudidi has created fascist wolves in the name of Islam. A party which does not hesitate from fabricating an incident about burning of the Koran for its political ends, how would it shun making false cases against its political opponents or trapping them; and now indeed it is absurd to mention the workers of this party, since a party which has created assassins in the name of God, the party which has the blood of thousands of East Pakistanis on the hands of its workers, it is useless to hope for any type of decency or principles from them.

A LETTER WHICH WAS NOT POSTED

Just now I have written a letter to Maulana Maudidi sitting in the Haram Sharif! Like that my relations with and obedience to the Maulana are from before the creation of Pakistan, when the Maulana was in Pathankot; so whenever he came to Lahore, Khwaja Abdul Waheed organized some occasion or the other for him and there would be parties at friends; so I would also be part of them. Pakistan was created and the Jamaat-e-Islami began to fully participate in politics so despite all disagreements the Communist Party and the Jamaat-e-Islami ran a campaign for civic freedoms and made arrangements for holding meetings; so I kept participating in these meetings as a representative of the Communist Party and Maulana Maududi himself kept addressing the meetings as the Emir of Jamaat-e-Islami. Then one kept meeting him in the field of journalism but in all conditions the respect of the Maulana remained and whenever I got the privilege of meeting him, I always met him very much with obedience, since decency and respect in politics should nevertheless be a compulsory and permanent quality and one should never leave its grasp. So my feelings have always been the same and I always expressed obedience to the Maulana under the same feelings. Therefore when he arrived ill in London so I too was in London in those days and unfortunately was ill myself and was in a hospital in London; I wrote a letter to the Maulana and sought an apology for being unable to visit him and he answered me with kindness. So when I got to know about these things from Abdullah Attas, I wrote a letter to Maulana Maududi but when I read this letter to Ayesha (wife) *she forbade from posting it, the reason she gave was that if this letter came in the custody of the Saudi government, some further calamity might be raised and besides, what would be its use? But the reality is that this matter really disturbed me so I also wrote an article in English for 'Outlook' with the title "Hajj and Politics" but I did not send that as well.*

Dated 28 January 1973
Mecca   Respected Syed Maududi sahib
Salam! I am sending these lines in your service with respect. I hope that you will reflect on these objections. Whatever be my political beliefs and however

much you may disagree with them, you or any of your supporters do not have the right principally and morally, that they doubt my Islam or my Hajj obligation, or attempt to make me a target of the rage and fury of the Saudi government by spreading jealousy among the ummal (agents) *of the Saudi government against me using your influence and approach.*

I have said these introductory lines, now coming to the real story. I request forgiveness for the length of the talk, but anyways I want to definitely deliver my full story to you.

I alongwith with my wife reached here via plane on December 28, while coming I had brought a letter of introduction composed of 3–4 lines from Mr Ehsan Elahi Zaheer addressed to the Muallim Aqeel Attas. So I reached here and gave this letter to Abdullah, the son of Aqeel Attas who now runs the business of this firm. Then me and my wife resided here after renting a room. Afterwards our contact with the Muallim was rare, us husband and wife spent more time in the Haram and remained busy in fulfilling the obligation for which we had come. Meanwhile when the ceremonies of Hajj began, I met Mian Shafi in Mina, I had no information about his arrival; he began to say that he came to know of my arrival through Iqbal Suhail. Well the matter was forgotten, he said I was searching for you, Iqbal Suhail wants to meet you, I too was desirous of meeting him. So at that very time after Isha we went to Iqbal Suhail's place where we talked for 3 to 4 hours, while going I asked details about Iqbal Suhail from Mian Shafi, so he mentioned the former's whole family and belief, I asked what is his arrangement for livelihood, so Mian Shafi said that he works for the Saudi government but does not want to express it so do not mention it.

We sat for a long time at Iqbal Suhail's. On our return, Mian Shafi asks me that you had brought the letter of Ehsan Elahi Zaheer; I said that how do you know, you have arrived from Pakistan before me, he said that Iqbal Suhail told me, he must have been told by your Muallim because he belongs to Jamaat-e-Islami. I said OK. Until that time, I had no knowledge about my Muallim, nor I tried to find out his political affiliation, the truth is that these things were not even in my remote thought; since I had arrived here with a totally different objective and different condition. However I was saddened by this matter. A few days too passed after this thing, one day after Isha I went to look for mail so Abdullah spontaneously began to say that the letter of Ehsan Elahi Zaheer which you had brought was lying here; it used to be seen by the Jamaat-e-Islami folks daily, now they have lifted it off because it's not in my drawer. I said what difference does it make?

In the morning today I came out of my room so Abdullah was sitting outside near the shopkeeper. He began to say that do tell me details about yourself in that after all who are you; why are the people of Jamaat-e-Islami so worried about you and daily ask me why have you arranged for him to stay, he is not a Muslim with proper beliefs, he is a communist. First they kept looking at the letter of Ehsan Elahi Zaheer, then one day they began to say that do you need this letter? Now doubts would be expressed upon this letter, then afterwards the officials of the Saudi government began calling, their ummal came and demanded your passport; after this the secret police of the Saudi government watched you for two days.

All these things have been told to me by Abdullah Attas, he is a great adherent of yours, though he does not have a good opinion about Khalil Hamidi, etc and was saying that these are the pensioners of our government and are professionals but Maududi is a mujahid and a scholar.

Now you tell me that is this fascism or not? Will one have to come with permission from your people for Hajj in future and be screened by them and now are these people of yours insistent upon fulfilling the duties of the Gestapo for the government of Saudi Arabia? Maulana, the 'enmities' in the field of politics indeed do not fall principally within the category of enmity, in fact come under the category of disagreements; but the people of your party have transformed these disagreements into enmities. This very enmity took them to the witness-box of police witnesses against me in the Martial Law case. Is this same the political training of these people, every sport has some rules, whoever deviates from these rules whether done by a socialist or a person of Jamaat-e-Islami will be deemed a criminal.

Maulana again I seek forgiveness for the length of the conversation but I thought to make you aware of the situation, since despite all disagreements I still have faith upon your knowledge and principles. I have dared write these lines based on this very faith.

Yours obediently,
Malik Abdullah
Note: All translations are by the writer.

Index[1]

---

[1] Note: Page numbers followed by 'n' refer to notes.

Milton Keynes UK
Ingram Content Group UK Ltd.
UKHW051625011023
429657UK00006BA/229